Property and Trust Law in Ireland

Property and Trust Law in Ireland

Second Edition

Una Woods

This book was originally published as a monograph in the International Encyclopaedia of Laws/Property and Trust Law.

Founding Editor: Roger Blanpain
General Editor: Frank Hendrickx
Volume Editors: Alain Verbeke & Vincent Sagaert

Wolters Kluwer

Published by:
Kluwer Law International B.V.
PO Box 316
2400 AH Alphen aan den Rijn
The Netherlands
Website: lrus.wolterskluwer.com

Sold and distributed in North, Central and South America by:
Wolters Kluwer Legal & Regulatory U.S.
7201 McKinney Circle
Frederick, MD 21704
United States of America
Email: customer.service@wolterskluwer.com

Sold and distributed in all other countries by:
Air Business Subscriptions
Rockwood House
Haywards Heath
West Sussex
RH16 3DH
United Kingdom
Email: international-customerservice@wolterskluwer.com

ISBN 978-90-411-9480-0

e-Book: ISBN 978-90-411-9501-2
web-PDF: ISBN 978-90-411-9523-4

The Author

Una Woods BCL (University College Cork), LLM (Queens University Belfast), PhD (Queens University Belfast), Solicitor is a Senior Lecturer with the School of Law, University of Limerick, Ireland. She teaches land law, comparative property law and the law of trusts and has written extensively on these subjects. Her articles have been published in national and international journals, and she was the author of the third edition of *Irish Conveyancing Law* (2005). In November 2006, she was appointed by the Minister for Justice as a member of the Property Registration Authority (which manages the Irish Land Registry and the Registry of Deeds), and she served two four-year terms in this Authority. She has acted as a consultant to the Law Reform Commission on the law in relation to cohabitants and adverse possession.

The Author

Table of Contents

Table of Contents

List of Abbreviations

AC/App Cas	Appeal Cases
All ER	All England Law Reports
B & A	Barnewall & Adolphus' King's Bench Reports
B & C	Barnewall & Cresswell's King's Bench Reports
BCLC	Butterworths Company Law Cases
Ball & B	Ball & Beatty's Reports
Beav.	Beavan's Rolls Court Reports
CC	Irish Circuit Court (unreported)
Ch/Ch D	Reports of the Chancery Division
CLR	Commonwealth Law Reports
Co Rep	Coke's King's Bench Reports
Cox Eq Cas/ Cox	Cox's Equity Cases
Cr & Ph	Craig & Phillips' Chancery Reports
De GF & J	De Gex, Fisher & Jones' Chancery Reports
Dick	Dicken's Chancery Reports
DLR	Dominion Law Reports
EG	Estates Gazette
EGLR	Estates Gazette Law Reports
EHRR	European Human Rights Reports
Ex D	Law Reports, Exchequer Division
HC	Irish High Court (unreported)
HLC	Clark & Finnelly's House of Lords Reports New Series
ICLR	Irish Common Law Reports (2nd Series)
IEHC	High Court of Ireland [Neutral Citation]
IESC	Supreme Court of Ireland [Neutral Citation]
ILRM	Irish Law Reports Monthly
ILT/ILTSJ	Irish Law Times

ILTR	Irish Law Times Reports
IR	Irish Reports
Ir Ch R	Irish Chancery Reports (2nd Series)
IR CL	Irish Reports, Common Law (3rd Series)
Ir Jur Rep	Irish Jurist Law Reports
Ir LR	Irish Law Reports (1st Series)
KB	Law Reports, King's Bench
Lev	Levinz's King's Bench and Common Pleas Reports
LJQB	Law Journal Reports, Queen's Bench New Series
LR Ir	Law Reports, Ireland (4th Series)
LR Eq/LR Eq R	Law Reports, Equity Cases
LR Ex	Law Reports, Exchequer Cases
LR HL	Law Reports, English & Irish Appeals
LT	Law Times Reports
Mac & G	Macnaghten & Gordon's Chancery Reports
Macq	Macqueen's Scotch Appeal Cases
Mol	Molloy's Chancery Reports
Mood & R	Moody & Robinson's Nisi Prius Reports
NI	Northern Ireland Law Reports
NSWLR	New South Wales Law Reports
NZLR	New Zealand Law Reports
PCC	Palmer's Company Cases
QB	Law Reports, Queen's Bench (3rd Series)
QBD	Law Reports, Queen's Bench Division
Russ	Russell's Chancery Reports tempore Eldon
RVR	Rating & Valuation Reporter
Salk	Salkeld's King's Bench Reports
SC	Irish Supreme Court (unreported)
Sch & Lef	Schoales & Lefroy's Irish Chancery Reports
Sel Cas Ch	Select Cases in Chancery tempore King
SLR	Scottish Law Reporter
UKHL	United Kingdom House of Lords [Neutral Citation]
US	United States Supreme Court Reports
Ves	Vesey Chancery Reports

List of Abbreviations

WLR	Weekly Law Reports
WN	Weekly Notes of Cases

General Introduction

§1. General Background

I. Territorial Scope

1. The island of Ireland is divided into two separate political units: the Republic of Ireland, comprising twenty-six counties, and Northern Ireland which is made up of the remaining six counties and forms part of the United Kingdom of Great Britain and Northern Ireland. Although the Republic of Ireland and Northern Ireland are separate jurisdictions, their legal systems are derived from the same source and because certain English land law reforms were not replicated for Northern Ireland, the land law of both jurisdictions on the island of Ireland had, until recently, more in common with each other than with the land law of England. However, the Land and Conveyancing Law Reform Act 2009 introduced substantive reforms to the law in the Republic which have not, to date, been replicated in Northern Ireland.[1] This monograph is solely concerned with the law of property and trusts in the Republic of Ireland.

II. Geography, Climate and Culture

2. The island of Ireland has a total area of 84,421 sq km and the Republic of Ireland occupies 70,282 sq km of the island. Ireland lies in the Atlantic Ocean in the extreme north-west of the European continent and its nearest European neighbour, the United Kingdom, is located across the Irish Sea to the east of the island. The climate of Ireland is mild, with a lack of temperature extremes, as it lies in the path of the Gulf Stream which has a warming effect throughout the year. The mean daily winter temperatures vary from 4°C to 7.6°C, while mean daily summer temperatures vary from 12.3°C to 15.7°C. The weather is generally moist and changeable. Most of the eastern half of the country gets between 750 mm and 1,000 mm of rainfall in the year. Rainfall in the west generally averages between 1,000 mm and 1,400 mm. In many mountainous districts, rainfall exceeds 2,000 mm per year.[2] Although Irish (or *Gaeilge*) was the original language of the Irish people, it is now spoken as a first language by only a small minority of the Irish population. However, it is widely considered to be an important part of the island's culture and heritage and enjoys constitutional status

1. Note, however, that a similar overhaul of the land law of Northern Ireland has been proposed, *see* Northern Ireland Law Commission *Report Land Law* (NILC 8, 2010).
2. For more details, *see* <www.met.ie/climate-ireland/climate-of-ireland.asp>, 28 Feb. 2017.

as the national and first official language of the Republic of Ireland.[3] Ireland's second official language, English, is spoken by most of the population. The preliminary results of the most recent census, conducted in 2016,[4] recorded the population of the Republic of Ireland as 4,757,976 persons, revealing a population growth of 3.7% since 2011. During the 2011 census, 84.2% of the population recorded themselves as members of the Roman Catholic Church. Ireland has become an increasingly diverse society over the last decade, and in April 2011, 544,357 non-Irish nationals were recorded as resident in Ireland. A substantial proportion of such non-Irish residents were from Poland and the United Kingdom.

§2. Introduction to the Law of Property and Trusts

I. Real Property and Personal Property

3. In contrast with the civil law distinction between immoveable and moveable property, in Ireland, as is the case in many other common law systems of property law, property may be classified as either real property (also known as 'realty') or personal property (also known as 'personality' or 'chattels'). Real property includes land, buildings and certain other items attached to land known as 'fixtures'. Personal property is a residual category comprising everything else. This classification stems from an early procedural distinction. While most common law actions would result in an award of damages and were known as personal actions, actions to recover land resulted in an order for its return and were known as real actions. Land came to be called real property and all other property came to be called personal property, reflecting the types of action available. The owner of a lease of land was precluded from bringing a real action and it was not until a special action known as 'ejectment' was introduced in the fifteenth century that an ousted lessee was able to recover possession of the land. At that point, leases became known as 'chattels real', reflecting both its historical association with personal property and the new type of action available. Before the enactment of the Succession Act 1965, the classification of property was more important as on an intestate death, the deceased's real property passed to the heir-at-law identified by the rules of primogeniture, while personal property passed to the deceased's next of kin. The rules governing the devolution of both real and personal property on death were assimilated by the 1965 Act. In modern times, whether an item can be classified as a chattel or a fixture (which the courts determine by examining the degree and mode of its annexation to land and the purpose of the annexation[5]) continues to be of relevance in identifying which items pass under a conveyance of land, in the absence of a specific contractual provision dealing with the issue. Unlike civil law systems of property law, where property provisions are distributed throughout the codes and taught in courses on private law, in common law jurisdictions, the law governing real and personal

3. *Constitution of Ireland* (1937), Art. 8.
4. *See* <http://www.cso.ie/>, accessed 28 Feb. 2017. Note that comprehensive results for the 2016 census will become available during 2017.
5. *See Leigh v. Taylor* [1902] AC 157; *D'Eyncourt v. Gregory* (1866) LR 3 Eq 382.

property tends to receive separate treatment by legislators and textbook writers.[6] Ireland is no exception to this rule and the law governing realty and real transactions could generally be described as more sophisticated or complicated than the law governing personal property.

II. Land Law, Conveyancing Law and the Law of Trusts

4. The law in relation to real property can be subdivided into two separate branches known as land law and conveyancing law. Although they are two separate subjects, land law and conveyancing law are closely related and interdependent. Land law is generally understood as defining the types of ownership (known as 'estates') or other interests which arise in relation to land, while conveyancing law is more concerned with the procedures that owners should follow to dispose of their interests and the precautions that purchasers should take in acquiring such interests. As is the case in all common law systems of property law, the trust, which can be created over real and personal property, plays an important role in Irish family and commercial life and for the purposes of giving to charity. Part I of this monograph sets out the Irish law governing real property, Part II deals with the Irish law concerning personal property, while Part III is devoted to the Irish law of trusts. It is important to note that while this monograph attempts to set out the most distinctive features and developments of the law of property and trusts in Ireland, numerous textbooks are available which focus exclusively on these individual areas and therefore provide a more in-depth review of the law. The most important of these are listed in the Selected Bibliography.

§3. History of Irish Land Law

I. The Brehon Law

5. The development of Irish land law is inextricably linked with our political and legal history and therefore any treatment of the subject must refer to that history. Before the invasion of Ireland by the Anglo-Normans in the twelfth century and the introduction of the feudal system, Ireland operated a decentralized system of government. The country was organized into tribes or political units. Each tribe (or *tuath*) was ruled by a chieftain and several of these tribes would often be ruled by an overlord, for example, the King of Leinster. The indigenous legal system was a customary set of laws administered by travelling jurists, known as the Brehons. A concept known as *tanistry* governed the succession to the chieftaincy and any lands associated with the chieftaincy. The eldest and worthiest male relative of the chieftain would be identified

6. Merryman partially attributes the paucity of literature dealing with comparative property law to the absence of a comparative field of study in relation to property law matters in civil law jurisdictions, relative to the strong emphasis placed on this area of law in common law jurisdictions, *see* Merryman, 'Ownership and Estates (Variations on a Theme by Lawson)', *Tulane Law Review* 48 (1974–1974): 916, 916–918.

as the *tanist* during the lifetime of the chieftain. Another succession law concept known as *gavelkind* allowed for the equal division of land owned by a father between his sons on his death. Illegitimate sons were allowed to succeed under this system but daughters had no inheritance rights.[7] These concepts would later come into direct conflict with the heirship rules of primogeniture which operated under the feudal system and favoured the eldest son.

II. The Feudal System in England

6. To understand the feudal system of tenure (or landholding) which was introduced in Ireland, it is necessary to give an overview of its operation in England.[8] The Normans, led by William ('The Conqueror'), invaded and conquered England in 1066. King William I claimed the throne by right of conquest and took the land of his opponents from them and made grants of it to his followers subject to the performance of certain services and sporadic rights and entitlements known as incidents. These recipients were called *tenants in chief* and they in turn made subgrants, subject to services and incidents to intermediate tenants known as *mesne tenants.* The process, known as 'subinfeudation', continued until it concerned a grant in favour of *tenants in desmesne* who were in occupation of the land. The services which had to be performed by a tenant for his immediate lord provided the lord with a regular source of income. The type of tenure determined the terms under which the tenant held the land. The two main types of feudal tenure were military tenure, which involved the provision of soldiers, and tenure in free and common socage, which involved the provision of agricultural produce. Eventually these services were replaced by monetary payments. Tenure in free and common socage subsequently became known as 'freehold' and survives today without any of its original feudal attributes. Incidents were rights and entitlements which a lord could claim from time to time. For example, the incident of 'relief' was a tax payable to the immediate lord on the death of a tenant before his heir could take control of the land and 'escheat' was the right of the immediate lord to take possession of the land if the tenant died without an heir or if he committed a felony. Under the feudal system of tenure, no land was allodial (without a lord) as all land ownership derived ultimately from the King. Therefore, the concept of absolute ownership (or *dominium*) which dominates civil law jurisdictions was an alien concept.

III. The Doctrine of Estates

7. The doctrine of estates, which is a distinctive feature of the common law approach to land law, developed because of the feudal notion that the King owned the underlying title to all land. The problem was that if the King owned the underlying title to the land, it was not clear what the occupier of the land under the grant owned.

7. *See* Wylie, *Irish Land Law,* 5th edn (Dublin: Bloomsbury Professional, 2013), paras 1.11–1.15.
8. *See* Zweigert & Kotz, *An Introduction to Comparative Law,* 3rd rev. edn (Oxford: Clarendon Press, 1998), Ch. 16; Wylie, *Irish Land Law,* 5th edn (Dublin: Bloomsbury Professional, 2013), paras 2.06 et seq.

The solution was to come up with an abstract entity called the 'estate'; the occupier owns an estate in land, not the land itself. The type of estate determines the duration of the holder's ownership rights in relation to the land. It is believed that the earliest type of estate was the life estate or ownership for the lifetime of the occupier or another person (i.e., a life estate *pur autre vie*). The fee simple estate, which has the potential to last forever, emerged following the recognition of inheritance as a right by Henry II in the Assize of Northampton, 1176. Since the enactment of Quia Emptores in 1290, restrictions cannot be placed on the sale of a fee simple estate and the Statute of Wills, enacted in both England and Ireland in 1634, allowed the fee simple owner to leave it by will to whomever he wished on his death. Either action would effectively disinherit the heir as identified by the rules of primogeniture, and so henceforth the heir could only be described as having a hope of inheriting the estate (a *spes successionis*). The fee tail estate, which was also capable of being inherited but only by the direct descendants of the original holder of the estate as identified by the rules of primogeniture, was introduced by the statute De Donis Conditionalibus in 1285. It was designed to keep land within the family and was often used in conjunction with the life estate to create a strict settlement over land. The doctrine of estates could be used in this manner to allow ownership to be fragmented over time. The doctrine of estates does not exist in civil law jurisdictions where there can only be one owner whose rights relate to the land itself.[9]

IV. The Birth of the Common Law

8. The introduction of the feudal system of landholding also led to the development of the common law.[10] The King and his council were responsible for ensuring that all feudal dues were paid by feudal inferiors. This council gradually developed into a court of the exchequer which decided all legal questions connected with feudal dues. It was important that there was peace in the land to ensure the regular payment of dues and, therefore, the court became involved in settling disputes of a civil and criminal nature. The King, as the source of all justice, began to send travelling justices out into the provinces during the twelfth century to hold court in the name of the King. The justices abided by the doctrine of precedent which allowed a unified or common law to develop. This unified system of law was the main reason why codification was never of such concern to the English, unlike France and Germany where diverse legal systems operated across different localities.

---

9. *See* Merryman, 'Ownership and Estates (Variations on a Theme by Lawson)', *Tulane Law Review* 48 (1974–1974): 916. Note, however, that the life estate has been compared to the civilian usufruct, *see* McClean, 'The Common Law Life Estate and the Civil Law Usufruct: A Comparative Study', *International and Comparative Law Quarterly* 12 (1963): 649.
10. *See* Zweigert & Kotz, *An Introduction to Comparative Law*, 3rd rev. edn (Oxford: Clarendon Press, 1998), Ch. 16.

V. Development of Equity

9. In the middle ages, the litigation process was founded on writs. The writs were issued by the Chancellor[11]. In order to be allowed to proceed with a case, it was necessary to bring the case within some established form of writ. The only alternative was to appeal to the King for relief. The King transmitted these appeals to the Chancellor, and the decisions the Chancellor made developed into a new branch of law known as equity which was soon administered by another court, the court of chancery. Equity developed new remedies such as the injunction and specific performance. It recognized the use, or trust as it later became known, which led to the fragmentation of property rights into legal and equitable. Equity developed to supplement and complement the common law system and following the enactment of the Judicature Act 1873 in England, and in 1877 in Ireland, both systems of law were administered by the one court. Although the institutional duality was abolished, the conceptual duality remains, especially in the area of land law as proprietary rights in land can be legal or equitable. The most significant effects which equity had on property law was the recognition of the use, the medieval precursor of the modern-day trust and the development of the equitable doctrine of notice, an important rule which operates in the context of transactions relating to land.

VI. The Origin of the Trust

10. The modern trust developed from a medieval device known as the 'use'.[12] To create a use, the land was transferred to a person known as the *feoffee to uses* who was directed to hold it to the use or for the benefit of a person known as *cestui que use*. Although the *feoffee* was regarded as the owner by the common law, the courts of chancery required him to exercise his ownership as was intended and, as a result, *cestui* was recognized as having equitable or beneficial ownership. The use became popular for numerous reasons: It could be used to avoid certain feudal dues; it also allowed an owner to make a settlement of land on his wife,[13] or to leave it to someone other than the heir-at-law on his death.[14] Efforts made to restrict the impact of the use through the Statute of Uses (Ireland) 1634, which operated to execute the use by vesting the legal ownership in the person intended to receive the beneficial ownership, failed as conveyancers simply inserted an extra use (known as a 'use-upon-a-use' or a 'conveyance to uses') to exhaust the effects of the Statute and recreate the division between legal and equitable ownership.[15] The use-upon-a-use evolved into the modern trust. The Statute of Uses (Ireland) 1634 was repealed by the Land and Conveyancing

11. *See* Biehler, *Equity and the Law of Trusts in Ireland,* 6th edn (Dublin: Roundhall, 2016), Ch. 1. Wylie, *Irish Land Law,* 5th edn (Dublin: Bloomsbury Professional, 2013), paras 3.01–3.06.
12. *See* Biehler, *Ibid.*, 59–61; Wylie, *Ibid.*, paras 3.07–3.32.
13. A man and his wife were regarded as one person for the purposes of the law and because of the common law rule that a man could neither convey property to himself nor could he convey it to his wife.
14. It was not possible to make a will of land in Ireland until the Statute of Wills (Ireland) 1634.
15. *See Sambach v. Dalston* (1635) 163 Tothill 168.

Law Reform Act 2009[16] which also eliminated the need for the use-upon-a-use or the conveyance to uses.[17]

11. Many trusts are expressly created by a trust deed or in a will.[18] Although they are often created for the benefit of persons, it is also possible to create a trust for charitable purposes and such trusts are enforced by the Charities Regulatory Authority.[19] In addition, the law recognizes that certain circumstances may give rise to a resulting trust[20] or a constructive trust.[21] For example, a purchase money resulting trust arises if someone contributes the purchase price of land bought in the name of another.[22] In such circumstances, the legal owner is required to hold the property on resulting trust for those who contributed to the purchase price. The equitable shares of the beneficiaries reflect their respective contributions. The courts recognize a constructive trust if it is necessary in the interests of justice and good conscience. It is long established, for example, that when a purchaser enters into an enforceable contract to purchase land, the vendor is deemed to hold the land on constructive trust for the purchaser.[23]

VII. The Feudal System in Ireland

12. In theory, the introduction of the common law and the feudal system of tenure began in Ireland with the Anglo-Norman invasion of Wexford in 1169, led by Richard Fitzgilbert deClare or 'Strongbow'.[24] In 1171, King Henry II visited the country and held a King's Council in Waterford which was of symbolic value in asserting English authority. In 1172, Hugh de Lacy was appointed as the first Justiciar of Ireland to represent the King. He was authorized to issue writs in 1204 and the Irish courts were instructed to apply the English common law. A number of grants of land were made by the King to tenants in chief, and Strongbow received the first feudal grant of the entire Kingdom of Leinster. However, a special feature of these early Irish grants was that the territories in question had not yet been conquered. The grants were of little practical significance until this happened. The application of the feudal system of landholding, government and law was only gradually extended to the entire country. Up until the seventeenth century, the feudal influence waxed and waned and, at one stage, the feudal system could only be described as operating effectively around Dublin and in relation to a strip of land along the East Coast of Ireland that became known as 'the Pale'. Many of the original Normal invaders intermarried with native Irish noble families, and it was said that they became 'more Irish than the Irish themselves'.

13. However, with the dawning of the seventeenth century, came the demise of the native system of law and government. A process of confiscation of land from the

16. Land and Conveyancing Law Reform Act 2009, s. 8.
17. Land and Conveyancing Law Reform Act 2009, s. 62(2).
18. *See* Part III, Ch. 2 below.
19. *See* Part III, Ch. 4 below.
20. *See* Part III, Ch. 5 below.
21. *See* Part III, Ch. 6 below.
22. *See C v. C* [1976] IR 254.
23. *See Tempany v. Hynes* [1976] IR 101; Land and Conveyancing Law Reform Act 2009, s. 52(1).
24. *See* Wylie, *Irish Land Law,* 5th edn (Dublin: Bloomsbury Professional, 2013), paras 1.16–1.34.

native Irish nobles followed by a re-grant of the holdings under the feudal system was initiated by Henry VIII during the 1540s. This approach was replaced by the plantation process during the reign of Mary I and William III under which the land of rebellious Irish landowners was forfeited for treason and re-settled with immigrants. This resettlement of Irish lands accelerated in the aftermath of a failed rebellion by certain noble landowners in the north of Ireland. These noblemen fled the country in 1607, an event referred to as 'the Flight of the Earls', and a large portion of the province of Ulster was re-settled with Scottish and English settlers as part of the Ulster Plantation. In addition, the Irish courts rejected the Brehon law rules of succession encapsulated by *gavelkind* and *tanistry*,[25] thereby establishing the dominance of the English common law.

14. Throughout the seventeenth century, rebellions occurred across Ireland and resettlements of land were made in many provinces, culminating with the conquest of Ireland led by Cromwell's army between 1649 and 1652 and a large-scale confiscation and resettlement of land in favour of Cromwell's soldiers and adventurers. Although some land was restored to certain Irish Catholic landowners who could prove that they were not involved in these rebellions, this resulted in the dissatisfaction of the Protestant settlers who had to surrender some of their land. Dissatisfaction on both sides led ultimately to the Battle of the Boyne in 1690 which saw the defeat of the Catholics led by King James II by the Protestant King William III, known as William of Orange. This event is still commemorated by a series of parades held across Northern Ireland annually on 12 July. In the early part of the seventeenth century, Catholics had owned about three-fifths of the land in Ireland but, by the end of the century, they held less than one-seventh of the land.

VIII. The Decline of Feudalism

15. It is perhaps ironic that by the time the feudal system came to be imposed over most of Ireland, many features associated with this system of land ownership had disappeared in England, primarily due to an increase in the value of land as a commodity.[26] In medieval times, there were two main methods of conveyancing: substitution, whereby the purchaser stepped into the shoes of the tenant and took over his obligations in relation to services and incidents, and subinfeudation, whereby the tenant created a new layer in the feudal pyramid by granting land to the purchaser in return for services and incidents. Although the lord's consent was required before a tenant could substitute, it was not necessary for a grant in subinfeudation. As land became more valuable, it became common for tenants to subinfeudate for a lump sum payment equivalent to the market value of the land and to impose only nominal services, such as the presentation of a rose at mid-summer to the lord. Although the original tenant was still liable for the services to his lord, his means of production may have been dramatically reduced. This practice also meant that the incidents attached to the land were of less value to the lord.

25. *See Case of Gavelkind* (1605) Dav 49; *Case of Tanistry* (1607) Dav 28.
26. Wylie, *Irish Land Law*, 5th edn (Dublin: Bloomsbury Professional, 2013), paras 2.35–2.66.

16. The Magna Carta was passed in 1217 which prohibited tenants from selling so much land that the part retained was insufficient to yield the services owing to the lord. Quia Emptores, a statute passed in 1290, was a more serious effort to meet the concerns of the feudal lords. It abolished subinfeudation for an estate to be held in fee simple and granted tenants the right to sell all or part of their land by substitution without the lord's consent. Where only part of the land was sold, the services were to be apportioned between the parts.

17. The ban on subinfeudation marked the beginning of the end of the feudal system as it led to a gradual shrinkage of the feudal pyramid through escheat.[27] The Tenures Abolition Act (Ireland) 1662 abolished most forms of tenure prevalent in Ireland, and all existing tenures were converted into free and common socage or 'freehold' as it became known. It also abolished most incidents. One remnant of the feudal system, escheat, remained in force in Ireland until its abolition by the Succession Act 1965 which replaced it with a declaration of the State as the ultimate intestate successor.[28]

18. In the Irish context, it is important to note that the prohibition on subinfeudation imposed by Quia Emptores did not apply to the Crown. This facilitated the resettlements of land which occurred during the seventeenth century. These feudal grants were made by letters patent which reserved a rent known as a 'quit rent' and often contained a *non obstante* clause which permitted the tenant in chief to subinfeudate notwithstanding Quia Emptores. The grant of a fee simple estate subject to the payment of a rent is a hybrid estate which combines freehold and leasehold features and such grants are known as fee farm grants. Although feudal fee farm grants are more common in Northern Ireland, they may still be found in certain urban areas of the Republic of Ireland.[29]

19. It should be mentioned that after the abolition of subinfeudation in fee simple, an alternative type of tenure, known as leasehold, began to emerge which mimicked feudal tenure in certain respects. It involved a landlord (or 'lessor') granting possession of the land to a tenant (or 'lessee') for a term subject to a rent.[30] Many of the English who received large grants of land were not tempted to settle in Ireland due to the widespread unrest and chose instead to remain absentee landlords and employ agents to run their land holdings. The agents engaged by the absentee landlords sought to earn as much profit from the land as possible and thereby increase their commission. As a result, many of the large estates were subdivided through leases. A peculiarly Irish phenomenon was the popularity of special types of leases known as renewable leases for years and renewable leases for lives. These leases were perpetually renewable on the payment of a fine on the expiry of the initial term or the death of a nominated life thereby maximizing profit for the landlord.

20. The legal and economic position of the small tenant farmer in the eighteenth century was particularly bleak. The possibility of eviction and starvation were constant worries and the plots were too small to yield enough income to support his family and to pay the rent. Towards the end of the eighteenth century, bands of men had formed

---

27. *See* para. 6 above.
28. Succession Act 1965, ss 11(3) and 73(1).
29. *See* Wylie, *Irish Land Law,* 5th edn (Dublin: Bloomsbury Professional, 2013), para. 4.61.
30. *See* Part I, Ch. 6 below.

groups which roamed the country, causing agrarian disturbances and threatening those who co-operated with the landlords and their agents. By the beginning of the nineteenth century, two causes dominated Irish politics: the call for Home Rule and the resolution of the land problem.[31]

IX. Home Rule

21. The desire for Home Rule emerged followed the enactment of the Act of Union in 1800. The Act of Union disbanded the Irish parliament which had been operating out of Dublin between 1783 and 1800 and established the Westminster Parliament as the principal legislative body for the United Kingdom of Great Britain and Ireland. Although the liberal Prime Minister Gladstone supported the campaign for home rule, there was strong opposition from the Unionist party which represented the Ulster Plantation settlers. The cruel suppression of a rebellion by nationalists in Easter 1916, cemented support for the nationalist cause represented by the Sinn Fein Party and, in the 1918 General Election to the Westminster Parliament, Sinn Fein received widespread support. The elected candidates refused to take their seats and instead set up a national parliament, called Dáil Éireann. An army formed by the nationalists engaged in a campaign against British Rule, called the War of Independence, which culminated in the negotiation of the Anglo-Irish Treaty towards the end of 1921. In January 1922, the Treaty was approved by the Dáil and two political units were created on the island of Ireland: Northern Ireland and the Irish Free State. The Free State was conferred with dominion status and members of the legislature were required to swear an oath of loyalty to the Crown. In 1949, Ireland declared itself a Republic.

X. The Resolution of the Land Problem

22. Agitation for land reform increased following the failure of the potato crop, a staple of the Irish peasant diet, in 1845–1847. By the mid-nineteenth century, it had become clear that tenants in Ulster were better off than tenants in the rest of Ireland. This was due to development of a custom by the settlers on the Ulster Plantation which provided the tenant with three basic rights: the right to remain in possession of the land (provided he paid his rent and performed his obligations) with reasonable limits being placed on increases in rent for improvements made by the tenant; the right to sell his interest without having to get the consent of the landlord; and the right to compensation on eviction or the termination of his tenancy. The Liberal Prime Minister, Gladstone, was sympathetic to the Irish case for land reform, and the enactment of the Landlord and Tenant (Ireland) Act 1870 gave legal recognition to the Ulster custom and similar customs operating in other parts of the country. The major flaw in this legislation was that it failed to protect tenants from eviction which the landlords could achieve by simply increasing the rents. In 1879, Michael Davitt formed the Land League which campaigned for the reduction of rents and the utopian dream of the right

31. *See* Wylie, *Irish Land Law*, 5th edn (Dublin: Bloomsbury Professional, 2013), paras 1.38 et seq.

of tenants to purchase the land outright. A campaign for 'the three Fs' – fair rent, free sale and fixity of tenure, led to the enactment of the Land Law (Ireland) 1881. This Act established the Land Commission and gave tenants the right to apply to the county courts or the Commission to have a fair rent fixed. They were also conferred with a renewable fifteen-year judicial tenancy and the right to sell their interests, subject to the right of the landlord to buy the land himself or make reasonable objections to the sale. This led to substantial reductions in rents across the country, although administratively it proved to be very demanding.

23. In the meantime, the notion of facilitating the purchase by tenants of their landlords' interest in the land became more popular. The Landlord and Tenant (Ireland) Act 1870 included provisions which allowed the Landed Estates Court to conduct sales to tenants with the State advancing a proportion of the purchase price. The Land Law (Ireland) Act 1881 conferred a power on the Land Commission to purchase an entire estate to sell off parts to its tenants, if a proportion of those tenants were willing to buy their holdings. Early efforts to facilitate the purchase of land by tenants were not generous enough; for example, the 1870 Act only advanced two-thirds of the purchase price to the tenants, while the 1881 Act increased the advance to three-quarters of the purchase price. However, a series of Acts passed in the late nineteenth and early twentieth century, known as the Land Purchase Acts[32] radically changed the face of Irish land ownership. The Land Commission could advance the entire purchase price of the holding to the occupying tenant, and the loan to the State was secured by an annuity charged on the lands repayable over a period of up to seventy-three years at a low-interest rate. An important development was the introduction of compulsory purchase of all tenanted agricultural land by the Land Act 1923, as previously the land purchase scheme had been a voluntary one. The Land Commission had also been given the task of relieving congestion in certain over-populated rural areas through compulsory purchase and resettlement. The problem of uneconomic smallholdings was taken very seriously, and up until recently, the permission of the Land Commission or the Minister for Agriculture was required to sub-divide or let an agricultural holding.[33] By the 1980s, the Land Commission had secured the purchase of 87% of agricultural land in Ireland and 20% of agricultural land had been structurally re-distributed to relieve congestion.[34] The Land Commission was dissolved in 1999.[35] These land purchases were effected by a vesting deed which had the effect of transferring a fee simple estate to the tenant farmer free and clear from all superior interests in the property which were converted into interests in the purchase money (a process known as 'overreaching'). The introduction of the land purchase scheme coincided with the introduction of the Local Registration of Title (Ireland) Act 1891 which imposed a requirement for compulsory registration on all holdings purchased under the Land Purchase Acts. As a result, most

32. For example, the Purchase of Land (Ireland) Act 1885, as amended by the Land Law (Ireland) Act 1887 and the Purchase of Land (Ireland) Amendment Act 1888; the Purchase of Land (Ireland) Act 1891; the Land Law (Ireland) Act 1896; the Land Act 1923; the Evicted Tenants (Ireland) Act 1907; the Irish Land Act 1909; the Land Act 1923; the Land Act 1933.

33. The Land Act 2005 eliminated the need to obtain such permission for transactions executed after 4 Nov. 2005.

34. 134 Seanad Debates, Col 970.

35. Land Commission (Dissolution) Act 1992.

agricultural land was quickly brought within the registration of title system, unlike England where a huge effort has been made in recent times to bring agricultural land onto the land register.

§4. MODERN IRISH LAND LAW

I. The Influence of English Land Law

24. Modern Irish land law is based on certain pre-1922 English common law and legislation passed by Westminster but only to the extent that it has not been altered by Irish case law or legislation. The famous English Birkenhead reforms of 1925[36] were not replicated in Ireland but, as has been noted elsewhere,[37] Ireland has since caught up in certain respects and it may not have been appropriate to replicate other reforms; for example, the introduction of a Land Charges Register would have been unnecessary, as Ireland operated a Registry of Deeds system[38] which England did not have. As regards the English reforms in relation to the registration of title and the administration of estates, Ireland has since modernized the law in these areas by the enactment of the Registration of Title Act 1964[39] and the Succession Act 1965. The English reforms in relation to strict settlements implemented in 1925, which were in any case of questionable benefit,[40] have since been swept away by the Trusts of Land and Appointment of Trustees Act 1996. The new approach to strict settlements adopted in the English 1996 Act is now replicated in Ireland by Part 4 of the Land and Conveyancing Law Reform Act 2009. Although the Irish law of trusts continues to be governed by the Trustee Act 1893, it has been amended on a few occasions,[41] and plans are afoot to consolidate the law in a modern statute.[42] It could be argued that the most substantial and lasting impact of the Birkenhead reforms in differentiating English Land law from Irish land law were the changes to co-ownership introduced by the English Law of Property Act 1925. The 1925 Act made it impossible to create a legal tenancy in common and instead imposed a statutory trust for sale (now a trust of land) vesting the legal interest in trustees as joint tenants so that only the equitable interest was held by the beneficiaries as tenants in common. Ireland has not seen fit to replicate this reform.[43]

---

36. Comprising six Acts: Settled Land Act 1925, Trustee Act 1925, Law of Property Act 1925, Land Registration Act 1925, Land Charges Act 1925 and Administration of Estates Act 1925.
37. Wylie, *Irish Land Law,* 3rd edn (Dublin: Butterworths, 1997), paras 1.81–1.82.
38. *See* para. 25 below.
39. As amended by the Registration of Deeds and Title Act 2006.
40. *See* Wylie, *Irish Land Law,* 3rd edn (Dublin: Butterworths, 1997), para. 1.82.
41. Trustee Act 1931; Trustee (Authorized Investments) Act 1958, Land and Conveyancing Law Reform Act 2009, Part 5; Charities Act 2009.
42. *See* Law Reform Commission, *Trust Law – General Proposals* (LRC 92–2008).
43. *See* Law Reform Commission, *Report on Land Law and Conveyancing Law: (7) Positive Covenants over Freehold Land and Other Proposals* (LRC 70–2003), para. 5.04; *Consultation Paper on Reform and Modernization of Land Law and Conveyancing Law* (LRC CP 34–2004), paras 6.02–6.05.

II. The Registration Systems

25. Ireland operates two mutually exclusive registration systems in relation to land: the Registry of Deeds and the Land Registry. The registration of deeds system permits the registration of deeds and other instruments affecting land in the Registry of Deeds. Registration does not guarantee the effectiveness of the deed and it is not compulsory, although it may afford priority over earlier unregistered transactions in relation to the same piece of land. Up until recently, the procedures to be followed to effect such registrations were governed by the antiquated Registration of Deeds Act (Ireland) 1707. The Registration of Deeds and Titles Act 2006 repealed the 1707 Act and facilitated the introduction of simplified and modernized procedures for the registration of deeds.[44] The registration of title system, governed by the Registration of Title Act 1964,[45] permits the registration of ownership and certain burdens affecting land in the Land Registry. The register is designed to be a mirror of the title of the registered owner and greatly facilitates the investigation of such titles for conveyancing solicitors. Once land has been registered for the first time in the Land Registry, a folio is opened which describes the property by reference to a map (known as a 'title plan') and sets out the owner and certain burdens (e.g., any charges or rights of way) affecting the property. The register provides a conclusive state guaranteed record of the title of the registered owner.[46] Future transactions in relation to such land are dramatically simplified for two reasons. First, it is much easier for the purchaser's solicitor to investigate vendor's title as a search of the Land Register will reveal whether he is the registered owner and most of the burdens affecting the land.[47] Second, the task of drafting the deed transferring ownership is more straightforward as a deed dealing with registered land must be submitted in a standardized form, known as a deed of transfer. A deed of transfer is shorter and less complicated than the deeds drafted in relation to unregistered land. An important feature of the registration of title system is that all subsequent dispositions must be registered in order to be effective. The Registration of Deeds and Titles Act 2006 established the Property Registration Authority[48] to manage both the Registry of Deeds and the Land Registry, and imposed a statutory obligation on the Authority to extend the registration of title system to the entire country. In recent times, huge efforts have been made to extend compulsory registration.[49] Once land is brought within a zone of compulsory registration, on the

---

44. Registration of Deeds and Title Act 2006, Part 3; Registration of Deeds Rules 2008 (SI 52/2008).
45. As amended by Registration of Deeds and Title Act 2006, Part 4.
46. Registration of Title Act 1964, s. 31. *See* Fitzgerald, *Land Registry Practice,* 2nd edn (Dublin: Roundhall, 1995).
47. However, the existence of 'overriding interests', which are interests that bind a purchaser even though they are not apparent from an inspection of the register, make it necessary for a purchaser to investigate certain other matters.
48. Registration of Deeds and Title Act 2006, Part 2.
49. Registration of Title Act 1964 (Compulsory Registration of Ownership) Order 1969 (SI 87/1969); Registration of Title Act 1964 (Compulsory Registration of Ownership) Order 2005 (SI 605/2005); Registration of Title Act 1964 (Compulsory Registration of Ownership) Order 2008 (SI 81/2008); Registration of Title Act 1964 (Compulsory Registration of Ownership) Order 2009 (SI 176/2009) have extended compulsory registration to the entire country with the exception of Dublin and Cork.

next sale of the property[50] the purchaser's solicitor is required to apply for first registration of the title to the property. Dublin and Cork, which contain the highest number of unregistered titles, were the last zones to be designated compulsory first registration areas from 1 June 2010.[51] Currently, about 93% of the land mass in Ireland is registered in the Land Registry and, it is envisaged that, in time, the Registration of Deeds system shall become defunct.

III. Recent Developments

26. The extension of the registered title system to the entire country is seen as essential in making progress towards an electronic conveyancing system.[52] An online paperless conveyancing system, which would reduce the inefficiencies and complexities in the current system, is part of the government's vision for the future, although its introduction lost momentum following the collapse in the property market. Recently, however, a task force on eConveyancing established by the Law Society of Ireland has made significant progress in devising a vision and developing a model for the introduction of eConveyancing[53] and it is expected that this project shall enter its implementation phase very soon. It is envisaged that information would be viewed and communications and data exchange would take place between solicitors, lenders, and the Property Registration Authority through a secure central electronic 'hub' or work area. In addition, the payment of the purchase price and the redemption of any existing charge would involve an electronic transfer of funds in real time with same day value. The introduction of eRegistration is viewed as a major component of an eConveyancing system and progress has also been made in this area. The Registration of Deeds and Title Act 2006 permits the register and maps to be maintained in an electronic format and provides a statutory basis for electronic communications and dealings with the Registry. The land register and map are now fully digitized and a number of online services are available through www.landdirect.ie and www.eregistration.ie. An eDischarges system was introduced in March 2009[54] which allows a borrower's bank to apply electronically to the Land Registry to remove a charge from registered land once it has been paid off. It is also possible for a charging order in favour of the Health Service Executive to be registered electronically where ancillary State support has been made available to persons in respect of long-term residential care.[55] Recently

50. Registration of Deeds and Title Act 2006, s. 53 amends Registration of Title Act 1964, s. 24 and facilitates an extension of the range of transactions which would trigger the requirement to apply for first registration.
51. Registration of Title Act 1964 (Compulsory Registration of Ownership) Order 2010 (SI 515/2010).
52. *See* Law Reform Commission, *Report on Reform and Modernization of Land Law and Conveyancing Law* (LRC 74–2005), para. 1.06; *eConveyancing: Modelling of the Irish Conveyancing System* (LRC 79–2006).
53. Law Society of Ireland, *eConveyancing: Back to Basic Principles; Vision of an Electronic System of Conveyancing ('eVision')*, March 2008, available at <https://www.lawsociety.ie/Documents/Media/eVision.pdf> accessed 28 Feb. 2017.
54. Land Registration Rules 2008 (SI 326/ 2008).
55. Nursing Homes Support Scheme Act 2009, s. 17(2).

a new range of services has been launched that allows legal practitioners to correspond electronically with the Property Registration Authority, draft Deeds of Transfer, circulate documents in a secure environment, interact with the Land Register (including the digital map) and pay registration fees by variable direct debit.

27. Another recent development was the enactment of the Land and Conveyancing Law Reform Act 2009 which came into force on 1 December, 2009.[56] The aim of this legislation was to simplify and modernize land law and conveyancing law. It repeals over 150 pre-1922 statutes, re-enacts certain legislative provisions in modern language and clarifies or abolishes other legislative and common law rules in line with Law Reform Commission recommendations.[57] Although it may be tempting to compare this major overhaul of the law in this area with the English Birkenhead reforms, or the introduction of a codification of the law (akin to the civilian approach), this would be an exaggeration of its scope.[58] Except for minor exceptions, the 2009 Act does not deal with areas covered by more modern legislation, for example, succession law, landlord and tenant law, the registration systems or the law of trusts. Similarly, it does not attempt to curtail the development or recognition of equitable doctrines or interests. It would also be inaccurate to refer to it as a consolidation of certain pre-1922 legislative provisions, as some of these have been incorporated with substantive amendments.[59] It is interesting to note the divergence from the English approach which has emerged in relation to certain reforms; for example, Ireland has abolished the rule against perpetuities, prohibited the unilateral severance of joint tenancies and, more relevant in the context of this discussion of the historical background to Irish land law, abolished the notion of feudal tenure.[60] The Law Reform Commission was of the view that this notion that all land is held from the State (which had replaced the position of the Crown in Ireland) was out of sync with the modern relationship between Irish citizens and the government.[61] Although the notion of feudal tenure is abolished, the 'estate', as the fundamental conception of ownership, is retained. In the United States, a similar move was made in many states following the Revolution and Declaration of Independence in 1776.[62]

56. *See* Wylie, *The Land and Conveyancing Law Reform Act 2009: Annotations and Commentary* (Dublin: Bloomsbury Professional, 2009).
57. *See* the Law Reform Commission, *Consultation Paper on Reform and Modernisation of Land Law and Conveyancing Law* (LRC CP 34–2004) and *Report on Reform and Modernization of Land Law and Conveyancing Law* (LRC 74–2005).
58. *See* Wylie, *The Land and Conveyancing Law Reform Act 2009: Annotations and Commentary* (Dublin: Bloomsbury Professional, 2009), 1–11.
59. *Ibid.*
60. Land and Conveyancing Law Reform Act, s. 9(2).
61. *See* the Law Reform Commission, *Consultation Paper on Reform and Modernization of Land Law and Conveyancing Law* (LRC CP 34–2004), para. 2.11.
62. *See* Wylie, *The Land and Conveyancing Law Reform Act 2009: Annotations and Commentary* (Dublin: Bloomsbury Professional, 2009), 51.

Part I. Irish Law of Real Property

Chapter 1. Legal and Equitable Estates

§1. The Types of Estates

28. As was mentioned in the General Introduction,[63] the doctrine of estates was developed in response to the feudal notion that the King owned the underlying title to all land. This doctrine facilitated the fragmentation of freehold ownership of land over time through the recognition of three types of estate: the fee simple, the fee tail and the life estate. All three estates could exist as 'interests in possession' (which the holder would be entitled to enjoy immediately) or 'future interests' (where the enjoyment was postponed until some point in the future) in the land. A future interest which is expressly created is known as a 'remainder' while a fee simple 'reversion' arises automatically on the expiry of a smaller estate (e.g., a life estate and, until recently, a fee tail) in the absence of a remainder. Leasehold ownership was recognized in more modern times and is dealt with in Chapter 6. Until recently, the fee simple, the fee tail and the life estate could be created as legal or as equitable estates. However, since the commencement of the Land and Conveyancing Law Reform Act 2009,[64] the only legal estates which may be created or disposed of are the fee simple 'in possession' and the leasehold estate. While the fee tail has been abolished,[65] the life estate and any future interests can only take effect as equitable estates under a trust of land which vests the power to deal with the legal fee simple in possession in trustees.[66]

§2. The Fee Simple

29. The fee simple, as the largest estate and the closest to absolute ownership, can exist as a fee simple absolute or a modified fee simple. A modified fee simple commences only on the satisfaction of a particular condition or terminates earlier than it would do naturally. Modified fee simples can be classified as determinable fee simples

63. *See* para. 7 above.
64. On 1 Dec. 2009.
65. *See* para. 41 below.
66. *See* paras 42 and 54 below.

or conditional fee simples. Typically, such modified fee simples are created by a testator through a devise in a will.

I. Determinable Fee Simple

30. A determinable fee simple is a fee simple which will terminate automatically on the occurrence of a stated event which may or may not occur. For example, land could be disposed of 'to A in fee simple until the land ceases to be used for agriculture'. In such circumstances, the grantor retains a possibility that the fee simple will revert to him if the event occurs, known as 'a possibility of reverter'. Section 11(2)(a) of the Land and Conveyancing Law Reform Act 2009 Act clarifies that a determinable fee simple is deemed to be a fee simple in possession. The possibility of reverter is not deemed to create a future interest in the land and so it does not give rise to a trust of land. Therefore, the owner of the determinable fee simple is free to dispose of the legal estate if he can find a buyer, although the risk of the occurrence of the determinable event may render it less marketable than a fee simple absolute.

II. Conditional Fee Simple

31. There are two types of conditional fee simple: a fee simple subject to a condition precedent and a fee simple subject to a condition subsequent. A condition precedent prevents the fee simple from vesting until the condition has been satisfied. For example, land could be disposed of 'to A in fee simple if he reaches the age of 18'. Since the commencement of the Land and Conveyancing Law Reform Act 2009, such a disposition must take effect under a trust of land as it creates a future interest, sometimes referred to as a 'springing interest'. A fee simple subject to a condition subsequent, for example 'to A in fee simple provided he remains on the roll of solicitors', creates a fee simple which may come to an end prematurely if the condition is satisfied. It does not come to an end automatically; however, and this is one feature which differentiates it from a determinable fee simple. In order to bring the fee simple to an end, the grantor or his successor in title must exercise 'a right of entry'. Section 11(2)(b) of the Land and Conveyancing Act 2009 provides that a fee simple subject to a right of entry is deemed to be a fee simple in possession and so it does not give rise to a trust of land. As is the case with a determinable fee simple, the owner of such a conditional fee simple can dispose of the legal estate.

III. The Distinction Between a Determinable Fee Simple and a Fee Simple Subject to a Condition Subsequent

32. It is sometimes difficult to distinguish a fee simple subject to a condition subsequent from a determinable fee simple. To create a determinable fee simple, it is advisable to use words which suggest a natural continuation up to a point, for example, 'while', 'during', 'as long as' or 'until'. Words which suggest an artificial interruption or cutting short of an interest, for example 'provided that', 'on condition that' or 'but if' are generally used to indicate a fee simple subject to a condition subsequent. Although the terminology suggests a very fine distinction, the consequences of creating one interest rather than the other can be serious.

33. In a determinable fee simple, the words describing the determining event are deemed to be part of the words of limitation, as they have the power to delimit the duration of the estate. This is why the estate comes to an end automatically on the occurrence of the event, with the effect that ownership automatically reverts to the grantor. In the case of a fee simple subject to a condition subsequent, the terms of the condition are deemed to be independent of the words of limitation. Therefore, the grantor or his successor in title has to exercise a right of entry before the estate comes to an end.

34. The distinction may be extremely significant in the event that the courts deem a condition or determining event to be void on the basis that it is contrary to law or public policy. It would be deemed to be contrary to law if it was repugnant to the estate granted (which is commonly the case with restraints on alienation[67]) or it was framed in too uncertain a manner. As we shall be demonstrated below,[68] public policy as a basis for invalidity is a more nebulous concept. If the court declares the condition or determining event invalid, the consequences are much more serious if the fee simple is classified as a determinable fee simple rather than a fee simple subject to a condition subsequent. In the case of a determinable fee simple, if the determining event is void, as it was part of the words of limitation, the whole grant is ineffective. In contrast, if the condition is void it is independent of the estate and can be severed from it to allow the grantee to take a fee simple absolute. As a result, the courts have been more reluctant to declare determining events invalid. The approach taken to restraints on marriage best illustrates this point.

IV. Restraints on Marriage

35. Wills which seek to impose marriage restrictions on a devisee of a fee simple are a common source of litigation.[69] Such restraints represent a clash between the testator's freedom of testation and the devisee's freedom to marry. A condition subsequent which imposes a total restraint on marriage would be considered to be contrary to public policy and therefore severed from the grant, so that the devisee takes a fee simple absolute. However, where such a restraint is phrased as a determinable fee simple, the determining event may be upheld as valid on the basis that its purpose was not to restrain the devisee from marrying but to provide for him for a certain length of time.[70] This more lenient approach is clearly based on the fact that if the court regards the determining event as void, the grant will be completely ineffective.

36. The validity or otherwise of a partial restriction on marriage is not as easy to predict. The court will have to decide whether the particular restraint is so restrictive

67. *See* para. 39 below.
68. *See* paras 35–39 below.
69. *See* Wylie, *Irish Land Law*, 5th edn (Dublin: Bloomsbury Professional, 2013), para. 4.54.
70. *Re Robson* [1940] IR Jur Rep 72; *Re King's Estate* (1892) 29 LR Ir 401.

that, in practical terms, it amounts to an absolute restraint, contrary to public policy.[71] Conditions designed to prevent a devisee from marrying a person of a particular religion have traditionally been upheld.[72] However, it is arguable that such a partial restraint may also be struck down as unconstitutional on the basis that it infringes the right to marry.[73]

V. Restraints on Religion

37. A condition which provides for the forfeiture of a gift if a person ceases 'to practice' a particular religion may be declared void on the basis that it is too uncertain.[74] In *Re Doyle*,[75] the devisee was required to be a Roman Catholic at the testator's death and to give an undertaking to her priest that she would remain one. The condition was held to be void on the basis that it was impossible to perform and also contrary to Article 44.1 of the Constitution which protects freedom of religion. In *Re Blake*,[76] the gift was conditional on the children being brought up in the Roman Catholic faith. The court held that the condition was void as it infringed the right of a parent to provide for the education of their children, protected by Article 42 of the Constitution.

38. Both *Re Doyle* and *Re Blake* are positive indications that Irish judges may be prepared to strike down restraints on marriage or religion in the future on the basis that they are unconstitutional. However, it would be unwise to be too dogmatic in this respect as some uncertainty exists over whether private breaches of constitutional rights, by individuals as opposed to State action, can be challenged. The same debate has arisen in relation to the European Convention on Human Rights which was recently incorporated into English law.[77] It may be possible to apply the approach adopted in the United States which renders discriminatory restrictions legal but unenforceable through the courts.[78] Alternatively, it could be argued that such restraints should be declared invalid on the basis that they are contrary to modern Irish public policy as reflected by the rights and freedoms protected by the Constitution.

VI. Restraints on Alienation

39. Since Quia Emptores, it has been a policy of our land law that the fee simple must be freely alienable. Although Quia Emptores was repealed by section 8 of the

---

71. *Keily v. Monck* (1795) 3 Ridge PC 205.
72. *Duggan v. Kelly* (1847) 10 Ir Eq R 295; *Re McKenna* [1947] IR 277.
73. The right to marry is protected as an unenumerated right by Art. 40.3 of the Constitution of Ireland, 1937, *see Murray v. Ireland* [1985] IR 532.
74. *Re Burke's Estate* [1951] IR 216.
75. Unreported, HC, 1972.
76. [1955] IR 89.
77. Human Rights Act 1998. *See* Grattan, 'Perpetuating Prejudice from Beyond the Grave: Testamentary Conditions in Restraint of Religion', in *Modern Studies in Property Law – Volume 1*, ed. Cooke (Oxford: Hart Publishing, 2001).
78. *Shelley v. Kraemer* (1948) 334 US 1.

Land and Conveyancing Law Reform Act 2009, section 9(2) clarifies that a fee simple remains freely alienable. Testators have, however, continued to attempt to restrict the powers of alienation of their successors in title. The courts have developed two distinct approaches to such restrictions. The first approach is based on the doctrine of repugnancy and has considerable support in Ireland. Under the doctrine of repugnancy, as freedom of alienation is an essential attribute of a fee simple estate, any total or partial restraint on alienation is void as it is repugnant to the nature of the fee simple granted.[79] The courts have, on occasion, considered the restriction from a public policy point of view which traditionally facilitated a more flexible approach, whereby conditions that did not wholly or substantially fetter the owner's capacity to dispose of his land were upheld.[80] However, in *Re Dunne's Estate*,[81] a more unusual take on the public policy approach was adopted by O'Hanlon J. The testator left his property to a couple subject to a condition that it should not 'be sold or otherwise conveyed or transferred by them or either of them, their successors or assigns, to any member of the Meredith families of O'Moore's Forest, Mountmellick'. O'Hanlon J held that the condition was void[82] as it was contrary to public policy in that it tended 'to perpetuate old family resentments and antagonisms'.[83]

§3. The Fee Tail

40. The fee tail was created by the Statute De Donis Conditionalibus 1285 in response to the demands of landowners for an estate which would be retained within the family and could not be sold by their descendants. The fee tail, like the fee simple, was an estate of inheritance, but succession under a fee tail was confined to the direct descendants of the original holder of the estate known as 'the tenant in tail'. The descendants were identified by the ancient heirship rules of primogeniture, which favoured the eldest son, although in the absence of a son, daughters could inherit as co-owners.[84] The fee tail frequently formed part of a strict settlement which settled the land on the current owner for life, remainder to the owner's eldest son in fee tail. The tenant in tail could not leave the land to someone else by will and if the holder of a fee tail attempted to sell the land, the purchaser would only acquire a life estate to

79. *Byrne v. Byrne* (1953) 87 ILTR 183; *Re McDonnell* [1965] IR 354.
80. *Re Macleay* (1875) LR 20 Eq 186; *Re Brown* [1954] Ch 39.
81. [1988] 1 IR 155.
82. The condition was also held to be void for uncertainty; the judge said that it would be difficult to pinpoint when a descendant of the present families could be regarded as no longer falling within the category.
83. Coughlan, in his article, 'Restraint on the Alienation of Fee Simples – A Repugnant Policy?', *Dublin University Law Journal* 12 (1990): 147 submits that O'Hanlon J should have decided this case using the doctrine of repugnancy which precludes partial restraints on alienation. He maintains that conditions which purport to qualify an essential attribute of an estate should be decided strictly on the basis of the doctrine of repugnancy, whereas conditions which qualify personal rights, such as the right to marry or practice a particular religion, should be considered in light of public policy.
84. It was also possible to create a fee tail special which would further restrict the class of descendants, so that only male heirs or the descendants of a tenant in tail by a particular spouse could inherit.

last the lifetime of the vendor. On the vendor's death, the descendants of the vendor would inherit. Land subject to a fee tail was, therefore, a less valuable commodity and conveyancers began to devise methods of allowing landowners to sell their entailed land as a fee simple, in a process known as 'barring the entail'.

41. In the fifteenth century, through fictitious court proceedings known as 'fines' and 'recoveries', a tenant in tail was enabled to transfer an estate known as a 'base fee' to the purchaser, which would last as long as the fee tail would have lasted (i.e., as long as there were direct descendants of the original holder of the estate living). If the tenant in tail was in possession (i.e., if the life tenant under the strict settlement was dead) or if he had the consent of the life tenant in possession, he could go further and actually transfer a fee simple to the purchaser, which meant that the rights of the fee simple reversioner or remainderman were also barred. Fines and recoveries were abolished by the Fines and Recoveries (Ireland) Act 1834 which introduced a new conveyancing device known as the 'disentailing assurance' to achieve the same effect. By executing a disentailing assurance, with the consent of the protector of the settlement (typically, the life tenant in possession) or after his death, and enrolling the deed in the High Court within six months of its execution, a tenant in tail could confer the fee simple on the purchaser. If the consent of the protector of the settlement was not forthcoming, or the deed was not enrolled, the purchaser would receive a base fee instead.[85] The fee tail has been unpopular for many years for tax reasons[86] and it has been suggested that the estate may be unconstitutional due to the manner in which it discriminates on the basis of gender.[87] The Law Reform Commission recently described the estate as an anachronism which should be consigned to history.[88] Section 13(1) of the Land and Conveyancing Law Reform Act 2009 prohibits the creation of new fee tails. Any attempt to do so will instead vest a fee simple estate in the grantee. Section 13(3) automatically converts any existing fee tails and base fees into fee simples, provided the protectorship has ended.[89] There is no longer any need to execute a disentailing assurance and the Fines and Recoveries Act (Ireland) Act 1834 has been repealed.[90]

§4. The Life Estate

42. The life estate is an estate which lasts only for someone's life. The life in question may be that of the grantee or it may be the life of someone else, which is

85. Such a base fee could, however, be converted into a fee simple in a number of ways, *see* Wylie, *Irish Land Law,* 5th edn (Dublin: Bloomsbury Professional, 2013), paras 4.142–4.144.

86. *See* Law Reform Commission, *Consultation Paper on Reform and Modernization of Land Law and Conveyancing Law* (LRC CP 34–2004), para. 2.28, n. 85 (referring to Capital Gains Tax liability).

87. *See* Lyall, *Land Law in Ireland,* 3rd edn (Dublin: Roundhall, 2010), 248–249.

88. *See* Law Reform Commission, *Consultation Paper on Reform and Modernization of Land Law and Conveyancing Law* (LRC CP 34–2004), para. 2.28.

89. This condition was inserted in order to avoid any constitutional difficulties, *see* Mee, 'The Fee Tail: Putting Us Out of Its Misery', *Conveyancing and Property Law Journal* 10, no. 1 (2005): 4.

90. Land and Conveyancing Law Reform Act 2009, s. 8.

referred to as a life estate *pur autre vie*. Since the commencement of the Land and Conveyancing Law Reform Act 2009, a life estate can only exist as an equitable interest behind a trust of land.[91] To protect those entitled to equitable future interests in the land, the life tenant is subject to limitations on the use he may make of the land, known as the rules of waste. Section 18(4) of the 2009 Act provides that the conversion of the life estate into an equitable interest does not affect the holder's liability for waste. A reversioner or a remainderman may be able to apply to the court for an injunction to restrain wastes being committed or to claim damages if he has suffered loss as a result of the waste. A life tenant will not usually be liable for permissive waste (an injury to the land caused by inaction, such as a failure to keep a building in good repair) unless the terms of the grant specify that he is impeachable for waste;[92] this is rarely the case. However, a tenant for life will be liable for voluntary waste (an injury to the land caused by a positive act, for example, the removal of earth from the land[93]) unless the terms of the grant specify that he is unimpeachable for waste. However, even the existence of such an exemption, will not allow a life tenant to commit equitable waste or wanton acts of destruction.[94]

§5. Fee Farm Grants

43. A Fee Farm Grant is a conveyance of a fee simple subject to payment of a perpetual rent by the grantee and his successors in title to the grantor and his successors in title.

I. Feudal Fee Farm Grants

44. As has already been mentioned, certain fee farm grants creating a feudal relationship between the grantor and the grantee were created in Ireland during the seventeenth century in derogation of Quia Emptores 1290.[95] If any of these survive in modern times they are more likely to be found in urban areas. They have been expressly preserved by the Land and Conveyancing Law Reform Act 2009 which abolished the notion of feudal tenure.[96] The most common fee farm grant to be found in Ireland is one creating a leasehold relationship between the grantor and the grantee and its prevalence has been described as a peculiarly Irish phenomenon.[97] There are two types of leasehold fee farm grant: Conversion Grants and Deasy's Act Grants.

91. Land and Conveyancing Law Reform Act 2009, ss 11(1) and 11(6) and 18.
92. *Re Cartwright* (1889) 41 Ch D 532.
93. *Shaftesbury v. Wallace* [1897] 1 IR 381.
94. Since *Doherty v. Allman* (1873) 3 AC 709, it is clear that the courts will not grant an injunction to prevent ameliorating waste (an action which benefits or improves the property). Such activity is instead regulated by planning and environmental legislation.
95. *See* para. 18 above.
96. Land and Conveyancing Law Reform Act 2009, ss 9(2) and 9(3)(c).
97. *See* Wylie, *Irish Land Law,* 5th edn (Dublin: Bloomsbury Professional, 2013), para. 4.58. In some parts of England, a fee farm grant which creates a perpetual rent charge is quite common.

II. Conversion Fee Farm Grants

45. These fee farm grants came about through legislation designed to avoid the need for perpetually renewable leases for lives or leases for years. During the eighteenth and nineteenth centuries, it became common[98] for large landowners to grant leases for lives renewable forever. Typically, the term would last for the lives of three named persons but when necessary and on payment of a fine to the landlord, a new life could be nominated. During the nineteenth century, it was estimated that up to one-seventh of the land in Ireland was subject to this arrangement.[99] During the same period, it was also common to find clauses in leases which provided that when the term of years expired, the lessee on payment of a fine, would be entitled to the grant of another term of years. These renewable leases for years were often designed to get around statutory limits on the duration of leases which certain institutions, such as the Church of Ireland and Trinity College Dublin, could grant.

46. The renewals of such leases involved considerable expense and inconvenience and legislation was introduced to convert them into fee farm grants. The Church Temporalities Act 1833 and the Trinity College Dublin Leasing and Perpetuity Act 1851 gave lessees under renewable leases for years granted by the Church and Trinity College the right to demand a conversion fee farm grant within a certain time frame. However, the main source of conversion fee farm grants is the Renewable Leasehold Conversion Act 1849 which applied to both renewable leases for years and leases for lives. Section 37 of the Renewable Leasehold Conversion Act 1849 provided that where a grant executed after 1 August 1849 purported to create a perpetually renewable lease for years or lives, a fee farm grant would vest in the grantee provided the grantor had the power to convey a fee simple. Lessees under perpetually renewable leases granted prior to the specified date were given the right to demand a fee farm grant from their lessors. The fee farm rent was calculated by reference to the existing rent and the fines which the lessors would have to forgo[100] and the grantor had the same remedies for non-payment of rent which were available to a landlord,[101] such as ejectment for non-payment of rent.[102] Section 1 of the 1849 Act provided that the covenants and conditions which existed under the lease continued to bind the fee farm grantee, except those in relation to renewal. Some initial confusion existed over whether a covenant which restricted the power of alienation of the lessee would continue to bind the fee farm grantee who now held a fee simple. It was eventually clarified that a restraint on alienation would apply to such a conversion fee farm grant, as the doctrine of repugnancy did not apply to this special fee simple arising under a statutory entitlement which expressly provided that the new estate remained subject to the covenants and conditions contained in the original lease.[103]

---

98. They may have become popular as they conferred the grantee with a right to vote in the days when a landlord could expect his tenant to vote for him or his nominee, *see* Wylie, *Ibid.*, para. 4.175.
99. Lyne, *Leases for Leaves Renewable for Ever* (1837), 1.
100. Renewable Leasehold Conversion Act 1849, s. 2.
101. Renewable Leasehold Conversion Act 1849, ss 20 and 21.
102. *See* para. 160 below.
103. *Re Naul's Estate* [1902] 1 IR 114.

47. As very few lessees under renewable leases made before 1849 demanded a fee farm grant under the 1849 Act, section 74 of the Landlord and Tenant (Amendment) Act 1980 set out that a lessee under a lease for lives renewable forever which was not converted into a fee farm grant under the 1849 Act now holds a fee simple. The fee simple is deemed to be a graft on the previous interest and, therefore, it is still subject to the covenants which existed under the lease.[104]

III. Deasy's Act Grants

48. Section 3 of the Landlord and Tenant (Amendment) Act 1860 or Deasy's Act, which specified that it was not necessary to have a fee simple reversion in order to create the relationship of landlord and tenant, made it possible to expressly create leasehold fee farm grants. Where someone transferred a fee simple to another who agreed to pay rent, the relationship of landlord and tenant arose between them and the benefit and burden of covenants contained in the deed would bind successors in title of both parties.[105] As a result, such fee farm grants were commonly used to avoid the rules which prevented positive covenants affecting freehold land being enforceable against successors in title.[106] As shall be discussed in Chapter 5, the rules in relation to freehold covenants have since been made less restrictive,[107] obviating the necessity for such fee farm grants in the future. The Law Reform Commission has also argued that fee farm grants are confusing for the general public who would not associate a fee simple with an obligation to pay rent.[108]

49. Section 12 of the Land and Conveyancing Act 2009 Act prohibits the creation of new fee farm grants and sets out that any instrument purporting to create a fee farm grant shall take effect as a fee simple, freed from any obligation to pay rent, but otherwise subject to the covenants contained in grant which are consistent with a fee simple. This provision seems to imply that restrictions on alienation will no longer be treated as valid. However, existing fee farm grants will remain in force and may be disposed of.[109]

§6. Successive Ownership and Trusts of Land

50. As has already been mentioned, the life estate and the fee tail were frequently used in conjunction to create what was known as a strict settlement over land,[110] a

104. Whether such an interest is still subject to the obligation to pay rent has caused some controversy, *see* Wylie, *Irish Land Law,* 5th edn (Dublin: Bloomsbury Professional, 2013), para. 4.84, cf. Lyall, *Land Law in Ireland,* 3rd edn (Dublin: Roundhall, 2010), 235.
105. *See* para. 147 below.
106. *See* para. 136 below.
107. *See* para. 137 below.
108. *See* Law Reform Commission, *Consultation Paper on Reform and Modernization of Land Law and Conveyancing Law* (LRC CP 34–2004), para. 2.18.
109. Land and Conveyancing Law Reform Act 2009, s. 12(5).
110. *See* para. 40 above.

device which was designed to keep land within the family. If land was settled on the settlor for life, remainder to his eldest son in fee tail, the eldest son could not bar the entail without his father's consent while the father was still living. In order to provide an income for the eldest son when he came of age, the father and the son would co-operate to bar the entail, raise an annuity which would become a charge on the land and re-settle it so that the father and son took successive life estates and a fee tail remainder (known as a 'contingent remainder'[111]) was created in favour of the son's eldest son. Such settlements often made provision for annual or lump sum payments (called jointures and portions) to other members of the family which also became a charge on the land. This process of settlement and resettlement led to the gradual deterioration of the land and the impoverishment of its owners. Over time, the income produced from the land became insufficient to discharge the various payments charged on it. The life tenant was restricted by the rules of waste in relation to the changes he could make to the land and, in any case, it was impossible to raise a loan of money to carry out improvements or repairs as all the life tenant could offer by way of security was a precarious life estate.

51. Parliament intervened with the enactment of legislation which allowed encumbered estates to be sold through the courts[112] and subsequently, the Settled Land Acts 1882–1890,[113] which conferred the life tenant with extensive powers to deal with land subject to a strict settlement, including the right to sell the fee simple.[114] The interests of the future owners under the settlement were 'overreached', which meant that they detached from the land and attached instead to the capital money received by the life tenant. The purchaser therefore received a fee simple freed from the interests under the settlement. The life tenant, in exercising his powers, was required to have regard to the interests of all parties entitled under the settlement[115] and the proceeds of sale had to be paid to the trustees of the settlement or into court,[116] another provision designed to protect those entitled to future interests under the settlement. The Settled Land Acts were criticized on the basis that the powers to deal with the land were too restrictive[117] but also vested too much control in the tenant for life, who was too self-interested to have due regard for the others entitled under the settlement.[118] It has also been argued that the Settled Land Acts should not have been extended to a succession of interests created behind a trust for sale, as this unduly curtailed and complicated the powers of the trustees.[119]

111. *See* para. 55 below.
112. Incumbered Estates (Ireland) Act 1849.
113. Wylie, *Irish Land Law,* 5th edn (Dublin: Bloomsbury Professional, 2013), paras 9.18 et seq.
114. Settled Land Act 1882, s. 3.
115. Settled Land Act 1882, s. 53.
116. Settled Land Act 1882, ss 22 and 46(2).
117. *See* Law Reform Commission, *Consultation Paper on Reform and Modernization of Land Law and Conveyancing Law* (LRC CP 34–2004), para. 4.12.
118. *See Wheelwright v. Walker* (1883) 23 Ch D 752.
119. Settled Land Act 1882, s. 62 as amended by Settled Land Act 1884 ss 6 and 7. *See* Wylie, *Irish Land Law,* 5th edn (Dublin: Bloomsbury Professional, 2013), paras 8.43-8.50.

52. The Law Reform Commission recommended that the Settled Land Acts scheme should be replaced by a new scheme[120] akin to that currently operating in England and Wales.[121] Part 4 of the Land and Conveyancing Law Reform Act 2009 implemented this proposal and imposes a trust of land to facilitate dealings with land which is subject to any succession of interests (i.e., the traditional strict settlement) or any kind of trust[122] (except a charitable trust[123]). It also applies whenever land is vested in a minor.[124] As has already been mentioned, a life estate and any future interests in land can only take effect as equitable estates since the commencement of the 2009 Act. Full power to deal with such land is now vested in trustees, subject only to the duties of a trustee, and any restrictions imposed by legislation, the general law of trusts, the trust instrument or a court order relating to the land.[125] Provided the statutory requirements are met, a sale by the trustees operates to overreach any equitable interests in the land and confer a legal fee simple on the purchaser freed and discharged from such equitable interests, regardless of whether the purchaser had notice of them.[126] Provision is also made for the resolution of disputes between trustees and beneficiaries in relation to the performance of the functions of the trustees and the nature or extent of any beneficial interest in the land. The court may make whatever order it thinks fit in the circumstances of the case, but is directed to have regard to the interests of the beneficiaries as a whole and the purposes which the trust is intended to achieve, the interests of any minor or other beneficiary subject to any incapacity, the interests of any secured creditor of a beneficiary and any other matter the court considers relevant.[127]

§7. Future Interests

53. As we have just seen, from very early on landowners wanted to control who would own their land in the future and how it would pass through successive generations. The courts developed rules to limit the extent to which they could create future interests over their land. The most important of these were the common law remainder rules and the rule against perpetuities.

54. The Land and Conveyancing Law Reform Act 2009 has radically reformed the law in this area in two ways. First, section 15 provides that henceforth, future interests can only take effect in equity behind a trust of land and second, section 16 abolishes the common law remainder rules and the rule against perpetuities. The

120. *See* Law Reform Commission, *Consultation Paper on Reform and Modernization of Land Law and Conveyancing Law* (LRC CP 34–2004), para. 4.13.
121. Trusts of Land and Appointment of Trustees Act 1996.
122. Land and Conveyancing Law Reform Act 2009, ss 18(1) and (2).
123. Land and Conveyancing Law Reform Act 2099, s. 18(9).
124. Land and Conveyancing Law Reform Act 2009, s. 18(1)(c).
125. Land and Conveyancing Law Reform Act 2009, s. 20.
126. Land and Conveyancing Law Reform Act 2009, s. 21.
127. Land and Conveyancing Law Reform Act 2009, 22. Cannon, in her article, 'Life Estates, Leases for Lives and Rights of Residence after the Land and Conveyancing Law Reform Act 2009', *Conveyancing and Property Law Journal* 20, no. 4 (2015): 91 argues that practitioners should now consider the creation of a general right of residence instead of a life estate where the client wishes to gift or bequeath someone a right to possession of the property for their lifetime.

abolition of the rules is retrospective, unless property had already been distributed based on the rules or someone relied to his or her detriment on the application of the rule.[128] Therefore, it will still occasionally be important to understand the rules and such understanding is also necessary to understand the impact of their abolition.

55. As has already been mentioned,[129] a person may have an interest in possession or a future interest in the property. A future interest arises if the enjoyment of the interest in land is postponed to sometime in the future, if that enjoyment is ever going to occur at all. This section is concerned with remainder interests, where the grantor expressly sets out to whom the land will pass in the future and, more particularly, 'contingent remainders', as opposed to remainder interests which are 'vested in interest'. A remainder is vested in interest if the person entitled to the interest can be identified by name and there are no outstanding conditions to be satisfied before that person is entitled to possession, except for the expiry of any prior interests in the land. A remainder is contingent if some condition has to be satisfied before it can be said to be vested or if it is not as yet possible to ascertain who will get the interest (because, perhaps, they have not yet been born).

I. The Common Law Remainder Rules

56. The early common law was concerned that there should be no abeyance of seisin (i.e., no gap in freehold possession). If there was a contingent remainder, it could be difficult to identify who was seized of the land at a given time. This was important for the feudal lords who needed to know who to demand their services from. Therefore, the common law developed four strict rules, known as the common law remainder rules, to regulate contingent remainders. Although the original reason for the creation of these rules is no longer relevant, they were deeply embedded in the law up until recently. The main principle underlying these rules was to ensure that there would always be someone entitled to a freehold estate in possession. The rules were as follows: a remainder is void unless it is supported by a prior freehold estate; a remainder must not cut short a prior freehold estate; there can be no remainder after a fee simple; and a remainder must vest during or immediately on the determination of a prior freehold estate.[130]

57. Note that the remainder rules did not apply to gifts arising out of a will. Also, these were common law rules which only applied to legal remainders. It was possible to avoid the common law remainder rules by conveying land to uses. For example, where a disposition was made 'to A to the use of B when he becomes a solicitor' the common law remainder rules would not apply to the equitable remainder in favour of B. After the Statute of Uses (Ireland) 1634, the use in favour of B would be executed to vest B with a legal remainder.[131] These legal remainders which came about through the Statute of Uses were known as legal executory interests and the common law remainder rules did not apply to them either. Neither did the rules apply

128. Land and Conveyancing Law Reform Act 2009, s. 17.
129. *See* para. 28 above.
130. *See* Wylie, *Irish Land Law,* 5th edn (Dublin: Bloomsbury Professional, 2013), paras 5.12–5.17.
131. *See* para. 10 above.

where a future trust was created, for example, if a disposition was made unto and the use of T on trust for B when he becomes a solicitor.

II. The Rule Against Perpetuities

58. This rule was devised to deal with the wholesale avoidance of the common law remainder rules which was made possible through devising the land by will, the creation of legal executory interests or future trusts. The rule applied to interests created by will, legal executory interests and equitable interests, but all other contingent remainders continued to be governed by the common law remainder rules.

59. The rule laid down limits on the grantor's power to postpone the vesting of the ownership of his property in the future. The main justification for the rule was the reduced marketability of land subject to contingent remainders. The rule stated that any future interest in any property, real or personal, was void from the outset if it *may possibly vest after the perpetuity period has expired.* The perpetuity period consisted of any life or lives in being together with a period of twenty-one years (and any relevant period of gestation). If there was no life in being, the period was simply twenty-one years.

60. The rule did not require the interest to vest *in possession* within the perpetuity period; it was sufficient if it vested *in interest*. It did not matter if the contingency was never satisfied (this was a feature of all contingent remainders), but if there was a possibility that the contingency would be satisfied outside the perpetuity period, the gift was void. Whether there was compliance with the rule against perpetuities was considered at the date the gift took effect. For example, if the gift was created by will you looked at the issue on the date of the death of the testator. The courts strictly applied this rule so that it was generally not possible to wait and see whether the interest might vest within the perpetuity period.[132]

61. The gift had to vest within twenty-one years of the death of the life in being or the death of the last survivor of the lives in being. A life could be implicitly or expressly selected as a relevant life. It was implicitly selected by the terms of the disposition. A person was a relevant life in being if he was alive at the time of the disposition and either he had to satisfy the condition himself or he had an impact on whether the condition or contingency was satisfied. It was also possible to expressly select any group of people who were alive at the time of the gift to be the relevant lives in being,[133] provided it was possible to identify with certainty when the last survivor would die.[134]

62. Even if it was highly improbable that the gift would vest outside the perpetuity period, the slightest possibility would invalidate the gift. In England, this was carried to extremes, with the courts disregarding physical impossibilities in what Professor

132. *See Re Wood* (1894) 3 Ch 381.

133. Royal lives clauses were very popular, *see Re Villar* [1929] 1 Ch 243.

134. *Re Moore* [1901] 1 Ch 936.

Barton Leach called the 'fertile octogenarian' and the 'precocious toddler cases'.[135] Before legislative intervention which introduced certain statutory rebuttable presumptions in relation to fertility,[136] the English courts had refused to regard a woman as incapable of having children, irrespective of how old she may be, or of clear medical evidence of infertility for the purposes of the rule.[137] The Irish courts did not, however, seem inclined to follow the approach taken by the English courts in this regard. In *Exham v. Beamish*,[138] Gavan Duffy J expressed the view, *obiter*, that he would not invalidate such a gift if medical evidence could be submitted demonstrating that such a child could not be born in the ordinary course of nature to the woman mentioned in the disposition.[139]

63. It was possible to save a gift from invalidity under the Rule against Perpetuities by using a saving clause and a number of exceptions to the operation of the rule had evolved.[140] However, in 2000 the Law Reform Commission[141] decided against recommending the more moderate reforms which were made to the operation of the rule in Northern Ireland and in England[142] and instead recommended that the rule be completely abolished. The Report pointed out that the rule tends to disrupt innocent settlements and, as it can easily be avoided by using a saving clause, it simply acts as a trap for the unwary or inexperienced solicitor.[143] The Commission devoted a chapter of the Report to the negative impact the rule could have on certain commercial transactions where future easements and options to purchase are created.[144] Subsequently, the Law Reform Commission also recommended the abolition of the Common Law Remainder Rules,[145] in light of the reforms which would be introduced by the Land and Conveyancing Law Reform Act 2009. Under the 2009 Act, future interests would take place in equity behind a trust of land, which would immediately vest the legal fee simple in possession in trustees, avoiding the abeyance of seisin issues mentioned earlier.[146]

135. *See* Leach, 'Perpetuities in a Nutshell', *Harvard Law Review* 51 (1938): 638; 'Perpetuities in Perspective: Ending the Rule's Reign of Terror', *Harvard Law Review* 65 (1952): 721; 'Perpetuities: Staying the Slaughter of Innocents', *Law Quarterly Review* 58 (1952): 35.
136. Perpetuities and Accumulations Act 1964, s. 2.
137. *Jee v. Audley* (1787) 1 Cox Eq Cas 324; *Re Dawson* (1888) 39 Ch D 155. *See also Re Gaite's Will Trusts* [1949] 1 All ER 459 as an example of a precocious toddler case.
138. [1939] IR 336.
139. Mee comments that although Gavan Duffy J's approach was probably the better one, it may have been undermined by advances in medical science, *see* Mee, 'Land Law – The Rule against Perpetuities Return of the Fertile Octogenarian', *Dublin University Law Journal* 14 (1992): 182.
140. *See* Wylie, *Irish Land Law,* 5th edn (Dublin: Bloomsbury Professional, 2013), paras 5.78–5.88.
141. *Report on the Rule Against Perpetuities and Cognate Rules* (LRC 62–2000).
142. The Perpetuities Act (NI) 1966; (English) Perpetuities and Accumulations Act 1964; (English) Perpetuities and Accumulations Act 2009.
143. *Report on the Rule Against Perpetuities and Cognate Rules* (LRC 62–2000), Ch. 4.
144. *Report on the Rule Against Perpetuities and Cognate Rules* (LRC 62–2000), Ch. 3.
145. *Consultation Paper on Reform and Modernization of Land Law and Conveyancing Law* (LRC CP 34–2004), paras 3.02–3.03.
146. *See* para. 56 above.

Chapter 2. Co-ownership

§1. Types of Co-ownership

64. Having discussed the Irish law governing successive and future ownership, it is necessary to discuss the rules governing co-ownership; that is where two or more owners are simultaneously entitled to possession of the land. In keeping with the common law tradition of property law, two types of co-ownership prevail in Ireland in modern times: the joint tenancy and the tenancy in common. Two other types of co-ownership, the tenancy by entireties and coparceny,[147] have been rendered redundant by changes in the law, although they have not been expressly abolished. The tenancy by entireties was a special type of joint tenancy which applied to married couples and recognized the sole legal personality of the husband. In Ireland, it seems to be generally accepted that the *Married Women's Property Act 1882*, which recognized the legal capacity of married women with respect to property, prevented the creation of any new tenancy by entireties after 1882.[148] The tenancy by entireties still survives in many jurisdictions in the United States.[149] A coparcenary arose under the ancient heirship rules of primogeniture, if no sons and two or more daughters survived the deceased. The daughters collectively constituted the 'heir' and took the land as coparceners. Section 11(1) of the Succession Act 1965 abolished primogeniture as the mode of intestate descent for real property except in so far as these rules would continue to apply to a fee tail estate. Therefore, a coparcenary could only have arisen in the context of a fee tail,[150] which had become a rarity in modern times. Section 13 of the Land and Conveyancing Law Reform Act 2009 has abolished the creation of new fee tails and automatically converts most existing fee tails into fee simples, thereby rendering the existence of coparcenaries in Ireland even more unlikely.

65. The joint tenancy bears a resemblance to the French institution of the *tontine* while the tenancy in common roughly corresponds with ownership *en indivision*.[151] The main distinguishing feature of a joint tenancy is the right of survivorship which means that the co-ownership share of a deceased joint tenant passes automatically to the surviving joint tenant(s). Through this process, one joint tenant may ultimately become the sole owner of the land. In contrast, when a tenant in common dies, the co-ownership share passes into his or her estate and is distributed in accordance with his will or the rules governing intestacies. Another feature associated with the joint tenancy is the presence of the four unities: unity of title (the co-owners acquire their title from the same source); unity of time (title vests in the co-owners at the same time); unity of interest (the interest acquired by each is the same in terms of its nature,

147. Wylie, *Irish Land Law,* 5th edn (Dublin: Bloomsbury Professional, 2013), paras 8.51–8.63.
148. Wylie, *Irish Land Law,* 5th edn (Dublin: Bloomsbury Professional, 2013), para. 8.63.
149. Carrozzo, 'Tenancies in Antiquity: A Transformation of Concurrent Ownership for Modern Relationships', *Marquette Law Review* 85 (2001–2002): 423, 445–446.
150. *See* paras 40–41 above.
151. *See* Dyson, 'Joint Ownership of Land in France', *Solicitors Journal* 133, no. 3 (1989): 68.

extent and duration); and unity of possession (each co-owner is entitled to possession of the entire premises). The only unity which is necessary in the case of a tenancy in common is unity of possession. Tenants in common are said to hold in 'undivided shares'. Each tenant in common holds a distinct share in the property, although the share is undivided in the sense that his share in the land is not subject to physical boundaries. The shares held by tenants in common may be equal or unequal.

§2. Presumptions at Common Law and Equity

66. If a deed fails to specify whether two or more purchasers took the legal and equitable ownership of the property as joint tenants or as tenants in common, it may be necessary to rely on certain legal presumptions to clarify the nature of the co-ownership relationship.[152] To complicate matters, different presumptions may arise at common law and in equity, as the common law favoured the joint tenancy while equity was said to 'lean in favour of a tenancy in common'. The common law presumes a joint tenancy, unless one of the four unities is missing or 'words of severance' are used in the deed. Words of severance are words which suggest that the co-owners were intended to take distinct shares in the property, such as 'in equal shares' or 'to be divided between'. Even if the presumption of a legal joint tenancy applies or if the deed expressly states that the purchasers take as joint tenants, in certain situations, equity presumes that the equitable interest is held by them as tenants in common, for example, if the purchasers contributed to the purchase price in unequal shares[153] or the property was acquired as part of a business arrangement.[154] In such circumstances, the equitable ownership in the property is held by the purchasers in shares proportionate to their contributions to the purchase price and on the death of one co-owner, the legal interest in his or her share will pass under the right of survivorship to the surviving co-owner(s) who are deemed to hold it on trust for the deceased co-owner's estate.

§3. Severance of a Joint Tenancy

67. The severance of a joint tenancy results in its conversion to a tenancy in common and the destruction of the right of survivorship. A formal transaction in relation to the land resulting in the destruction of one or more of the four unities will result in a severance at common law. Until recently, it was possible for one joint tenant to unilaterally effect a severance through the acquisition of an additional interest in the property or the transfer of his or her interest in the land to a third party. In fact, a joint tenant could convert his interest into one held on a tenancy in common by executing a conveyance to a nominal third party to hold to his or her own use. The conveyance

152. *See* Wylie, *Irish Land Law,* 5th edn (Dublin: Bloomsbury Professional, 2013), paras 8.15–8.25.
153. If the purchasers contribute in equal shares, this gives rise to a presumption of a beneficial joint tenancy which can be rebutted by evidence demonstrating that they intended to hold as beneficial tenants in common, *see O'Connell v. Harrison* [1927] IR 330.
154. *McCarthy v. Barry* (1859) 9 Ir Ch R 377.

to uses, when executed by the Statute of Uses (Ireland) 1634,[155] operated to vest the legal interest back in the transferor but as a tenant in common, given the destruction of the unity of title. Section 30(1) of the Land and Conveyancing Law Reform Act 2009, in a somewhat controversial move,[156] has abolished unilateral severance. The Law Reform Commission was of the opinion that where each joint tenant has the chance of ending up as the sole owner through the right of survivorship, it is unfair if he can be deprived of this chance through the unilateral actions of one of the joint tenants.[157] Henceforth, any conveyance (or contract for a conveyance) of land held in a joint tenancy or acquisition of another interest in such land by a joint tenant without the prior written consent of the other joint tenant(s) shall be void, although a court order dispensing with such consent may be obtained if it has been unreasonably withheld.[158] The 2009 Act also provides that the registration of a judgment mortgage against the interests of a joint tenant does not sever the joint tenancy, with the result that the judgment mortgage will be extinguished on the death of the judgment debtor.[159] A joint tenancy may also be severed in equity by mutual agreement or conduct of all the joint tenants which suggests a mutual intention to sever.[160] Recently, it was clarified that the unlawful killing of one joint tenant by another joint tenant effects a severance

---

155. *See* para. 10 above.
156. *See* Mee, 'The Land and Conveyancing Law Reform Bill 2006: Observations on the Law Reform Process and a Critique of Selected Provisions – Part II', *Conveyancing and Property Law Journal* 11, no. 4 (2006): 91; Woods, 'Unilateral Severance of Joint Tenancies – The Case for Abolition', *Conveyancing and Property Law Journal* 12, no. 2 (2007): 47; Conway, 'Leaving Nothing to Chance?: Joint Tenancies, the 'Right' of Survivorship and Unilateral Severance', *Oxford University Commonwealth Law Journal* (2008): 45.
157. *See Consultation Paper on Judgment Mortgages* (LRC CP 30–2004), para. 5.09.
158. Land and Conveyancing Law Reform Act 2009, s. 31(2)(e).
159. Land and Conveyancing Law Reform Act 2009, s. 30(3). This deals with an inconsistency in the pre-existing law: although a severance took place if a judgment mortgage was registered against the interest of one joint tenant over unregistered land, *see Containercare v. Wycherly* [1982] IR 143, the registration of a judgment mortgage against the interest of one joint tenant over registered land did not effect a severance, *see Irwin v. Deasy* [2006] IEHC, [2011] IESC 15; *Judge Mahon v. Lawlor* [2010] IESC 58.
160. Land and Conveyancing Law Reform Act 2009, s. 30(4). Previously, a contract for sale executed by one joint tenant dealing with his or her share of the property would effect a severance in equity. The abolition of unilateral severance is replicated for the law governing a severance in equity.

in equity as a result of the imposition of a constructive trust which requires the offender to hold the victim's share on trust for the victim's estate.[161]

68. Until recently, there was confusion over whether a situation known as 'commorientes' gave rise to a severance of a joint tenancy. This arose where two joint tenants died in circumstances, such as a car crash, where it was unclear if one survived the other. Section 5 of the Succession Act 1965 provides that where two persons have died in circumstances rendering it uncertain which of them survived the other, they shall be deemed to have died simultaneously. However, until recently, section 5 failed to set out the implications of such a simultaneous death if the deceased persons held property as joint tenants. Early case law suggested that in such circumstances, the heirs of the deceased joint tenants took their interests as joint tenants (i.e., there was no survivorship and the joint tenancy continued).[162] Of course, the ancient laws of heirship or primogeniture, which typically identified one heir, have long since been replaced by intestacy rules. These intestacy rules would commonly result in a number of relatives acquiring the interest of the deceased joint tenant, perhaps in unequal shares, through an assent by the personal representative, thereby destroying unity of title and interest. Logically, such circumstances seem, therefore, to give rise to a severance.[163] A recent amendment to section 5 of the Succession Act 1965[164] clarifies that where two or more joint tenants are deemed to have died simultaneously they shall be deemed to have held the property immediately prior to their deaths as tenants in common in equal shares.

§4. TERMINATION OF CO-OWNERSHIP AND DISPUTE RESOLUTION

69. A co-ownership relationship will come to an end if the property becomes vested in only one of the co-owners through the operation of the right of survivorship or if one co-owner buys out the interests of the other co-owners. Alternatively, the

---

161. *See Cawley v. Lillis* [2012] 1 IR 281. In her judgment Laffoy J recommended the introduction of legislation which prescribes the destination of co-owned property in the event of the unlawful killing of one of the co-owners by another co-owner. The Law Reform Commission has since published a *Report on Prevention of Benefit from Homicide* (LRC 114 – 2015) which makes a number of recommendations for legislative clarification of the law in this area. The primary recommendation is for the enactment of legislation providing for a legal and equitable severance where a joint tenant murders, attempts to murder or commits manslaughter of the other joint tenant. Although the victim's estate shall after severance hold at least a half share of the property, it also recommends that there should be judicial discretion to reduce the share that the offender will take as tenant in common if, for example, the offender has benefited from the early discharge of the mortgage or a mortgage protection policy. It also recommends that the court should have discretion to modify or disapply the rule if the death was caused by manslaughter and it was provoked or the offender was suffering from diminished responsibility.

162. *See* Lord Thurlow LC's statement in *Bradshaw v. Toulmin* (1784) Dick 633: 'if two persons, being joint tenants, perish by one blow, the estate will remain in joint tenancy, in their respective heirs'.

163. This argument was eloquently made by Mee in, 'Commorientes, Joint Tenancies and the Law of Succession', *Northern Ireland Legal Quarterly* 56, no. 2 (2005): 171.

164. Civil Law (Miscellaneous Provisions) Act 2008, s. 68.

relationship will be terminated by the partition of the co-owned property between the co-owners so that each becomes the sole owner of a portion of the land. The co-owners may voluntarily enter into a deed of partition. Alternatively, any co-owner or person with an interest in co-owned property may apply for an order for partition or an order for the sale of the land and the distribution of the proceeds of sale pursuant to section 31(2) of the Land and Conveyancing Law Reform Act 2009. This jurisdiction was previously exercised by the courts pursuant to the Partition Acts 1868–1876 which was weighted heavily in favour of the co-owner seeking an order for sale. It remains to be seen how this new jurisdiction will be exercised, as the courts have not been given any guidelines for the purposes of deciding whether such an order should be made.[165] Section 31(2) of the 2009 Act also permits the court to make an order directing that accounting adjustments be made between the co-owners, or any other order which the court considers to be just and equitable in the circumstances of the case.

165. *See* Conway, *Co-Ownership of Land: Partition Actions and Remedies* 2nd edn. (Dublin: Bloomsbury Professional, 2012), paras 7.55–7.59.

Chapter 3. The Transfer of Land

§1. Priorities

70. The recognition of equitable interests in land led to a proliferation of the types of real (or proprietary) interests which a landowner could create over the land and considerably complicated dealings with it. Real interests are interests which are capable of binding future owners of the land, while personal interests only bind the contracting parties. Transactions with different people in relation to the same piece of land may give rise to disputes over which transaction has priority. For example, a person who purchases land by way of a deed of conveyance may be unclear as to whether he is bound by earlier or subsequent transactions entered into by the vendor creating legal or equitable interests in the land. The same piece of land could be subject to a lease,[166] a mortgage,[167] a right of way or a freehold covenant[168] and these rights are capable of existing as legal or equitable interests. In addition, it could be subject to an express trust, a purchase money resulting trust (which confers an equitable interest on a person who contributed to its purchase price), or a constructive trust (if, for example, the vendor executed a contract for sale in favour of a different purchaser).[169] Finally, the existence of a 'mere equity' (i.e., a right to pursue an equitable remedy, such as, to have a deed in relation to the land set aside for undue influence) may also give rise to a priority dispute. In modern times, the resolution of such priority disputes will typically depend on the order of registration of the interests or, if the older interest was not registrable, whether its owner was in actual occupation of the property.

71. Before the introduction of both registration systems in Ireland, priority disputes were resolved by two equitable maxims and the equitable doctrine of notice. The maxims generally ensured that where successive legal or successive equitable interests were created over land, priority was afforded to the earlier transaction[170] and where a legal transaction was followed by the creation of an equitable interest, the legal interest had priority.[171] The superiority of legal interests was also recognized by the fundamental principle governing land transactions: 'legal interests bind the world, while equitable interests bind everyone except the bona fide purchaser for value without notice'. The latter part of this statement is known as the equitable doctrine of notice and means that a purchaser or mortgagee of a legal estate who can prove that they had no actual, constructive or imputed notice of the existence of a pre-existing equitable interest shall take the legal estate free from such an interest. The element of constructive notice deems purchasers and mortgagees to have notice of all equitable interests that they would have discovered if they had made the enquiries and inspections they should

166. *See* Ch. 6 below.
167. *See* Ch. 7 below.
168. *See* Ch. 5 below.
169. *See* Part III below.
170. Where the equities are equal, the first in time prevails.
171. Where the equities are equal, the law prevails.

reasonably have made. In addition, purchasers and mortgagees are imputed with notice of all matters which their solicitors discovered or would have discovered if they had made reasonable enquiries. Traditionally, the doctrine of notice required a purchaser/mortgagee or his solicitor to inspect the title offered and also the land and to make further enquiries if an inconsistency with the title offered was revealed. If anyone, other than the vendor, was in occupation of the land, the doctrine of notice required the purchaser/mortgagee or their solicitor to make enquiries to clarify if the occupier of the property had any interest in the land.[172] One obvious danger was the possibility that the occupier may have contributed to the purchase price of property put in the vendor's sole name giving rise to an equitable interest under a purchase money resulting trust. As was held in *Northern Bank Ltd v. Henry*,[173] a mortgagee who fails to make enquiries, in such circumstances, is fixed with constructive notice of the equitable interest and its mortgage is therefore postponed to the interest of the owner in equity.

§2. THE IMPACT OF THE REGISTRATION OF DEEDS SYSTEM

72. The operation of the maxims and the doctrine of notice made conveyancing risky as the existence of earlier transactions and equitable interests could not always be easily detected. The introduction of the registration of deeds system by the Registration of Deeds Act (Ireland) 1707 helped to reduce this risk. Part 3 of the Registration of Deeds and Title Act 2006 replaced the archaic procedures set out in the 1707 Act and a deed may now be registered by lodging an application containing certain essential details in relation to the deed with the Property Registration Authority. Registration is not compulsory but registered deeds are assigned a serial number and, as per section 38(1) of the 2006 Act, the priority of deeds or other documents is determined by the serial numbers assigned. It does not matter which deed was executed earlier or whether it created a legal or an equitable interest, as priority is governed by the order of registration. An unregistered deed is void as against a registered deed.[174] The Registry of Deeds also operates a search facility to identify earlier registered transactions in relation to land. Therefore, before completing a transaction, a solicitor acting for a purchaser can identify the interests which will bind his client or, in the worst-case scenario, whether the vendor has already disposed of his interest in the property. After the transaction has been completed, such a solicitor may also, by promptly registering the deed in favour of his client, ensure that any subsequent transactions entered into by the vendor are not afforded priority.

73. The registration of deeds system does not eliminate entirely the old rules which are used to resolve priority disputes as they continue to apply if neither deed was registered. Also, this system of registration is only applicable if both interests were created by a deed or a document. An equitable interest which arose under a purchase money resulting trust would not be registrable and the doctrine of notice continues to apply in such circumstances. Finally, section 38(3) of the Registration of

172. The rule in *Hunt v. Luck* [1901] 1 Ch 45 provided that a tenant's occupation is notice of all that tenant's rights, including an option to purchase the landlord's interest.

173. [1981] IR 1.

174. Registration of Deeds and Title Act 2006, s. 38(2).

Deeds and Title Act 2006 preserves the common law exception that the registration of a deed does not secure priority for a purchaser who had actual knowledge of an earlier unregistered deed at the time of the transaction, or who had such notice imputed to him through the actual notice of his or her agent. This exception is designed to prevent a statute being used as an instrument of fraud.

§3. The Impact of the Registration of Title System

74. If the title to the land is registered in the Land Registry, a purchaser is generally only bound by interests which were registered as burdens affecting the land. Section 69 of the Registration of Title Act 1964 sets out a list of registrable burdens, which includes charges, easements and leases exceeding twenty-one years. The purchaser's solicitor may carry out a Land Registry search to clarify that the vendor is in fact the registered owner of the land and to identify any section 69 burdens. Although a trust cannot be registered as a burden, a beneficiary may protect his or her interest by registering a caution or an inhibition. While the land register is designed to be a mirror of the title, the existence of 'overriding interests' imposes a duty on a purchaser to investigate the land and to make enquiries, akin to that imposed by the doctrine of notice. Such interests bind a purchaser even though they do not appear on the register and the list of such interests set out in section 72(2) of the Registration of Title Act 1964 includes the interest of a lessee under a lease for a term not exceeding twenty-one years where the lessee is in occupation[175] and any interest acquired or in the process of being acquired by adverse possession.[176] Also, if the land is subject to an equitable interest, it will qualify as an overriding interest if the owner of the equitable interest is 'in actual occupation of the land, save where upon enquiry made of such a person the interest is not disclosed'.[177] Therefore, as is the case with unregistered land, a purchaser of registered land will be bound by an equitable interest arising under a purchase money resulting trust if its owner is in actual occupation of the land.[178]

75. Although the doctrine of notice and the existence of overriding interests place quite a heavy burden to make enquiries on those wishing to enter into land transactions, the advantage of the current law is that it extends a degree of protection to the more vulnerable owners of certain interests which arise informally. The original version of section 21 of the Land and Conveyancing Law Reform Bill 2006, if it had been enacted, would have introduced a very radical reform to the law in this area. It aimed to completely eradicate the doctrine of notice to clarify and simplify the position of a purchaser of land subject to a trust of land. A purchaser would not be bound by any equitable interest in land, regardless of whether he had notice of it unless it had been registered in the Registry of Deeds or the Land Registry, as appropriate. The equitable interest would instead be overreached (i.e., it would detach from the land and attach instead to the proceeds of sale). In response to criticisms of the potential

175. Registration of Title Act 1964, s. 72(2)(i).
176. Registration of Title Act 1964, s. 72(2)(p).
177. Registration of Title Act 1964, s. 72(2)(j).
178. *See Williams and Glynn's Bank v. Boland* [1981] AC 487.

impact of such a reform,[179] the overreaching provisions were scaled back so that they now only apply to the trust of land which arises out of a succession of interests or the ownership of a minor.[180] The overreaching provisions shall not apply if the purchaser is dealing with a single trustee or owner of the legal estate and the equitable interest qualifies as an overriding interest under section 72(1)(j) or, in the case of unregistered land, would qualify as such if the land were registered.[181] Therefore, purchasers will continue to be bound by the equitable interests of those in occupation of the land.

76. Finally, the doctrine of notice has, since the enactment of the Family Home Protection Act 1976, played a significant role in transactions which relate to the family home of a married couple and, recently, this protection was extended to the family home of a same-sex couple who have entered into a civil partnership.[182] Section 3 of the 1976 Act provides that any conveyance or mortgage of a family home without the prior consent in writing of the non-owning spouse is void unless it was made in favour of a purchaser for value without notice of the fact that it was a family home. Again, notice includes actual, constructive and imputed notice. This legislation places a heavy onus on the purchaser to make enquiries[183] and has greatly influenced conveyancing practice.[184]

§4. The Conveyancing Transaction

I. General Characteristics

77. The transfer of real property in Ireland is governed by an abstract system. In the case of unregistered land, the transfer of ownership is effected through the execution and delivery of a deed but, in the case of registered land, the purchaser does not become the owner until the deed of transfer is registered in the Land Registry. Although a valid contract for sale is not a prerequisite for the transfer of ownership, most sales are preceded by a contract, which governs the rights and obligations of the parties during the period before completion. A conveyance of a residential property will often culminate in a deed conferring a fee simple on the purchaser, although apartments have to date generally been sold by means of a grant or assignment of a very long lease. Recent changes in the law governing the enforceability of freehold

179. *See* Mee, 'The Land and Conveyancing Law Reform Bill 2006: Observations on the Law Reform Process and a Critique of Selected Provisions – Part 1', *Conveyancing and Property Law Journal* 11, no. 3 (2006): 67, 69–72.
180. *See* para. 52 above.
181. Land and Conveyancing Law Reform Act 2009, s. 21(3)(b)(iii).
182. Civil Partnership and Certain Rights and Obligations of Cohabitants Act 2010, Part 4.
183. *See Somers v. Weir* [1979] IR 94.
184. *See* Wylie & Woods, *Irish Conveyancing Law*, 3rd edn (Dublin: Tottel Publishing, 2005) paras 16.48–16.59.

covenants,[185] coupled with the enactment of the Multi-Unit Development Act 2011,[186] may make freehold apartment ownership schemes (or 'flying freeholds') a more realistic prospect in the future. In contrast, commercial conveyancing relies heavily on the Full Repairing and Insurance Lease. The remainder of this chapter outlines the main steps in a standard residential conveyancing transaction.[187]

II. Pre-contract Stage

78. A person who wishes to sell a house typically engages an estate agent and a solicitor. An interested buyer is usually asked to pay a booking deposit to the vendor's estate agent who instructs the vendor's solicitor to draft the contract for sale. In the meantime, the purchaser goes to his bank to negotiate a mortgage loan and engages a different solicitor to act on his or her behalf. There are ethical difficulties with allowing one solicitor to act for both parties[188] and from 1 January 2013, solicitors are prohibited from acting for both a vendor and a purchaser in a conveyancing transaction except in specified circumstances.[189] Although theoretically the parties are not obliged to engage a solicitor and could act for themselves, the complexity of such transactions and the requirements of lenders make this a very unrealistic prospect.

79. The vendor's solicitor will have to examine the vendor's title before he will be in a position to draft the contract for sale. If the land is registered in the Land Registry, the vendor's solicitor can apply for an up-to-date folio and title plan, but if it is unregistered, he will have to examine the title deeds. If there is a mortgage on the property, the title deeds will be with the bank. In such circumstances, the vendor's solicitor will have to obtain the client's authority to take up the deeds and give an undertaking to the bank that he will not part with the deeds without discharging the outstanding loan affecting the property.

80. The vendor's solicitor invariably uses the Law Society Contract for Sale[190] which includes standard conditions on issues, such as, the timetable for the rest of the transaction, the evidence of title required and the penalties for breaching any of the conditions. Two copies of the contract for sale are sent to the purchaser's solicitor who usually makes a number of pre-contract enquiries. For example, if the house is in the countryside, he will seek to establish whether there is access to a public road and if the services (e.g., a well or septic tank) are within the boundaries of the property. The

185. *See* para. 137 below.

186. This Act addresses certain practical issues which have been the source of much dispute between developers and apartment owners, such as transferring common areas, the completion of developments, the duties of management companies and service charges. The Act specifically sets out a procedure for the resolution of disputes and will apply, not only to new developments completed after the commencement of the Act, but also to existing multi-unit developments.

187. For a more detailed exposition of the law in this area, *see* Wylie & Woods, *Irish Conveyancing Law*, 3rd edn (Dublin: Tottel Publishing, 2005).

188. Law Society of Ireland, *Guide to Professional Conduct of Solicitors in Ireland,* 3rd edn (Dublin: Law Society of Ireland, 2013).

189. Solicitors (Professional Practice, Conduct and Discipline – Conveyancing Conflict of Interest) Regulation 2012 (SI 375/2012).

190. Law Society of Ireland, *General Conditions of Sale* (2017 Edition).

purchaser's solicitor also negotiates the terms of the contract on behalf of his client. If, for example, the purchaser is buying a site in order to build a house, it may be possible to negotiate the insertion of a condition which makes the sale subject to planning permission being obtained. If a second-hand property is being purchased, the purchaser's solicitor will advise his client to engage an engineer or architect to carry out a structural survey of the property, as the basic rule in relation to structural defects is *caveat emptor* or 'let the buyer beware'. The purchaser's solicitor will also find out how his client intends to finance the purchase. If the purchaser is obtaining a loan from his bank, the purchaser's solicitor shall also typically be acting on behalf of the bank and will be required to do the work necessary to complete the mortgage in favour of the bank.

81. Although technically the vendor's duty to prove (or deduce) his title only arises after the contracts have been executed,[191] typically a special condition is included in the contract for sale setting out the title being furnished and copies of certain title documents are sent with the contracts to the purchaser's solicitor. As a result, the purchaser's solicitor usually investigates the vendor's title before the contracts have been executed. As mentioned earlier, this investigation of title is greatly simplified in the case of registered land as the ownership and most burdens affecting the property are revealed by the register. If the vendor's title is unregistered, the purchaser's solicitor's task in investigating the vendor's title is more challenging. The purchaser's solicitor will seek to establish if the vendor has a good and marketable title to the property from the copy title documents sent with the contracts for sale. The purchaser's solicitor usually insists on proof of fifteen years title commencing with a 'good root'. A conveyance for value which adequately identifies the property will be considered a good root. If the contract does not deal with title issues (e.g., if it was drafted without the help of a solicitor), it is described as an 'open contract' and the purchaser is entitled to insist on proof of fifteen years title commencing with a good root under the Land and Conveyancing Law Reform Act 2009.[192]

82. From time to time, a sellers' market will prevail and the possibility of 'gazumping' becomes a concern for purchasers at the pre-contract stage. This danger arises because of the statutory formalities required to create an enforceable contract.[193] Until there is a written contract or at least written evidence of the essential terms of the contract[194] which has been signed by the vendor or his agent, the agreement usually cannot be enforced and the vendor is free to negotiate more favourable terms with another purchaser. Most communications between solicitors at the pre-contract stage are headed 'Subject to Contract/Contract Denied' as otherwise there is a risk that the court could treat the communication as sufficient to satisfy the formalities required. The Law Reform Commission published a report in 1999 investigating proposals to deal with the problem of gazumping.[195] It rejected certain radical proposals, such as

191. *Reeve v. Berridge* (1888) 20 QBD 523, per Fry LJ, 528.
192. Land and Conveyancing Law Reform Act 2009, s. 56 which replaced the requirement for proof of forty years title under the Vendor and Purchaser Act 1874, s. 1.
193. Land and Conveyancing Law Reform Act 2009, s. 56.
194. The written evidence must identify the parties, the price, the premises and any other terms which were considered by the parties to be essential elements of the contract.
195. *Report on Gazumping* (LRC 59–1998).

making 'subject to contract' agreements binding, on the basis that gazumping was a temporary and infrequent phenomenon. Instead, it recommended legislation designed to ensure that purchasers were better informed and which would regulate the payment of booking deposits. The Property Services (Regulation) Act 2011 provides the framework necessary to implement these proposals and an information guide for purchasers is now available.[196] It should be noted that when a buyers' market prevails, the tables are turned and sellers are at risk of 'gazundering', which occurs when a purchaser demands a reduction in price just before the contracts are signed.

83. Once the purchaser signs both copies of the contract, they are sent to the vendor's solicitor with a deposit, usually 10% of the purchase price. The vendor then signs both copies and one copy is returned to the purchaser. In most cases, the deposit is held by the vendor's solicitor and is not released to the vendor until the sale has been completed.

III. Informal Contracts

84. If the parties entered into an oral agreement for the sale of land and there is insufficient written evidence of the agreement to satisfy the statutory formalities, it may still be possible for a purchaser to enforce the contract under the doctrine of part performance.[197] The court may order the vendor to perform the contract (known as an order for 'specific performance') if, for example, the purchaser moved into possession of the property[198] or carried out improvements to it[199] and the vendor encouraged such actions or stood by while they were taking place. Alternatively, the purchaser may be entitled to a remedy under the doctrine of proprietary estoppel[200] if it can be proved that the vendor made a representation that the purchaser would have an interest in the land and the purchaser relied to his detriment on that representation in circumstances where it would be unconscionable for the vendor to insist on the strict legal position.[201]

IV. Post-contract Stage

85. Once both parties have executed the contracts, the next stage of the conveyancing process begins. The purchaser's solicitor makes certain standard enquiries about the property, known as 'requisitions on title'. These requisitions are designed to elicit information on practical and title matters in relation to the property such as: whether all developments on the property were carried out in compliance with planning

---

196. *See A Guide for Users of Property Services Providers in Ireland* (Property Services Regulatory Authority, 2016), in particular, Part III.
197. Wylie & Woods, *Irish Conveyancing Law*, 3rd edn (Dublin: Tottel Publishing, 2005), paras 6.48–6.60.
198. *Callaghan v. Pepper* (1840) 2 Ir Eq R 399 per Pennefather B, 401.
199. *Re Sullivan's Estate* (1889) 23 LR Ir 255 per Monroe J, 256.
200. Biehler, *Equity and the Law of Trusts in Ireland*, 6th edn (Dublin: Roundhall, 2016), Ch. 18.
201. *See Courtney v. McCarthy* [2007] IESC 58; *An Cumann Peile Boitheimach Teoranta (Bohemians Football Club) v. Albion Properties Ltd & Others* [2008] IEHC 447.

and building regulations; whether there is any litigation pending in relation to the property; whether the property is a family home;[202] whether someone other than the vendor made a financial contribution to its purchase or acquired an interest in the property by an agreement or arrangement; whether the property is let; whether any tax incentives apply, and so on. It also allows the purchaser's solicitor to list the documents which he will require on completion. The purchaser's solicitor is usually responsible for drafting the deed, and it is sent to the vendor's solicitor for approval with the requisitions on title. Once the vendor's solicitor has satisfactorily replied to the requisitions and approved the draft deed, the parties are in a position to complete the transaction.

V. Contractual Remedies

86. If one party fails to complete the transaction, the other may be able to get an order for specific performance of the contract. If the purchaser is in default, the vendor may choose instead to forfeit the deposit and resell the property. If a loss is made on the re-sale, it may be recovered from the purchaser. If the vendor refuses to complete, the purchaser may, instead of trying to enforce the contract, seek the return of the deposit and damages for breach of contract.

87. If the purchaser was induced to enter the contract as a result of a misrepresentation or if the contract contains a misdescription, he may be entitled to rescind the contract and recover the deposit or to proceed with the transaction and sue for damages, depending on the nature of the misrepresentation or misdescription.

88. The Law Society Contract for Sale includes specific provisions dealing with the consequence of a delay in completing the transaction. For example, a delaying purchaser is liable to pay interest on the balance purchase price from the closing date. Also, if a completion notice has been served requiring the delaying party to complete within twenty-eight days and the notice has expired, the other party may be entitled to treat the contract as rescinded and to forfeit or seek recovery of the deposit, as appropriate.

VI. Completion of the Sale

89. If the purchase is being financed by a mortgage, the purchaser's solicitor arranges for the loan cheque to be sent by the bank in time for completion. He also carries out certain title searches in the Land Registry or the Registry of Deeds to ensure that the vendor has not engaged in any undisclosed recent transactions which could have priority over the transaction in favour of his or her client.[203] The vendor's solicitor is required to satisfactorily explain any transactions which are revealed by these searches. The completion of the transaction or 'closing' typically occurs in the vendor's

202. *See* para. 76 above.

203. *See* paras 72 and 74 above. The purchaser's solicitor also carries out a bankruptcy office and a judgments office search, *see* Wylie & Woods, *Irish Conveyancing Law*, 3rd edn (Dublin: Tottel Publishing, 2005), paras 15.39–15.48.

solicitor's office. The closing documents and the keys to the property are exchanged for a bank draft for the balance purchase price. If there is an existing mortgage on the property, the vendor's solicitor gives an undertaking to the purchaser's solicitor to discharge it out of the sales proceeds.

VII. Post-completion Stage

90. The purchaser's solicitor arranges for stamp duty to be paid on the deed and then for the deed to be registered in the Registry of Deeds or the Land Registry, as appropriate. Recently, the requirement to apply for first registration of unregistered land following a sale was extended to the entire country.[204] If the purchase was financed by a mortgage, once registration has taken place, the solicitor will forward the title documents to the lender together with a 'certificate of title', whereby the solicitor certifies that the borrower has acquired a good marketable title to the property.

VIII. The Impact of eConveyancing Proposals

91. The introduction of eConveyancing in Ireland is likely to dramatically alter the steps and procedures to be followed in conveyancing transactions in relation to registered land. The Law Society of Ireland's eConveyancing Task Force suggests that it could reduce the time taken to complete a residential conveyancing transaction to only 5 days and it argues that the introduction of an eConveyancing system should be coupled with an overhaul of the entire conveyancing process.[205] In its *'eVision'*, the Task Force proposes the removal of certain administrative burdens on solicitors unrelated to the transfer of title, the replacement of the principle of caveat emptor by a principle of vendor disclosure and the abolition of overriding interests. It envisages that information would be viewed, data would be exchanged and communications would take place between solicitors, lenders and the Property Registration Authority through a central electronic 'hub' or work area. A typical residential sale would only require the execution of an eContract by digital signature and completion would involve the simultaneous electronic transfer of funds and a direction to the Property Registration Authority to register the purchaser as owner. The registration of an eDeed or eLease would only be necessary where the transaction required the creation of new easements or covenants. It is anticipated that this project shall shortly enter an implementation phase.

---

204. *See* para. 25 above.

205. Law Society of Ireland, *eConveyancing: Back to Basic Principles; Vision of an Electronic System of Conveyancing ('eVision')*, March 2008, available at <https://www.lawsociety.ie/Documents/Media/eVision.pdf> accessed 28 Feb. 2017.

Chapter 4. The Acquisition of Title and Other Interests Through the Passage of Time

§1. ADVERSE POSSESSION

I. The Limitation Period

92. A person who enters into possession of land without the consent of the owner is a trespasser and may be evicted by the owner. However, eventually, through the passage of time, that trespasser may succeed in extinguishing the title of the owner and acquiring title by adverse possession. The statutory provisions which govern the law on adverse possession are set out in the Statute of Limitations Act 1957. Section 13 of the 1957 Act provides that an action to recover land must be brought by the owner within the requisite limitation period, which is usually twelve years, although if a State authority is seeking to recover land or part of the foreshore, a limitation period of thirty or sixty years is applicable. In circumstances of fraud[206] or a legal disability on the part of the owner,[207] the limitation period may be extended. On the expiry of the limitation period, section 24 of the 1957 Act provides that the title of owner is extinguished.

II. Human Rights Concerns and Justifications

93. The loss of title through adverse possession may seem harsh from the owner's perspective, and the doctrine appears to reward the wrongful behaviour of the adverse possessor (sometimes referred to as the squatter). It is unsurprising, therefore, that the doctrine occasionally sparks controversy. However, the Grand Chamber of the European Court of Human Rights recently ruled in *JA Pye (Oxford) Ltd v. United Kingdom*[208] that the English law on adverse possession (as it applied to registered land before recent reforms were enacted by the Land Registration Act 2002) was compatible with the European Convention on Human Rights. Overruling the Chamber decision, the Grand Chamber declared that there was no infringement of the right to property of the owner as protected by Article 1 of the First Protocol to the Convention.[209]

94. A number of justifications are traditionally given for the existence of the doctrine. As is the case with all statutes of limitation, the doctrine is designed to protect

---

206. Statute of Limitations 1957, s. 71.
207. Statute of Limitations 1957, ss 48–49.
208. (2007) 46 EHRR 1083.
209. The similarities between the English law and the Irish law on adverse possession had prompted the Irish Government to make a third-party submission to the Grand Chamber outlining the various public interests served by the doctrine in Ireland.

defendants from stale claims[210] and it encourages plaintiffs not to sleep on their rights. The doctrine is also justified on the basis that it brings abandoned land back onto the market and rewards the person who puts it to productive use. One of the strongest justifications for the doctrine is the role it plays in 'quieting'[211] or clarifying men's titles. It may not be possible to resolve the problems created by a defect in a deed which forms part of the chain of title proffered by a vendor and, in such circumstances, the doctrine provides a degree of reassurance to a purchaser that any adverse rights have probably been barred.[212] The doctrine, therefore, facilitates the functioning of the unregistered conveyancing system. In the case of registered land, the doctrine may play a role in regularizing informal transactions in relation to the land.[213] It may also be used to resolve boundary disputes.[214] Finally, in Ireland, the doctrine has frequently been used to regularize the ownership of land forming part of unadministered intestate estates. In the past, a grant of representation was rarely taken out if the owner of a small farm died intestate. Instead, one child remained in possession of the farm and the other children, who were entitled to shares on intestacy as co-owners, went to live elsewhere. The child in possession eventually acquired title through adverse possession and could update the land register accordingly.[215]

95. In a report published in 2005,[216] the Irish Law Reform Commission noted that the doctrine of adverse possession had become the subject of increasing controversy. It referred to doubts which had been expressed by English courts at different levels, before the ruling of the European Court of Human Rights in the *Pye* case, about the compatibility of the doctrine of adverse possession with the European Convention on Human Rights. The Commission argued:

> It must be recognized that on occasion the doctrine may operate unfairly, especially where it appears to enable a person, who deliberately sets out to take advantage of it, to use it as a means of obtaining ownership of someone else's land without paying any compensation. The same applies where it appears to exact a very severe penalty on a landowner (the loss of the land) through a mere oversight or mistake.[217]

---

210. *Dundee Harbour Trustees v. Dougall* (1852) 1 Macq 317, 321.
211. *See* Ballantine, 'Title by Adverse Possession', *Harvard Law Review* 32 (1918): 135.
212. For a discussion of the role played by adverse possession and other remedies in curing title defects *see* Woods, 'Adverse Possession, Unregistered Land and Title Defects: A Fly in the Ointment of Irish Reform' in *Modern Studies in Property Law: Volume 9* ed. Conway and Hickey (Oxford: Hart Publishing, forthcoming 2017).
213. *See* Woods, 'Adverse Possession and Informal Purchasers'. *Northern Ireland Legal Quarterly* 60 no. 3 (2009): 305.
214. *See* Woods, 'Adverse Possession and Boundary Disputes: Lessons for Ireland from Abroad'. *International Journal of Law in the Built Environment*, 8 no. 1 (2016): 56.
215. *See Gleeson v. Feehan* [1993] 2 IR 113. For a discussion of whether this justification for the doctrine continues to be relevant and achieves a fair result, *see* Woods, 'Adverse Possession and Unadministered Estates: An Unfair Solution to a Redundant Irish Problem', *Northern Ireland Legal Quarterly* 67 no. 2 (2016): 137.
216. *Report on Reform and Modernization of Land Law and Conveyancing Law* (LRC 74–2005).
217. *Ibid.*, para. 2.06.

The Commission included a number of provisions[218] in the draft Land and Conveyancing Law Reform Bill set out in its report which were clearly intended to confer added protection on the owner and to hone the operation of the doctrine so that it would continue to apply only where necessary to restore the marketability of abandoned land, to clarify title or in circumstances where reliance on the doctrine was perceived as fair. The proposals were jettisoned in response to critical submissions made to the government by the Law Society's Conveyancing Committee, mostly related to the workability of the proposed scheme and its prematurity, given that the Grand Chamber had yet to deliver its ruling in the *Pye* case. The Land and Conveyancing Law Reform Bill 2006 was published, and in turn the 2009 Act was enacted, without the inclusion of any reforms dealing with the law on adverse possession. Although the Grand Chamber ruling in *Pye* eliminates the possibility that the Convention will act as a catalyst for change in the immediate future, the law on adverse possession and more particularly the doctrine's potential to operate unfairly may be given further consideration in a future Law Reform Commission publication.[219] Recently, in *Dunne v Irish Rail*[220] Laffoy J commented that the doctrine of adverse possession remains controversial and stated: 'There would seem to be a need for a review of the recommendations made by the Law Reform Commission in 1989, 2002 and 2005 with a view to bringing clarity to the law in this area.'

III. Proving Adverse Possession

96. The owner of the land must have been dispossessed or discontinued possession[221] and someone else must be able to prove adverse possession for the limitation period.[222] The acts of possession of the person claiming adverse possession must be exclusive, non-consensual,[223] strong and unequivocal.[224] If the owner continues

218. *Ibid.*, draft Land and Conveyancing Law Reform Bill, ss 29–30.
219. Over the last few decades, concerns have been expressed in law reform circles across the common law world in relation to the fairness of the doctrine of adverse possession. The principal concerns relate the doctrine's failure to confer adequate protection on owners against the danger of inadvertently losing title by adverse possession and the extent to which it permits squatters who know they do not own the land (deliberate or 'bad faith' squatters) to acquire title. In England and Wales, the reforms introduced by the Land Registration Act 2002 purported to address both concerns. Additional protection is conferred on the registered owner who may veto an adverse possession application. However, the qualifications to the veto system preserve the operation of the doctrine for certain adverse possessors (for example, a good faith adverse possessor of boundary land) in the interest of fairness.
220. [2016] IESC 47, para. [23].
221. Statute of Limitations, s. 14.
222. Statute of Limitations s. 18.
223. *Bellew v. Bellew* [1982] IR 447.
224. *See Doyle v. O'Neill* [1995] IEHC 4.

to engage in acts of possession in relation to the land[225] or if the squatter is only engaged in occasional or temporary acts of user,[226] the claim will be defeated. The adverse possessor must also be able to demonstrate *animus possidendi* (i.e., an intention to possess the land and to exclude the true owner and all others from it). This mental element will typically be proved by examining the statements[227] and actions of the adverse possessor (such as erecting gates or fences). It is generally accepted that an adverse possessor who believes he owns the land can satisfy the requirement for *animus possidendi*.[228] The periods of possession of successive adverse possessors may be added together to make up the limitation period.[229] However, the limitation period will stop running if the owner recovers possession or commences legal proceedings[230] or if the adverse possessor abandons the property or makes a written and signed acknowledgement of the owner's title to the owner or his agent.[231]

97. Although there are conflicting High Court authorities on this issue,[232] most, recent *obiter* judicial commentary suggests that the doctrine in *Leigh v. Jack*[233] no longer applies in Ireland.[234] This doctrine provided that if the owner had future plans for the land, any possession which was not inconsistent with those future plans could not amount to adverse possession. It would seem safer to assume that adverse possession can take place in such circumstances, unless evidence is adduced that the possessor only intends to use the land on a temporary basis until the owner is in a position to implement those plans.

225. *See Browne v. Fahy* (HC) 24 Oct. 1975; *Mulhern v. Brady* [2001] IEHC 23 *Kelleher v. Botany Weaving Mills Ltd* [2008] IEHC 417. In a more controversial case, *Feehan v. Leamy* [2000] IEHC 118 it was held that the owner continued to engage in acts of possession by looking over the hedge or gate onto his land, *see* Woods, 'The Position of the Owner under the Irish Law on Adverse Possession', *Dublin University Law Journal* 30 (2008): 298. *See also Dunne v Irish Rail* [2007] IEHC 314 and *Dooley v Flaherty* [2014] IEHC 528, critiqued by Mee in 'A minimal approach to adverse possession', *The Conveyancer and Property Lawyer* 79 no. 5 (2015): 455.
226. *See Doyle v. O'Neill* [1995] IEHC 4.
227. In *Feehan v. Leamy* [2000] IEHC 118 the requirement was not proved where the defendant notified the gardaí that the land belonged to someone living in America.
228. *See Murphy v. Murphy* [1980] IR 183; cf. *Kelleher v. Botany Weaving Mills Ltd* [2008] IEHC 417.
229. *Mount Carmel Investments Ltd v. Peter Thurlow Ltd* [1988] 3 All ER 129.
230. Sending a solicitor's letter threatening legal action will not suffice, *see Mount Carmel Investments Ltd v. Peter Thurlow Ltd* [1988] 3 All ER 129.
231. Statute of Limitations 1957, ss 51 and 58. If the owner sends a letter to the adverse possessor asserting ownership, this will not stop time running against him, *see Mahon v. O'Reilly* [2010] IEHC 103.
232. *See Cork Corporation v. Lynch* [1995] 2 ILRM 598; *Durack (Seamus) Manufacturing Ltd v. Considine* [1987] IR 677.
233. Named after the English case reported at (1879) 5 Ex D 264, 272.
234. *Tracey Enterprises MacAdam Limited v. Drury* [2006] IEHC 381; *Dunne v. Irish Rail* [2007] IEHC 314, paras 4.6–4.7; *Kelleher v. Botany Weaving Mills Ltd* [2008] IEHC 417, para. 16. *See also* Woods, 'The Position of the Owner under the Irish Law on Adverse Possession', *Dublin University Law Journal* 30 (2008): 298.

IV. Adverse Possession Against Future Owners and Lessors

98. Where the current owner is only entitled to a life estate in the land, the limitation period runs against the life tenant and not against the fee simple reversioner or remainderman. Section 15(2)(a) of the Statute of Limitations 1957 provides that the reversioner or remainderman has twelve years from the date the adverse possessor took possession or six years from the date the life estate comes to an end, whichever is longer, in which to bring an action. A life estate and future estates now take place behind a trust of land[235] but this does not change the law on this issue as the same rules in relation to limitation periods apply to equitable estates as apply to legal estates.[236]

99. During the term of a lease, a lessee's possession can rarely be adverse to the title of the lessor. Even if the lessee fails to pay rent, the relationship of landlord and tenant continues to exist and so his possession is not inconsistent with the title of the lessor.[237] The lessor may, however, lose the right to recover some of the rent, as section 28 of the Statute of Limitations Act 1957 provides that no action can be brought to recover arrears of rent after the expiration of six years from the date the arrears became due. However, if the tenant holding under a written lease which reserves an annual rent of at least IEP 1 (i.e., EUR 1.37) pays the rent to a person wrongfully claiming to be the landlord, this is equivalent to adverse possession by the tenant against the landlord.[238] The landlord's title will be barred after twelve years and he will be unable to recover possession from the tenant when the lease expires.

100. Once the term of a lease comes to an end, the possession of the lessee becomes adverse and the lessor's title shall be extinguished unless he brings an action to recover the land within twelve years. Section 17 of the 1957 Act provides that in the case of a periodic tenancy (e.g., from week to week or month to month) where there is no written lease, the tenancy is deemed to determine on the expiry of the first period for which no rent is paid.[239]

V. Adverse Possession Against a Lessee

101. Although section 24 of the Statute of Limitations 1957 provides that on the expiration of the twelve-year limitation period the title of the owner is extinguished, it fails to state what type of title the adverse possessor acquires. This has raised particular complications where adverse possession takes place against the owner of a leasehold interest in the land. Originally, both the Irish and English courts adopted the parliamentary conveyance or assignment theory. In *Rankin v. McMurtry*[240] Holmes J stated:

235. Land and Conveyancing Law Reform Act 2009, s. 11(6).
236. Statute of Limitations 1957, s. 25.
237. *Re Shanahan* (SC) 5 Jul. 1968, per O'Dalaigh CJ.
238. Statute of Limitations 1957, s. 17(3).
239. *See Dooley v Flaherty* [2014] IEHC 528; Mee, 'A minimal approach to adverse possession' *The Conveyancer and Property Lawyer* 79 no. 5 (2015): 455.
240. (1889) 24 LR Ir. 290.

> The estate and interest the right to which is extinguished, so far as the original owner is concerned, became vested in the person whose possession has caused such extinction. The opposite conclusion would seriously affect leasehold tenancies in this country.[241]

As noted by the judge, this theory worked very well in the case of adverse possession of leasehold land as it meant that the adverse possessor acquired the interest of the lessee under the lease. The adverse possessor became liable on the covenants under the lease and the original lessee, who was no longer in possession, was no longer subject to any obligations under the lease. The landlord could collect the rent from the adverse possessor and ensure that the other covenants were complied with until the lease came to an end.

102. The problem with this viewpoint was that it does not sit comfortably with the wording of section 24 of the Statute of Limitations 1957 which states that the title of the owner is extinguished. Surely if the title is extinguished, there is nothing to transfer to the squatter. In England, the decision in *Tichborne v. Weir*[242] marked the end of the parliamentary conveyance theory. Lord Esher MR stated 'the effect of the statute is not that the right of one person is conveyed to another, but that the right is extinguished and destroyed'.[243] In that case, the court held that the adverse possessor could not be sued upon a covenant to repair contained in the lease.

103. This viewpoint was accepted *obiter* by the Irish Court of Appeal in *O'Connor v. Foley*[244] but the issue was more directly dealt with by the Supreme Court in *Perry v. Woodfarm Homes Ltd.*[245] This case concerned a small plot of ground at the back of a house held under a 999-year lease granted in 1947. The plaintiff had been in possession of the plot since 1955 and had extinguished the lessee's title by twelve years adverse possession. In 1970, the dispossessed lessee purported to assign the lease to the defendant, who then acquired the freehold reversion from the landlord. The defendant argued that the leasehold interest had merged with the freehold and, therefore, the company was entitled to immediate possession of the property. The majority of the Supreme Court rejected this argument and ruled that because the lessee's title was extinguished, he had nothing to surrender or assign. They refused to follow the English House of Lords ruling in *Fairweather v. St Marylebone Property Co. Ltd.*[246] on this point which provided that the title of the lessee, which is extinguished as against the squatter, remains good as against the landlord. Thus, in the *Fairweather* case, the court ruled that the lessee could surrender the lease to the landlord who would immediately become entitled to possession of the property. However, in the *Perry* case, the Supreme Court also rejected that there was a parliamentary conveyance or assignment from the lessee to the squatter on the expiry of the limitation period in the case of unregistered land. Griffin J stated as follows:

---

241. *Ibid.*, 301.
242. (1892) 67 LT 735.
243. *Ibid.*, at 737.
244. [1906] 1 IR 20.
245. [1975] IR 104.
246. [1963] AC 510.

> (W)hat the squatter has gained is a right to possession of the premises in dispute as against the fee simple owner ... for the unexpired portion of the term, subject to the risk and possibility of a forfeiture. During the currency of the term limited by a lease, the lessor has no right to possession of the property unless the lessee has incurred a forfeiture for breach of one or more of the covenants in the lease ... The ousted lessee continues to be contractually liable to the lessor upon the covenants in the lease.[247]

104. It is unclear whether the adverse possessor can protect himself from a forfeiture by personally performing the covenants,[248] although he may be able to establish a tenancy by estoppel against the landlord who engages in co-operative acts based on the terms of the lease.[249] In the aftermath of the *Perry* case, it was clear that the adverse possessor of unregistered leasehold land was in a very precarious position on the expiry of the limitation period and left with a title which was essentially unmarketable. However, in the same case, Walsh J expressed the view that the parliamentary conveyance theory does operate where adverse possession of registered land has taken place.[250]

105. In 2002, the Law Reform Commission pointed out that the insecurities of the adverse possessor on leasehold land are exacerbated in Ireland by virtue of the fact that a large proportion of urban land is held under long leases of unregistered land. The Commission recommended an amendment of section 24 of the Statute of Limitations to provide for a parliamentary conveyance or assignment of the owner's title to the adverse possessor on the expiry of the limitation period.[251] This would mean that where the land concerned was subject to a lease, the original lessee would no longer be bound by the covenants. The Commission also recommended that the adverse possessor, in such circumstances, should be entitled to a copy of the lease so that he can become familiar with the covenants it contains. If the adverse possessor was in possession of only part of the land subject to the lease, the Commission recommended that the court should have jurisdiction to order an apportionment of the rights and liabilities between the adverse possessor and the original lessee where they fail to reach an agreement in this respect.

106. These reforms were incorporated into the draft Land and Conveyancing Law Reform Bill set out in the Report published by the Law Reform Commission in 2005.[252] However, the entire section of the draft Bill setting out the reforms to the law on adverse possession[253] was omitted from the Land and Conveyancing Law Reform Bill which was published by the government in 2006 due to the controversy generated

---

247. [1975] IR 104, 129.
248. In England in *Tickner v. Buzzacott* [1965] Ch 426, it was held that the landlord could forfeit the lease for non-payment of rent by the original tenant, even if the squatter was paying it, and the squatter had no right to claim relief against forfeiture.
249. *See Ashe v. Hogan* [1920] 1 IR 159 where a squatter was estopped from denying that he was bound by the covenants in the lease when he had taken advantage of a proviso contained in it.
250. [1975] IR 104, 120.
251. *Report on Title by Adverse Possession of Land* (LRC 67–2002).
252. *Report on Reform and Modernization of Land Law and Conveyancing Law* (LRC 74–2005).
253. Part 11.

by the proposed substantive reforms designed to restrict the operation of the doctrine.[254] In the meantime, the position of the adverse possessor on unregistered leasehold land has been improved to a certain extent by section 50(d)(ii) of the Registration of Deeds and Title Act 2006. This provision amends the definition of a leasehold interest which may be registered in the Land Registry and allows an adverse possessor on unregistered leasehold land, after the expiry of the limitation period, to make an application for first registration to the Land Registry of that leasehold interest provided that at least twenty-one years of the term is unexpired at the date of registration. If there is less than twenty-one years left to run on the lease, the application will currently be rejected and *Perry v. Woodfarm Homes Ltd*[255] continues to govern the position of such an adverse possessor.

§2. PRESCRIPTION

107. The law on prescription allows a person to acquire an easement or a profit à prendre[256] through its long enjoyment. The other three methods of acquiring such a minor interest in land: by statute, by express grant or reservation and by implication of law, are discussed in Chapter 5. Even in the context of acquisition by prescription, the law preserved the fiction that all easements originate or 'lie in grant'; in this case the grant was presumed. The law on prescription has been radically reformed by sections 33–39 of the Land and Conveyancing Law Reform Act 2009.[257] To consider the impact of the reforms, it is necessary to outline the old law governing prescription. A familiarity with the old law will also be necessary to invoke the transitional provisions which require a claim to be brought based on the old law if the user period began prior to the commencement of the new provisions and the claim is brought within twelve years of such commencement (i.e., before 1 December 2021).[258] The amendments introduced by the 2009 Act do not change the law on whether a particular use of land is capable of being recognized as an easement which is discussed in Chapter 5.[259] Someone who wishes to claim an easement by prescription must be able to satisfy this initial requirement.

---

254. *See* para. 95 above.
255. [1975] IR 104.
256. *See* para. 119 below for an explanation of these terms.
257. These reforms have generated considerable controversy and negative commentary, *see* Mee, 'Reforming the Law of Prescription: A Cautionary Tale from Ireland' in *Modern Studies in Property Law* ed. Barr (Oxford: Hart Publishing, 2015: 31); Bland 'A "Hopeless Jumble": The Cursed Reform of Prescription', *Conveyancing and Property Law Journal* 16 no. 3 (2011): 54.
258. Land and Conveyancing Law Reform Act, s. 38, as amended by Civil Law (Miscellaneous Provisions) Act 2011, s. 38.
259. *See* paras 120–121 below.

I. The Old Methods of Prescription

108. Three methods of prescription came to be recognized over the years: prescription at common law, under the doctrine of lost modern grant and under the Prescription Act 1832. A common requirement running through all three types of prescription was the need to prove continuous 'user as of right' which was traditionally defined by reference to the Latin phrase *nec per vim, nec per clam, nec precario* (i.e., neither by force, secrecy nor by permission). The owner of the servient tenement[260] must have acquiesced to the user throughout the period[261] and if he continually and unmistakably objected to it, the claim will be defeated.[262]

109. At common law, the courts were prepared to presume that there had been an ancient grant of an easement or profit if the claimant could show that it had been enjoyed 'as of right' since time immemorial (i.e., the limit of legal memory). This date was fixed as 1189 by the Statute of Westminster 1. Although, in theory, the claimant had to prove that he and his predecessors had enjoyed the easement or profit continuously since 1189, in practice proof of twenty years' user raised a presumption of user since 1189. However, this presumption could be rebutted by showing that user must have commenced more recently. For example, if the user related to a building which did not exist in 1189, the claim could be defeated. The ease with which a claim could be defeated rendered it unsatisfactory and the courts developed a second method of prescription known as the doctrine of lost modern grant.

110. Under the doctrine of lost modern grant, proof of twenty years enjoyment allowed the courts to presume that a grant was made in modern times but that this grant had been lost and therefore could not be produced in court. This method of prescription also had flaws. For example, the claimant would fail if it could be shown that the making of a grant prior to the commencement of the twenty-year period would have been impossible because the owner of the servient tenement lacked legal capacity.

111. The difficulties associated with both methods of prescription prompted the enactment of the Prescription Act 1832, which was extended to Ireland by the Prescription (Ireland) Act 1858. Although the statute was intended to simplify the law in this area, in reality it made things more complicated by failing to abolish the previous methods of prescription and providing two additional bases for a claim. It has also been described as 'one of the worst drafted Acts on the Statute Book'.[263] It set out a short period of user (twenty years for easements and thirty years for profits) which may have been designed to replace the doctrine of lost modern grant and a long period of user (forty years for easements and sixty years for profits) which may have been designed to

260. The servient tenement is the land over which the easement is exercised.

261. It may be difficult to determine from the facts whether there has been acquiescence to the user or if it has been merely tolerated giving rise to the inference of a licence, *see Walsh v Sligo County Council* [2011] 2 IR 260; *Zopitar Ltd v Jacob* [2015] IEHC 790.

262. *Dalton v. Angus* (1881) 6 App Cas 740, 773 as per Fry J.

263. English Law Reform Committee, *Acquisition of Easements and Profits by Prescription*, Fourteenth Report (1966 Cmnd 3100), para. 40.

replace common law prescription.[264] In addition, separate provisions were introduced to govern the acquisition of a right to light.

112. Where an easement or profit had been enjoyed 'as of right' and 'without interruption' for the short period 'next before some suit or action' it could not be defeated merely by proof that user began after 1189. The period of user had to continue up until the institution of proceedings, which was one reason for the continuing popularity of common law prescription and the doctrine of lost modern grant which did not impose such a requirement.[265] Although the user period must have been 'without interruption', to qualify as an interruption which breaks the statutory prescription period, the claimant must have submitted to or acquiesced in the interruption for at least one year. In computing the shorter period it was necessary to deduct any periods during which the landowner was under a legal disability (such as infancy or insanity).

113. If user as of right could be demonstrated for the long period, the right claimed became absolute and indefeasible. Again, the period of user must have been next before some suit or action and without interruption. It was not necessary to deduct periods of disability in calculating the longer period. Also, there was a confusing provision which set out that written consent to the exercise of the right would prevent the long period from running. This was odd, because under the common law, any form of permission was fatal to a claim for prescription as it prevented user as of right. The courts have suggested that this provision implies that oral consent given at the beginning of the longer period would not be fatal to a claim. However, if oral permission was given during the period of enjoyment, it would be necessary to re-commence calculating the user period.[266]

114. Section 3 of the 1832 Act dealt specifically with acquiring a right to light through prescription. It provided that where access of light to a building had been actually enjoyed for twenty years without interruption, the right was deemed absolute and indefeasible, unless it was enjoyed by virtue of consent in writing. Therefore, it could be acquired even if oral consent was given during the period of enjoyment.

II. The New Method of Prescription

115. The Law Reform Commission recommended the reform of the law on prescription in a report published in 2002.[267] These reforms, with some changes inspired by an academic critique of the proposals[268] were implemented by sections 33–35 of the Land and Conveyancing Law Reform Act 2009. The old methods of prescription

---

264. Law Reform Commission, *Report On The Acquisition Of Easements And Profits À Prendre By Prescription* (LRC 66–2002), para. 1.11.
265. *See Orwell Park Management Ltd v. Henihan* [2004] IEHC 87 where the plaintiff relied on the doctrine of lost modern grant to establish a vehicular right of way in respect of a user period which had ended in 1972.
266. *Gardner v. Hodgson's Kingston Brewery Co Ltd* [1903] AC 229; *Agnew v Barry* [2009] IESC 45.
267. *Report on the Acquisition of Easements and Profits À Prendre by Prescription* (LRC 66–2002).
268. Mee, 'Reform of the Law on the Acquisition of Easments and Profits à Prendre by Prescription', *Dublin University Law Journal* 12, no. 1 (2005): 86.

will be abolished once the transitional period has elapsed (on 1 December 2021) and section 35 introduces a new streamlined method of acquiring easements and profits by prescription. It sets out a single prescriptive period of twelve years which applies to both easements (including a right to light) and profits. The desire was to align the law on prescription with the law on adverse possession. Consequently, a longer user period must be established to acquire an easement by prescription against the State or over the foreshore.[269] Also, the mental incapacity of the servient owner may in certain circumstances postpone the running of the prescription period for up to thirty years.[270] It should be noted that by reducing the user period the reforms have, in general, made it easier to acquire rights by prescription when some have argued for a more restrictive regime or its outright abolition.[271]

116. The 2009 Act also specifically defines certain essential elements of the doctrine by reference to the common law, clarifying certain ambiguities which have arisen. User must be enjoyed 'as of right' which is defined as use or enjoyment without force, without secrecy and without the oral or written consent of the servient owner,[272] thus eliminating any confusion in relation to the impact of oral consent on the running of the user period. The user period must be 'without interruption', defined as an interference with or cessation of the use or enjoyment of the easement or profit for a continuous period of at least one year,[273] and it must continue up until the commencement of the action.[274] However, the latter requirement may be waived if the court is satisfied that it is just and equitable to do so in all the circumstances of the case.[275]

117. Section 36 of the 2009 Act clarifies the law and removes certain inconsistencies in the application of prescription to leasehold land. Although in England, the law on prescription could only be relied on by a fee simple owner against a fee simple owner, the position adopted by the Irish judiciary in relation to prescription by or against tenants was not as strict, probably due to the prevalence of long leasehold estates. In Ireland, prescription could be claimed to benefit or burden leasehold land under the Prescription Act and in certain circumstances under the doctrine of Lost Modern Grant,[276] although the position under common law prescription was less certain. Section 36(1) confirms that where the dominant owner[277] is a tenant, any easement or profit acquired by prescription attaches to the dominant land and passes to the landlord once the tenancy ends. Section 36(2) provides that where prescription operates against a servient owner who is a tenant, the easement or profit will come to an end when the tenancy ends, although it may be extended if the tenancy is extended or renewed, and

269. Land and Conveyancing Law Reform Act 2009, s. 33(b).
270. Land and Conveyancing Law Reform Act 2009, s. 37.
271. *See* Bland, *Easements,* 3rd edn (Dublin: Roundhall, 2015), paras. 6.07–6.08; Bailey, 'Stuck in the Past—The Failure of the Land and Conveyancing Law Reform Act 2009 to Modernize the Law of Easements in Ireland', *Conveyancing and Property Law Journal* 15, no. 3 (2010): 52.
272. Land and Conveyancing Law Reform Act 2009, s. 33.
273. *Ibid.*
274. Land and Conveyancing Law Reform Act, s. 35(2).
275. Land and Conveyancing Law Reform Act s. 35(3).
276. *See Fahy v. Dwyer* (1879) 4 LR Ir 271; *Tisdall v. McArthur* [1951] IR 228; *Deeble Linehan* (1860) 12 ICLR 1.
277. The dominant owner is the owner of the land which benefits from the easement.

if the tenant subsequently acquires the landlord's superior interest, it will attach to that superior interest.

118. The original version of section 35(1) provided that an easement or a profit could only be acquired at law by prescription on registration of a court order in the Land Registry or the Registry of Deeds, as appropriate. Under the old law, an easement by prescription amounted to an overriding interest under section 72(1)(h) of the Registration of Title Act 1964. The registration requirement was included to make it easier for a purchaser to discover these types of easements[278] and to facilitate, in due course, the introduction of eConveyancing. Although, a court order was always required to establish the legal title to an easement by prescription, it is understood that transactions were occasionally completed on the basis of a statutory declaration by the dominant owner setting out the basis for a claim.[279] It has been argued that such a declaration may amount to evidence of an equitable easement[280] and, to reduce the necessity for litigation in such circumstances, section 35(1) was recently amended[281] to facilitate the establishment of an easement or profit by prescription by an application to the Property Registration Authority.[282] This procedure mimics the one which currently operates in relation to adverse possession claims which requires the owner to be notified of the application and permits the matter to be referred to court, if there is a dispute as to the facts or on a point of law, or any decision made to be appealed to court under section 19 of the Registration of Title Act 1964.

278. *Report on the Acquisition of Easements and Profits À Prendre by Prescription* (LRC 74–2005), para. 124.
279. *See* Wylie, The *Land and Conveyancing Law Reform Act 2009: Annotations and Commentary* (Dublin: Bloomsbury Professional, 2009), 138–139, n. 3.
280. *Ibid.*
281. Civil Law (Miscellaneous Provisions) Act 2011, s. 37.
282. Civil Law (Miscellaneous Provisions) Act 2011, s. 41, inserting Registration of Title Act 1964, s. 49A. *See* Bland, *Easements* 3rd edn (Dublin: Roundhall, 2015) Ch. 7.

Chapter 5. Easements, Profits and Freehold Covenants

§1. General Characteristics of Easements and Profits

119. Easements and profits à prendre may be described as minor interests in land, in contrast to the fee simple and leasehold estates which are major interests. Occasionally, easements and profits are referred to as servitudes due to their similarity to the praedrial servitude of Roman law and the influence that the civil law has had over the development of certain aspects of the law in this area.[283] They are also classified as incorporeal hereditaments (i.e., rights over land which are capable of being inherited but do not confer a right to physical possession of the land).[284] Crucially, they amount to real rights as opposed to personal rights. Real rights are capable of binding future owners of the affected land, while personal rights are only enforceable by and against the original parties to the agreement.

120. An easement can be defined as 'a right exercised for the benefit of land by obliging another owner of land to suffer a use of his land or refrain from using his land in a particular way'.[285] Thus, they can have a positive or a negative quality. Certain rights are long established as easements, such as rights of way, support, light and water. A profit à prendre entitles its owner to take some natural product (e.g., turf under a right of turbary) or creature (under fishing or sporting rights) from another person's land. While an easement must be appurtenant (or annexed) to some piece of land which benefits from it, a profit can be appurtenant to a piece of land or it can exist 'in gross' (i.e., independently of the ownership of land).

121. While the list of easements which is recognized by the law is not closed and new easements may be recognized to reflect modern demands, to ensure certainty and predictability in this area of law, the courts insist that such newly recognized rights share specific characteristics. In *Redfront Ltd v. Custom House Dock Management Ltd*,[286] the Irish High Court adopted Danckwerts J's statement of the four essential elements of an easement set out in *Re Ellenborough Park*.[287] First, there must be a dominant and a servient tenement. It must be possible to identify a piece of land which benefits from the easement (the dominant tenement) and a piece of land over which the easement is exercisable (the servient tenement). Although the tenements do not have to be adjacent, they must be sufficiently proximate to confer a real practical

283. For example, the rule in *Wheeldon v. Burrows* (1878) 12 Ch D 31; *see* Simpson, 'The Rule in *Wheeldon v. Burrows* and the Code Civile', *Law Quarterly Review* 83 (1967): 240; Bland, *Easements*, 3rd edn (Dublin: Roundhall, 2015), xvi–xvii.

284. *See* Wylie, *Irish Land Law*, 5th edn (Dublin: Bloomsbury Professional, 2013), para. 6.05 and Lyall, *Land Law in Ireland*, 3rd edn (Dublin: Roundhall, 2010), 798. Note that Bland describes this classification as fallacious and unhelpful and prefers to describe them as interests in an incorporeity, *see* Bland, *Easements*, 3rd edn (Dublin: Roundhall, 2015), para. 1.03.

285. Bland, *Easements*, 3rd edn (Dublin: Roundhall, 2015), para. 1.02.

286. [1998] IEHC 206.

287. [1956] Ch 131.

benefit on the dominant tenement. Second, an easement must accommodate the dominant tenement. It is not enough that the easement benefits the owner of the dominant land in his personal capacity, it must benefit the land itself. If the right benefits some business or other activity normally conducted on the dominant tenement, this will be sufficient.[288] Third, the dominant and servient tenements must be owned by different persons or, at least, occupied by different persons where the tenements are in common ownership. Finally, the right claimed must be capable of forming the subject matter of a grant. This means that the right claimed must be capable of being accurately described in a deed. For this reason, the courts have consistently refused to recognize vague rights such as the right to shelter from the weather[289] or a right to a view[290] as an easement.

122. The courts have also demonstrated a reluctance to recognize negative rights that prevent the servient owner from doing something on his land as new easements. In addition, a right which confers exclusive possession of the servient tenement on the dominant owner and leaves the servient owner with no use of the land may not be recognized as an easement. In recent times, the application of this approach, known as 'the ouster principle', has led to difficulties in determining whether a right to park in a dedicated space can exist as an easement.[291]

§2. Acquisition of Easements and Profits

123. Easements and profits may be acquired by statute, express grant or reservation, by implication of the law or by prescription. Statutory easements are frequently created in respect of electricity, water, sewage, gas and telecommunications services. The acquisition of easements and profits by prescription was discussed in Chapter 4.[292]

I. Express Grant or Reservation

124. Although a landowner may expressly create an easement or profit by deed,[293] typically it is created as part of a larger transaction. For example, a landowner may sell a site to a purchaser and include in the deed of conveyance a right of way over his retained land so that the purchaser can access the public road. It is also common for a landowner selling part of his land to reserve certain easements over the sold land. For example, he may reserve a right of way over the part of the land sold or a right to water flowing through pipes going through the land sold. Before the Land and

288. *See Hannon v. BQ Investments* [2009] IEHC 191; *Moody v. Steggles* (1879) 12 Ch D 261.
289. *See Cockrane v. Verner* (1895) 29 ILTSJ 571; *Phipps v. Pears* [1965] 1 QB 76.
290. *See Aldred's Case* (1610) 6 Co Rep 57b.
291. *See* Bland, *Easements,* 3rd edn (Dublin: Roundhall, 2015), para 11.16–11.19.
292. *See* paras 107–118 above.
293. Note that there is no longer any need to use words of limitation to ensure that an easement is granted in fee simple, *see* Registration of Deeds and Title Act 2006, s. 70 and Land and Conveyancing Law Reform Act 2009, s. 67. Unless the deed suggests otherwise, the largest estate shall pass.

Conveyancing Law Reform Act 2009, easements which were reserved to the vendor in such a deed of conveyance technically amounted to a re-grant of the right to the vendor by the purchaser. This meant that any ambiguity in its terms would be construed against the purchaser and it only had legal effect if executed by the purchaser. Section 69 of the Land and Conveyancing Law Reform Act 2009 makes a reservation in a conveyance fully effective without the need for execution by the purchaser and reverses the rule of construction just discussed. The express creation of an easement or a profit by deed must be registered as a burden affecting the servient land if that land is registered in the Land Registry.[294] A failure to register the right will result in a future registered owner taking the servient tenement free from such a right.[295]

II. Implied Grant or Reservation

125. Where an easement is not expressly created, there are certain circumstances in which the grant or reservation of an easement may be implied. Although, it is generally suggested that there are four categories of implied easement, the categories may overlap and all four appear to either give effect to the supposed intention of the parties or be based on the principle that a grantor cannot derogate from his grant (i.e., he cannot do something which prevents the land from being fit for the purposes for which it was sold).

126. An easement or way of necessity will be implied where a disposition of part of the land results in one portion becoming landlocked by reason of the absence of any access to the public road. It may arise by way of implied grant or reservation. However, it cannot arise if the landlocked tenement has an alternative means of access, regardless of its inconvenience.[296] Also, it cannot arise to burden the land of a third party to a conveyance.[297]

127. A grant or reservation of an easement will be implied by the law where necessary to give effect to the common intention of the parties to a deed that the land was to be used for a particular purpose. For example, in *Wong v. Beaumont Properties Trust Ltd*,[298] basement premises were leased for use as a Chinese restaurant but under public health regulations the basement could only be used for this purpose if the kitchens were vented to roof level. It was held that there was an implied easement to instal a ventilation duct through the upstairs floors retained by the landlord. In *Conneran v. Corbett and Sons Ltd*[299] where the lease to a tenant of a shopping mall contained an express right to use delivery doors in the car park and common areas for deliveries, the court implied an easement of common intention to pass and re-pass over the car park and loading area from the public road, as otherwise the express right would be ineffective.

294. Registration of Title Act 1964, s. 69(1)(j).
295. Registration of Title Act 1964, ss 52(1) and 55(1).
296. *See Donnelly v. Adams* [1905] 1 IR 154.
297. *See Byrnes v. Meakstown Construction Ltd* [2009] IEHC 123.
298. (1965) 1 QB 173.
299. [2004] IEHC 389.

128. Section 40 of the Land and Conveyancing Law Reform Act 2009 provides for the abolition of the rule known as the rule in *Wheeldon v. Burrows*[300] and its replacement with a rule which was intended to be clearer. The replacement rule provides that where a landowner disposes of part of his land (or all of it in parts) an easement will be implied for the benefit of the part(s) disposed of, over the part retained (or the parts simultaneously disposed of) if it is necessary for the reasonable enjoyment of the land, and it was reasonable for the parties to assume (or would have been if they had adverted to the matter) that it was included in the disposition. To appreciate the implications of this reform, it is necessary to briefly discuss the rule in *Wheeldon v. Burrows*. This rule facilitated the conversion of certain quasi-easements into easements proper on a subdivision of land. Quasi-easements are rights that the owner habitually exercises over his own land which could if exercised by someone else constitute an easement. The rule provided:

> On the grant by the owner of a tenement of part of that tenement ... there will pass to the grantee all those continuous and apparent easements (by which, of course, I mean quasi-easements), or which are necessary to the reasonable enjoyment of the property granted, and which have been and are at the time of the grant used by the owner of the entirety for the benefit of the part granted.[301]

The rule has been distilled into three separate requirements. The first requirement, that the exercise of the right had to be 'continuous and apparent', gave rise to some controversy.[302] Also, it was initially unclear whether the second requirement, that the right was necessary to the reasonable enjoyment of the property, had to be proved as an additional or alternative requirement to the first requirement. The third requirement meant that the quasi-easement had to be in existence at the time of the conveyance and was insisted upon as recently as 2004 by the Supreme Court in *Bennett Construction Ltd v. Greene*.[303] The uncertainties surrounding the operation of the rule in *Wheeldon v. Burrows* and its description as a specific application of the doctrine of non-derogation from grant[304] led the Law Reform Commission to recommend its replacement by the more general principle based on the latter doctrine set out in section 40 of the 2009 Act.[305] It has been argued that in the application of the new more general principle, the courts will have to grapple with many of the issues that created the very complexities that the Law Reform Commission sought to replace, but without the guidance of the authorities on the rule in *Wheeldon v. Burrows*.[306] Section 40(3) clarifies that the reform does not affect claims to an implied easement of necessity or to give effect to the

---

300. (1879) 12 Ch D 31.
301. *Ibid.*, at 49 per Theisger LJ.
302. Bland, *Easements*, 3rd edn (Dublin: Roundhall, 2015), para. 5.37.
303. [2004] 2 ILRM 96.
304. *Ibid.*
305. *Consultation Paper on Reform and Modernization of Land Law and Conveyancing Law* (LRC CP 34–2004), paras 7.22–7.23.
306. *See* Mee, 'Reform of the Law on the Acquisition of Easements and Profits à Prendre by Prescription', *Dublin University Law Journal* 27 (2005): 86; Bland, *Easements*, 3rd edn (Dublin: Roundhall, 2015), paras 5.29–5.37.

common intention of the parties, or the operation of the doctrine of non-derogation from grant in its wider context.

129. Finally, certain easements will be implied in a conveyance of land pursuant to section 71 of the Land and Conveyancing Law Reform Act 2009 which provides that a conveyance of land includes easements and profits appertaining or annexed to the land. It re-enacts the substance of section 6 of the Conveyancing Act 1881, which was repealed by the 2009 Act, and amounts to a word-saving device which eliminates the need to refer, in subsequent deeds, to easements and profits which have already been created. Certain aspects of the operation of section 6 of the 1881 Act proved controversial. There was some confusion over whether section 6 of the 1881 Act could be relied on to convert a quasi-easement into an easement proper. However, it was later clarified that it was inapplicable in the absence of diversity of ownership or occupation prior to the conveyance.[307] Similarly, recent case law had clarified that section 6 could not be relied on to enlarge or upgrade an informal arrangement over land into a full easement on a conveyance of the accommodated land.[308] Section 71(3) confirms these interpretations in relation to the new provision.

§3. Extinguishment of Easements and Profits

130. There are three main ways in which an easement or a profit can be extinguished. They can be extinguished by statute; for example, legislation will generally authorize the extinguishment of all easements and profits formerly attached to land which is compulsorily acquired.[309] An important development was the introduction of a special form of statutory extinguishment by section 39 of the Land and Conveyancing Law Reform Act 2009. It provides for the automatic extinguishment of prescriptive and implied rights which have not been exercised for a continuous period of twelve years unless they have been protected by registration in the Registry of Deeds or the Land Registry, as appropriate. This provision was designed to prevent purchasers from being burdened by easements which are no longer in use and may no longer be detectable. Section 39(2) clarifies that the section shall apply to extinguish prescriptive or implied easements which were acquired before 1 December 2009, provided there was a period of at least three years non-user after the commencement date, thereby providing a transitional period in which the dominant owner could protect the right by registration or resumption of user. Section 39 must be considered in the context of section 72(1)(h) of the Registration of Title Act 1964 which confers overriding status on all easements, except those which were created by express grant or reservation after the first registration of the land. Therefore, prescriptive easements acquired under the old regime will bind a purchaser without appearing on the register unless there has been a twelve-year period of non-user, while prescriptive easements which are acquired under the new regime must be registered pursuant to section 35 in order to bind a purchaser. Although there is no express requirement to register an implied easement, regardless of when it was created, non-user for twelve years will result in its automatic

307. *Bennett Construction Ltd v. Greene* [2004] 2 ILRM 96.

308. *Ibid.*

309. *See* the Planning and Development Act 2000, Part 14.

extinguishment. Therefore, a valuable right, which may not have been exercised for good reason over the relevant time period,[310] may be lost in circumstances where the owner of the right may not have known that his easement only arose by implication and could not possibly have been aware of the danger of non-user.

131. Just as easements and profits may be expressly granted by deed, they may also be expressly released by deed. The courts may be willing to imply a release if it can be shown that the conduct of the person entitled to the right shows an unequivocal intention never to use it again. Section 39(3) of the 2009 Act specifically preserves the jurisdiction of the court to declare that an easement or a profit, however acquired, has been abandoned or extinguished. This intention to abandon will not be readily inferred by the courts and, unlike the new method of statutory extinguishment which applies to prescriptive and implied easements, evidence of a long period of non-user will not necessarily suffice. In *Carroll v. Sheridan,*[311] most of a laneway had become overgrown and impassable because those entitled to the right of way had an easier method of accessing their land. Nevertheless, O'Hanlon J declined to infer the necessary intention to abandon their right to use it.

132. Finally, if the same person becomes entitled to ownership and possession of both the dominant and the servient tenements, one of the essential requirements of an easement is removed and any easements attached to those lands are extinguished.

§4. Freehold Covenants

133. A covenant is a promise contained in a deed. It may be enforced by the original parties to the deed under the ordinary rules of contract law, but in certain circumstances it may also be enforced by and against successors in title who were not privy to the original deed. Covenants will frequently be imposed in relation to freehold land where a vendor retains neighbouring land which benefits from the covenant or if the entire plot is sold in lots subject to identical covenants with the intention that all the purchasers would benefit from the arrangement. Therefore, freehold covenants, similar to easements, can be described as appurtenant rights which exist between neighbouring landowners. Two bodies of rules govern freehold covenants in Ireland: the traditional system which applies to the many freehold covenants which were entered into before 1 December 2009 and the new statutory system which applies to freehold covenants entered into after that date.

I. Traditional Rules Governing Old Freehold Covenants

134. In determining whether a covenant binds a successor in title, traditionally distinctions were made between covenants which affected leasehold and freehold land, between positive and restrictive covenants, between the running of the benefit and the burden of such covenants and between the approach taken by the common law and equity. While the benefit and burden of covenants contained in a lease which affect

310. *See* Bland, *Easements,* 3rd edn (Dublin: Roundhall, 2015), paras 20.08–20.09.
311. [1984] ILRM 451.

the land have traditionally run with such land,[312] in the case of covenants affecting freehold land, the law has not been so clear-cut. At common law, for the benefit of a freehold covenant to pass to a successor in title, it must touch and concern the covenantee's land[313] and the successor must have succeeded to the same legal estate as was held by the original covenantee.[314] Therefore, if the original covenantee had acquired a fee simple, his tenant could not enforce the covenant. At common law, the burden of a covenant affecting freehold land did not run with the land. However, the burden of a restrictive covenant (such as one restricting the user of the land or the extent to which it can be developed) was enforceable in equity against a successor in title with notice of its existence. This approach is known as the rule in *Tulk v. Moxhay*[315] and was developed by equity to preserve the value of the covenantee's land. In practice, the doctrine of notice has been replaced by a requirement to register the deed creating the restrictive covenant in the Registry of Deeds[316] or the Land Registry[317] to ensure that it will bind future owners of the land. For the benefit of such a restrictive covenant to run with the land, equity insists on the satisfaction of certain additional requirements: the plaintiff must own the land which is benefited by the covenant and be able to prove that the benefit of the covenant passed to him by assignment, by annexation or pursuant to an estate scheme.

135. The rule in *Elliston v. Reacher*[318] governs the running of the benefit of restrictive covenants affecting individual plots in an estate scheme. This rule ensures the mutual enforceability of such restrictive covenants by and against each purchaser and his successors in title of an individual plot, provided certain conditions are satisfied: The plaintiff and the defendant must derive title from a common vendor; the vendor must have laid out the land for sale in plots subject to restrictions intended to be imposed on all the plots or consistent only with such a scheme; the vendor must have intended the restrictions to benefit all the plots sold; the plots must have been purchased on the basis that the restrictions would benefit the other plots and the area covered by the estate scheme must be clearly defined.[319]

136. Unlike restrictive covenants, the burden of a positive covenant affecting freehold land is not enforceable against a successor in title to the original covenantor,[320] regardless of notice. This means that a freehold covenant to carry out repairs or pay a service charge for the maintenance of common areas cannot be enforced against a successor in title to the original covenantor. Although, certain conveyancing devices could be used with varying effectiveness to circumvent this rule,[321] it resulted in the

---

312. *See Spencer's Case* (1583) 5 Co Rep 16a; Landlord and Tenant Amendment Act 1860 (otherwise known as Deasy's Act), ss 12 and 13; Conveyancing Act 1881, ss 10 and 11.
313. It must be of direct relevance to the land and its enjoyment and cannot be purely of personal benefit.
314. *Gaw v. CIE* [1953] IR 232.
315. (1848) 2 Ph774.
316. *See* para. 72 above.
317. Registration of Title Act 1964, s. 69(1)(k).
318. [1908] 2 Ch 374. This rule has been applied in Ireland in *Fitzpatrick v. Clancy* (HC) 1964 and recognized in *Belmont Securities Ltd v. Crean* [1988] IEHC 20.
319. *Reid v. Bickerstaff* [1909] 2 Ch 305 at 319.
320. *See Austerberry v. Oldham Corp* (1885) 29 Ch D 750; *Rhone v. Stephens* [1994] 2 AC 310.
321. For example, a chain of covenants and indemnity agreements or a lease of easements.

widespread reliance on long leases or fee farm grants to ensure the enforceability of positive covenants against future owners of the land, particularly where apartment or duplex ownership schemes were concerned. Although Irish leasehold apartment ownership schemes have not been plagued by some of the problems facing such schemes in England which necessitated the introduction of commonhold,[322] it was nevertheless recognized by the Law Reform Commission that the law governing the enforceability of freehold covenants was anomalous.[323] The difficulties it created have been exacerbated by the restrictions imposed by ground rents legislation[324] on the use of the long lease for conveyancing purposes. It should also be noted that since the commencement of the Land and Conveyancing Law Reform Act 2009, it shall no longer be possible to create a fee farm grant to avail of the rules governing leasehold covenants.[325]

II. Statutory Rules Governing New Freehold Covenants

137. Sections 48–50 of the Land and Conveyancing Law Reform Act 2009 implement the Law Reform Commission's proposals for reform in this area which render freehold covenants attaching to appurtenant parcels of land enforceable by and against successors in title to the original covenantor and covenantee. It is important to note, however, that these new rules only apply to covenants entered into after the commencement of the 2009 Act[326] and the old law will, therefore, continue to govern covenants created under earlier deeds. Section 49(1) abolishes the current rules of common law and equity governing the enforceability of freehold covenants, including the rule in *Tulk v. Moxhay*. Section 49(2) provides that any freehold covenant which imposes an obligation in respect of servient land to do or refrain from doing any act or thing is enforceable by the current dominant owner against the current servient owner. The definition of a dominant owner includes a person deriving title from or under that owner, allowing a tenant or a mortgagee in possession to enforce such freehold covenants.[327] The definition of a servient owner includes a person deriving title from or under such an owner (except tenants for a period of less than five years) and, in the case of a restrictive covenant, it includes a licensee or a person in occupation of the land with or without the consent of the servient owner.[328] Section 49(2) also provides that freehold covenants may only be enforced by or against previous owners where a breach of covenant occurred during their period of ownership. Section 49(3) applies the rule in *Elliston v. Reacher* to development schemes, although the scope of the rule is now wider as it governs the enforceability of both the benefit and burden

322. Mainly because in Ireland the terms of such leases tend to be much longer, *see* Woods, 'Commonhold – An Option for Ireland?', *Irish Jurist* 38 (2003): 285.

323. *Report on Land Law and Conveyancing Law: (7) Positive Covenants over Freehold land and other proposals* (LRC 70–2003), para. 1.01.

324. *See* para. 175 below.

325. *See* para. 49 above.

326. 1 Dec. 2009.

327. Land and Conveyancing Law Reform Act 2009, s. 48.

328. Land and Conveyancing Law Reform Act 2009, s. 48.

of freehold covenants. Section 49(4) makes specific provision for the apportionment of any freehold covenants where the servient land is subdivided.

138. Another criticism which had been made of the law in this area was the absence of any comprehensive statutory scheme to facilitate the removal of obsolete restrictive covenants.[329] Section 69(3) of the Registration of Title Act 1964 permits the Property Registration Authority to discharge or modify a registered restrictive covenant if the consent of all persons interested in its enforcement is forthcoming or on the production of a court order. The court could make such an order if it was satisfied that one of the following conditions was satisfied: the covenant did not run with the land; it was not enforceable against the owner of the land; or its modification or discharge would be beneficial to the persons principally interested in its enforcement. This highly restrictive scheme had no application to unregistered land. Section 50 of the 2009 Act, which applies to all freehold covenants, both positive and restrictive and regardless of when they were created, has dramatically improved the law in this respect. It allows a servient owner to apply to court for an order discharging or modifying a freehold covenant on the basis that continued compliance with the covenant would constitute an unreasonable interference with the use and enjoyment of the servient land. In making this assessment the court is directed to have regard to a list of factors, including, the age of the covenant, any change in the character of the neighbourhood, the development plan for the area and any planning decisions in the relation to land in the vicinity, the extent to which the covenant secures a practical benefit to the dominant owner and whether compliance with the covenant has become unduly onerous for the servient owner. The court may make such an order conditional on the servient owner paying compensation to the dominant owner, if it results in a quantifiable loss. Just as the deed creating such a covenant should be registered in the Registry of Deeds[330] or the Land Registry,[331] as appropriate, so too must an order modifying or discharging such a covenant.[332]

329. *See* Law Reform Commission, *Report on Land Law and Conveyancing Law: (7) Positive Covenants over Freehold land and other proposals* (LRC 70–2003), paras 1.17–1.18.

330. Although a freehold covenant affecting unregistered land created after the commencement of the 2009 Act is a legal interest (*see* s. 11(4)(b) of the 2009 Act) capable of binding the world, to ensure priority the deed creating it should be registered in the Registry of Deeds.

331. Note that s. 129 of the Land and Conveyancing Law Reform Act 2009 inserts 'a freehold covenant within the meaning of section 48 of the Land and Conveyancing Law Reform Act 2009' into the list of burdens which must be registered to bind a purchaser of registered land, *see* s. 69(1)(kk) of the Registration of Title Act 1964.

332. Land and Conveyancing Law Reform Act 2009, s. 50(4).

Chapter 6. Tenancies

§1. General

139. As has previously been mentioned, leasehold ownership emerged following the decline of feudal tenure.[333] It involves the freehold owner or landlord making a grant of possession of land to a tenant for a term in consideration of rent. Although, this type of ownership was initially classified as personality, it was re-classified as a 'chattel real' following the recognition of the ejectment action which allowed a tenant to recover possession of the land.[334] In Ireland, following the confiscation of land in the seventeenth century, many of the English who received grants of land were unwilling to settle here and instead became absentee landlords who let the land through agents. As a result, the tenancy became a widespread feature of Irish society.[335] The terms 'lease' ('lessor', and 'lessee') and 'tenancy' ('landlord' and 'tenant') have, to date, been used interchangeably, although the Law Reform Commission has recommended that any new legislation should rely on 'tenancy' as a generic term and confine the term 'lease' to situations where a tenancy has been created by a written document.[336] A tenancy may be for any period of time or any recurring period,[337] although a tenancy for a fixed term and a periodic tenancy (such as from week to week or from month to month) are most common. The definition of a 'tenancy' set out in section 3 of the Land and Conveyancing Law Reform Act 2009 excludes a tenancy at will (a relationship more akin to a license) and a tenancy at sufferance (the name given to the occupation of a tenant who is overholding). The Law Reform Commission felt that although it was generally accepted that such tenancies did not give rise to the landlord and tenant relationship, this should be confirmed by legislation.[338]

140. It should be noted that although a Draft General Scheme of Landlord and Tenant Law Reform Bill[339] was published by the Department of Justice and Equality for consultation in 2011, the Bill has not, as yet, been initiated by the government. The proposed legislation is based on the draft Bill set out in a Law Reform Commission Report[340] and was underpinned by a number of guiding principles. It aims to repeal

333. *See* para. 19 above.
334. *See* para. 3 above.
335. *See* para.19 above.
336. Law Reform Commission, *Consultation Paper on General Law of Landlord and Tenant* (LRC CP 28–2003), para. 2.05.
337. Land and Conveyancing Law Reform Act 2009, s. 11(3).
338. *Consultation Paper on General Law of Landlord and Tenant* (LRC CP 28–2003), paras 1.24–1.25.
339. Draft General Scheme of Landlord and Tenant Law Reform Bill 2011 available at http://www.justice.ie/en/JELR/Draft%20GS%20of%20Landlord%20and%20Tenant%20Law%20Reform%20Bill%202011.pdf/Files/Draft%20GS%20of%20Landlord%20and%20Tenant%20Law%20Reform%20Bill%202011.pdf> accessed 28 Feb. 2017.
340. Law Reform Commission, *Report on the Law of Landlord and Tenant* (LRC 85–2007), Appendix B.

obsolete provisions and provisions which militate against commercial practice and the operation of free market choice; to recast certain legislative provisions to remove uncertainties in the law; to introduce new legislative provisions to meet gaps in the existing law; and also to consolidate existing legislation.[341]

§2. The Nature of the Relationship

141. Although the relationship between landlord and tenant has a common law basis, in Ireland, its nature must also be considered in light of section 3 of the Landlord and Tenant (Amendment) Act 1860 (more commonly referred to as 'Deasy's Act') which provides:

> The relation of landlord and tenant shall be deemed to be founded on the express or implied contract of the parties, and not upon tenure or service, and a reversion shall not be necessary to such a relation, which shall be deemed to subsist in all cases in which there shall be an agreement by one party to hold land from or under another in consideration of any rent.[342]

An important consequence of this definition was that in eliminating the requirement for a reversion, it facilitated a sub-lease of the entire term granted under the head lease, a practice which many agents acting for English landlords engaged in. It also paved the way for 'Deasy's Act' Fee Farm Grants which conferred a fee simple on the grantee but also created the relationship of landlord and tenant between the parties.[343] Founding the relationship on the agreement of the parties also seems to have facilitated the avoidance of the common law requirement of a term of certain duration or a term capable of being rendered certain[344] which has given rise to some controversy in England.[345] For example, leases for lives were widespread at one point.[346] The Law Reform Commission recently concluded that the agreement of the parties should remain the fundamental basis of the landlord and tenant relationship and recommended the substantive re-enactment of section 3 of Deasy's Act.[347] However, section 11(3) of the Land and Conveyancing Law Reform Act 2009 clarifies that the relationship also gives rise to an estate. The 2009 Act provides that the leasehold estate and the fee simple in

341. *Ibid.*, para. 2.
342. The Draft General Scheme of Landlord and Tenant Law Reform Bill 2011, Head 10(3) will, if enacted, render void the grant of a tenancy without a reversion. *See* Lyall, 'What difference does a day make? Leases, Reversions and a Disturbing Proposal', *Conveyancing and Property Law Journal* 19 no. 1 (2014): 6.
343. Note that Land and Conveyancing Law Reform Act 2009, s. 12 prevents the creation of new fee farm grants, although those which were created prior to commencement will remain in force, *see* para. 49 above.
344. *Prudential Assurance Co Ltd v. London Residuary Body* [1992] 2 AC 386.
345. *See* Bright, 'Certainty of Leases – Is it a Vice?,' *Legal Studies* (1993): 38.
346. It is no longer possible to create such leases, *see* Land and Conveyancing Law Reform Act 2009, s. 14.
347. *See* s. 10(1) of the draft Bill attached to the Law Reform Commission, *Report on the Law of Landlord and Tenant* (LRC 85–2007).

possession are the only two estates which can be created or disposed of as legal estates,[348] while recognizing that an equitable lease may still arise.[349]

142. One of the fundamental features of a tenancy is that it amounts to a real interest in land. Therefore, a tenant will typically be able to enforce his interest against a person who purchases his landlord's interest in the land. However, if the tenancy was created by deed for a term exceeding twenty-one years, the lease must be registered in the Registry of Deeds[350] or the Land Registry,[351] as appropriate, to ensure priority or to bind a newly registered owner. Shorter or equitable leases will bind a purchaser as an overriding interest in the case of registered land if the tenant is in occupation at the time of the transaction.[352] In the case of unregistered land, the issue of priority will depend on whether the lease was a legal interest (as legal interests bind the world) or equitable and, if equitable, whether the purchaser had actual, imputed or constructive notices of its existence.[353] Another consequence of its proprietary effect is that the tenant may dispose of his interest by way of an assignment or grant a sub-lease.[354]

§3. The Distinction Between a Lease and a License

143. It is important to distinguish a lease from a license. A license is usually defined as permission to do something which would otherwise be a trespass.[355] It creates a personal relationship between the parties which cannot be assigned and cannot bind a future owner of the land, unless it is coupled with an interest[356] or arises by means of an estoppel.[357] A licensee will also be unable to avail of the numerous protections and advantages which attach to both residential and business tenancies. The courts have been prepared to look beyond the label attached to the agreement in determining whether the parties intended to create a lease or a license.[358]

144. Traditionally, the presence or absence of exclusive possession by the occupier was determinative of the relationship. If present, the relationship was classified as a tenancy[359] and if not, it was classified as a license.[360] In more recent times, it has been recognized that although a tenancy cannot exist without exclusive possession, a

348. Land law and Conveyancing Law Reform Act 2009, s. 11(1).
349. Land law and Conveyancing Law Reform Act 2009, s. 11(6).
350. Registration of Deeds and Title Act 2006, ss 38 and 32(1). Note that section 32(1)(ii) permits the Minister for Justice and Law Reform to prescribe that leases for lesser periods are registrable.
351. Registration of Title Act 1964, s. 69(g).
352. Registration of Title Act 1964, s. 72(1)(i) and (j).
353. *See* para. 71 above.
354. *See* para. 147 below.
355. *See Kelly v. Woolworth & Co Ltd* [1922] 2 IR 448.
356. *See* Wylie, *Irish Land Law,* 5th edn (Dublin: Bloomsbury Professional, 2013), para. 22.04.
357. *Ibid.*, para. 22.07.
358. *Irish Shell & BP Ltd v Costello Ltd* [1981] ILRM 66; *O'Siodhachain v O'Mahony* [2002] 4 IR 147.
359. *See Lynes v. Snaith* [1895–1899] All ER 997.
360. *Peakin v. Peakin* [1895] 2 IR 359.

license agreement may also confer exclusive possession.[361] The presence of a clause which specifically or by implication negates the presence of exclusive possession continues to be an important factor in determining the nature of the relationship, as does the degree of control or dominion retained by the grantor over the premises.[362] For example, the occupation of lodgers, hotel guests or employees is classified as pursuant to a license due to the level of control retained by the owner.[363] In addition, the courts are more likely to decide that an arrangement amounts to a tenancy if rent, or an equivalent fee, was payable under the agreement.[364] Finally, the courts will seek to ascertain the intention of the parties as demonstrated by the express terms of the agreement or as implied by the circumstances. This factor has recently given rise to confusion in circumstances where it is expressly provided in the agreement that a tenancy is not created, but the conduct of the parties suggests that the license label is simply a sham to enable one party in a superior bargaining position to evade his obligations under landlord and tenant legislation. In *Kenny Homes & Co Ltd v. Leonard*,[365] the Supreme Court attached considerable weight to the express provisions of the agreement as evidence of what the parties intended and concluded that the occupation was pursuant to a license agreement. In contrast, in the High Court decision in *Smith v. Irish Rail*,[366] Peart J made no reference to the Supreme Court decision in

361. *See Gatien Motor Co. Ltd v. Continental Oil Co of Ireland Ltd* [1979] IR 406, 420 per Kenny J.
362. *See Governors of National Maternity Hospital v. McGouran* [1994] ILRM 521 where the hospital allowed the defendant to occupy part of the building for use as a coffee shop but retained the right to change the venue within the hospital. The agreement also expressly stated that exclusive possession was not conferred and provided that the hospital administrators were entitled to come into the coffee shop whenever they wished. The court concluded that the agreement amounted to a license. *See also Irish Shell & BP Ltd v. Costello Ltd* [1981] ILRM 66.
363. *See Carroll v. Mayo County Council* [1967] IR 364, 367 per Henchy J; *Moore v. Doherty* (1843) 5 Ir LR 449.
364. In *Gatien Motor Co Ltd v. Continental Oil of Ireland Ltd* [1979] IR 406, no rent was payable during the period governed by a caretaker agreement and this was one factor which influenced the court in reaching its conclusion that the arrangement did not amount to a tenancy. In *Irish Shell & BP Ltd v. Costello Ltd* [1981] ILRM 66, the majority of the Supreme Court ruled that hiring fees for the use of petrol tanks and other items supplied with the premises amounted in substance to rent and held that the agreement created a tenancy. Kenny J dissented on this point and held that as rent was not payable, a tenancy had not been created as this was an essential requirements set out by s. 3 of Deasy's Act.
365. [1997] IEHC 230.
366. [2002] IEHC 103.

Kenny Homes and instead relied heavily on the English case, *Street v. Mountford*.[367] He ruled that the agreement gave rise to a tenancy in spite of the express provisions of the agreement and the fact that the occupier, an experienced businessman who had engaged his own solicitors to negotiate the terms of the agreement on his behalf, admitted in evidence that he understood that he was only getting a license. In a recent High Court decision, *Esso Ireland Ltd v Nine One Ltd*,[368] McGovern J refused to follow Peart J's decision in *Smith*. The decision in *Smith* has also been criticized by the Law Reform Commission on the basis that it carries the courts' supervisory function too far and effectively rewrites a commercial agreement which had been negotiated at arms' length by the parties' solicitors.[369] It recommended the introduction of statutory guidelines which would require the courts to give effect to the parties' express agreement in this respect, provided they have each had the benefit of independent legal advice. If it can be established that no advice had been received, it would be open to the court to disregard an express provision, but only if the court is satisfied that it does not reflect the party in question's true intention and that its enforcement would prejudice that party.[370] This recommendation will be implemented if the Draft General Scheme of the Landlord and Tenant Law Reform Bill 2011[371] is enacted.[372] It should also be mentioned that the Law Reform Commission in its proposed re-enactment of section 3 of Deasy's Act stipulates that an obligation to pay rent, although broadly defined, is necessary to create the relationship of landlord and tenant.[373]

§4. Formalities

145. The grant of a tenancy may in certain circumstances be preceded by a contract to grant a lease. In such circumstances, the contract can only give rise to an

---

367. [1985] AC 809. The House of Lords ruled in this case that, save in exceptional circumstances, the offer and acceptance of residential accommodation with exclusive possession for a term at a rent, results in the creation of a tenancy. Wylie notes, however, that the English courts have increasingly emphasized that this approach should not necessarily be adopted in a commercial situation, particularly where the parties have had the benefit of independent professional advice, *see* Wylie, *Landlord and Tenant Law* 3rd edn (Dublin: Bloomsbury Professional, 2014), para 2.34; *National Car Parks Ltd v Trinity Developments Co (Banbury) Ltd* [2001] EWCA Civ 1686; *Clear Channel UK Ltd v Manchester CC* [2005] EWCA Civ 1304. *See also* Haley, 'Licences of Business Premises: Contract, Context and the Reach of Street v Mountford' *Northern Ireland Legal Quarterly* 64 no. 3 (2013): 425.
368. [2013] IEHC 514. McGovern J ruled that the agreement in question was a licence and stated: 'The court should be slow to look behind the clear terms negotiated by the parties at arm's length and in circumstances where each was legally represented.'
369. Law Reform Commission, *Consultation Paper on General Law of Landlord and Tenant* (LRC CP 28–2003), para. 1.30.
370. *Ibid.*, para. 1.31; *see* s. 11 of the draft Bill attached to the Law Reform Commission, *Report on the Law of Landlord and Tenant* (LRC 85–2007).
371. *See* s. 10(3) of the draft Bill attached to the Law Reform Commission, *Report on the Law of Landlord and Tenant* (LRC 85–2007).
372. Draft General Scheme of the Landlord and Tenant Law Reform Bill 2011, Head 11.
373. Draft General Scheme of the Landlord and Tenant Law Reform Bill 2011, Head 10.

equitable tenancy and the tenancy is only effective as a legal interest once a grant has been made. However, section 4 of Deasy's Act provides that, subject to certain exceptions, such grants must comply with specified formalities in order to be effective at law. The section 4 formalities do not apply to periodic tenancies from year to year, month to-month or week to week or a tenancy for a fixed term of less than one year. Despite some initial confusion, it also seems to be settled that the section 4 requirements do not apply to a tenancy for one year.[374] However, all other tenancies must be created by deed or a note in writing which is executed by the landlord or his authorized agent. Although the language used in section 4 appears to also apply these formalities to a contract to grant a lease, it is settled that such contracts are governed by alternative statutory formalities. Section 51(1) of the Land and Conveyancing Law Reform Act 2009, which re-enacts section 2 of the Statute of Frauds (Ir) 1695, provides that such a contract cannot be enforced unless it is evidenced by a written note or memorandum which is signed by the person being sued or his agent. The Law Reform Commission has recommended that section 4 of Deasy's Act should be recast in language which eliminates the uncertainties just discussed.[375] It proposed that the reference to contracts for the grant of a tenancy should be dropped. It also recommended clarification that any tenancy for a recurring period which does not exceed one year or any tenancy for a fixed period which does not exceed one year[376] may be created orally.

146. If the requisite section 4 formalities have not been complied with, but the tenant has gone into possession and started paying rent, the courts may imply a periodic tenancy based on how the rent is calculated.[377] Alternatively, if the parties had entered into a contract for a tenancy which failed to comply with the requirements of section 51(1) of the Land and Conveyancing Law Reform Act 2009, it may be possible to seek a remedy of specific performance based on the equitable doctrine of part performance. This approach, known as the rule in *Walsh v. Lonsdale*[378] allows an informal lease to be treated as a contract for a lease. On this basis it is sometimes suggested that a contract for a lease was as good as a lease, although clearly its equitable status makes it more precarious, as equitable remedies are discretionary and it may not bind a purchaser of a legal interest under the rules governing priorities.[379]

147. An assignment of a lease involves a transfer of the tenant's entire interest to the assignee so that the original tenant steps out of the picture and the assignee becomes the new tenant. It frequently requires the payment of a fine (i.e., a lump sum) to the assignor. A sub-letting typically involves the grant of a tenancy by the tenant for a term that is shorter than his own, so that the head (original) tenant retains a

374. Although it was held in *Wright v. Tracey* (1874) IR 8 CL 478 that a tenancy for one year certain was not less than a tenancy from year to year, this decision has been criticized by subsequent case law, *see Jameson v. Squire* [1948] IR 153, 165–166.

375. Law Reform Commission, *Consultation Paper on General Law of Landlord and Tenant* (LRC CP 28–2003), paras 2.10–2.15, *see* s. 12 of the draft Bill attached to the Law Reform Commission, *Report on the Law of Landlord and Tenant* (LRC 85–2007). *See also* Draft General Scheme of the Landlord and Tenant Law Reform Bill 2011, Head 12.

376. This would not apply to a tenancy with an option to renew which, if exercised, would result in the tenancy's combined periods exceeding one year.

377. *See* Wylie, *Irish Land Law*, 5th edn (Dublin: Bloomsbury Professional, 2013), para. 19.17.

378. (1882) 21 Ch D 9.

379. *See* paras 70–76 above.

reversionary interest and continues to be liable for rent to his own landlord under the head lease, while in receipt of rent from the sub-tenant. A sub-letting must comply with the formalities set out in section 4 of Deasy's Act as it creates a new relationship between landlord and tenant. However, section 9 of Deasy's Act requires an assignment of an oral or a written tenancy to be made by deed or instrument in writing signed by the assignor or his agent, by devise or bequest or by act and operation of law. It is beyond doubt that when an assignment of the tenant's interest or a conveyance of the landlord's interest takes place, the covenants in the lease bind the successors in title of the original parties to the lease and the original parties cease to be liable for any breach which occurs after the transaction. However, the duplication of statutory provisions governing this situation by sections 11–16 of Deasy's Act and sections 10 and 11 of the Conveyancing Act 1881 has given rise to a degree of confusion. Therefore, the Law Reform Commission has recommended the amalgamation of these rules into a single set of provisions governing the matter. It also recommended that these new statutory provisions should make comprehensive provision for part assignments to ensure clarity in respect of the rights and obligations of the respective parties.[380]

§5. The Obligations of Landlords and Tenants

148. The obligations of the landlord and tenant depend upon the covenants or terms contained in the lease or tenancy agreement. These covenants may be expressly agreed or implied by common law or statute. Some express covenants in a lease may not be enforceable in their existing format; they may be modified or even declared void by legislation. On the other hand, it may be possible to vary or exclude the operation of certain implied covenants by express provision. Although, in theory, the parties to a tenancy should be in a position to negotiate the terms of the lease to suit themselves, in practice, negotiations typically only take place in relation to commercial leases. In the case of a short-term residential tenancy, the inequality of bargaining power between the parties traditionally resulted in the lease being presented to the tenant on a 'take it or leave it' basis. This imbalance has recently been redressed by the Residential Tenancies Act 2004 which implies certain terms designed to protect tenants which cannot be modified, varied or excluded by express terms.[381]

I. Covenants Relating to Alienation, Change of User and Improvements

149. Landlords will frequently wish to restrict their tenants' freedom to assign or sub-let the premises. However, section 66(1) of the Landlord and Tenant (Amendment) Act 1980 provides that any express absolute prohibition or restriction on alienation

380. *See* Law Reform Commission, *Consultation Paper on General Law of Landlord and Tenant* (LRC CP 28–2003), Ch. 3; Part 4 of the draft Bill attached to the Law Reform Commission, *Report on the Law of Landlord and Tenant* (LRC 85–2007); and Draft General Scheme of the Landlord and Tenant Law Reform Bill 2011, Part 4.

381. Residential Tenancies Act 2004, s. 16.

contained in a lease of a tenement shall take effect as if it were a covenant prohibiting or restricting such alienation without the license or consent of the lessor.[382] Section 66(2) provides that such license or consent shall not be unreasonably withheld. To qualify as a 'tenement', the premises must comprise land wholly or partly covered by buildings and any land uncovered by buildings must be subsidiary and ancillary to those buildings.[383] What is reasonable, in the context of withholding consent, depends on the circumstances of the case and the onus of proving that consent has been unreasonably withheld lies on the tenant.[384] If there are genuine doubts over the solvency of the proposed assignee, the refusal of consent will be deemed to be reasonable.[385] However, this does not mean that a landlord can insist that the assignee is of equal or greater financial standing than the assignor.[386] It may, in certain circumstances, be reasonable to insist on a guarantee being put in place before consenting to the assignment, but not a draconian one.[387] The Law Reform Commission has recommended that the burden of proof associated with consent applications should be reversed to ensure that landlords deal expeditiously with such applications. In addition, it has recommended the introduction of a number of new procedural requirements, e.g., the landlord would be required to give reasons for a refusal of consent within a time limit.[388]

150. The proposed assignee may need to alter the user of the premises, and a lease will often include a covenant prohibiting such an alteration in user. Section 67 of the 1980 Act subjects such express covenants to a similar modification designed to ensure that such alterations can take place with the consent of the landlord, which cannot be unreasonably withheld.[389] Recent case law indicates that a landlord of a shopping centre may refuse such consent in the interests of good estate management where necessary to achieve a good mix of tenants. For example, in *OHS Ltd v. Green*

382. The landlord may, however, require the payment of a reasonable sum for legal or other expenses incurred.
383. Landlord and Tenant Amendment Act 1980, s. 5. Note that the Law Reform Commission has recommended the removal of this restriction, *see Consultation Paper on Business Tenancies* (LRC CP 21-2003), 3.43; Draft General Scheme of the Landlord and Tenant Law Reform Bill 2011, Part 6, Ch. 3.
384. Rice *and Kenny v. Dublin Corporation* [1947] IR 425.
385. *Burns v. Morelli* [1953–1954] IR Jur Rep 50.
386. *Extra-Vision Ltd v. Chevas Securities Ltd* (CC) 1 Mar. 2005.
387. *Gunne Estate Agents (Dublin) v. Pembroke Estates Management Ltd* (CC) 15 May 2000.
388. *See Consultation Paper on Business Tenancies* (LRC CP 21-2003), para 3.44–3.46 and 4.47; Draft General Scheme of the Landlord and Tenant Law Reform Bill 2011, Part 6, Ch. 3. Until these reforms are implemented, an aggrieved tenant will not be able to sue for damages to cover a loss caused by an uncooperative landlord in the context of a consent application, *see Meagher v Luke J Healy Pharmacy Ltd* [2010] IESC 40. However, the courts have recently insisted that the landlord must disclose all bona fide reasons for their decision to refuse consent. The landlord may not refuse consent for an improper motive and then attempt to rely on a new, good reason for refusal in court, *see Perfect Pies (In Receivership) and Pearse Farrell v Chupn Ltd* [2015] IEHC 692.
389. Note that the Law Reform Commission's recommendations in relation to applications for consent (*see* para 149, in particular, text accompanying fn. 388, above) apply to any provision of a tenancy which prohibits or restricts the doing of anything by the tenant in relation to the premises without the consent of the landlord.

Property Co Ltd,[390] a covenant restricted the user of the premises to a fruit and vegetable shop but the proposed assignee wished to run a building society from the premises. The landlord argued that such an alteration in user would result in too many 'dead frontages' in the shopping centre. The court was satisfied that the refusal of consent was reasonable.[391]

151. Sometimes a covenant will be included prohibiting the tenant from carrying out alterations or improvements to the premises, the landlord being anxious to preserve the identity of what is still 'his' property. A covenant in a lease which absolutely prohibits the making of improvements is not permitted and is modified by section 68(1) of the 1980 Act to take effect as if it were a covenant prohibiting or restricting the making of any improvement without the license or consent of the landlord, which cannot be unreasonably withheld.[392] Section 67(3) defines an improvement as any addition or alteration short of a change causing the building to lose its original identity. In *O'Neill v. Murphy*,[393] the court accepted that it was not unreasonable for a landlord to withhold consent if he was not provided with sufficient details of the improvements proposed. As shall be discussed later, the tenant may be entitled to compensation on the determination of the lease for such improvements.[394]

152. The reasonableness of the landlord's decision to refuse consent to alienation, a change of user or improvements will only be an issue in relation to tenancies which are not governed by the Residential Tenancies Act 2004. Section 16 of the Residential Tenancies Act 2004 imposes an obligation on residential tenants not to assign, sub-let, alter, improve or change the use of the dwelling without the landlord's written consent. However, in the case of residential tenancies, landlords are entitled to exercise their absolute discretion in refusing consent. The only exception is if the landlord refuses to consent to an alternation or improvement which consists only of repairing, painting or decorating; in such circumstances, the decision by the landlord must be reasonable.

II. Fixtures

153. A related matter is the extent to which tenants may remove fixtures at the end of the tenancy. The traditional rule at common law was that fixtures attached to the premises by the tenant belonged to the landlord and had to be surrendered along with the premises on determination of the tenancy. Gradually, the courts relaxed this rule[395] and the new position was recognized by section 17 of Deasy's Act which permits

390. [1986] IR 39.

391. *See* also *Wanze Properties (Ireland) Ltd v. Mastertron Ltd* [1992] ILRM 746; *Irish Glass Bottle Ltd v. Dublin Port* [2005] IEHC 89.

392. Note that the Law Reform Commission's recommendations in relation to applications for consent (*see* para. 149, in particular, text accompanying fn. 388, above) apply to any provision of a tenancy which prohibits or restricts the doing of anything by the tenant in relation to the premises without the consent of the landlord (with the exception of a proposal to carry out works on or to the premises which are more substantial than an improvement).

393. [1918] IR 72.

394. *See* para. 167 below.

395. *Poole's Case* (1703) 1 Salk 368.

the removal of 'personal chattels, engines and machinery and buildings accessorial thereto, erected and affixed to the freehold by the tenant at his sole expense for any purpose of trade, manufacture, or agriculture, or for ornament, or for the domestic convenience of the tenant' provided the removal shall not cause substantial damage to the property or the fixture and the agreement does not provide otherwise. The landlord is entitled to compensation for any damage that does occur. The fixture must be removed during the tenancy or if it determines due to an uncertain event, through no act or default of the tenant, within two months of its determination. The Law Reform Commission has recommended that the law relating to fixtures should be replaced by new statutory provisions which would allow for such matters to be dealt with by express provisions in the lease but also set out certain default provisions which would improve the current law and clarify certain ambiguities which have arisen.[396]

III. Covenants Relating to Good Title and Quiet and Peaceable Enjoyment

154. Section 41 of Deasy's Act implies a covenant on the part of the landlord that he has good title to grant the lease and that the tenant shall have quiet and peaceable enjoyment of the premises, without interference from the landlord or any person whomsoever for the duration of the lease, provided the tenant performs his obligations under the lease. The obligation to protect against disturbances by 'any person whomsoever' is extremely broad and appears to expose a landlord to liability for the actions of a person over whom he has no control. Therefore, it is typically modified by an express covenant on the part of the landlord which reduces his exposure in relation to such disturbances to his own acts or those of anyone for whom he is responsible. The Law Reform Commission has recommended that this implied covenant should be limited to reflect the more limited scope invariably adopted by express covenants.[397] In the case of a residential tenancy, the landlord is obliged to allow the tenant to enjoy peaceful and exclusive occupation of the building.[398]

IV. Covenants Relating to Repairs, Maintenance and Insurance

155. Express obligations on the part of the tenant to repair and insure the premises are very common in certain commercial leases, known as Full Repairing and Insuring Leases (or FRI leases). In contrast, in the case of short-term residential tenancies, the

---

396. Law Reform Commission, *Consultation Paper on General Law of Landlord and Tenant* (LRC CP 28–2003), para. 4.19; Part 5 of the draft Bill attached to the Law Reform Commission, Report on the Law of Landlord and Tenant (LRC 85–2007); Draft General Scheme of the Landlord and Tenant Law Reform Bill 2011, Part 5.

397. Law Reform Commission, *Consultation Paper on General Law of Landlord and Tenant* (LRC CP 28–2003), para. 6.05; s. 26(1)(b) of the draft Bill attached to the Law Reform Commission, *Report on the Law of Landlord and Tenant* (LRC 85–2007); Draft General Scheme of the Landlord and Tenant Law Reform Bill 2011, Head 26.

398. Residential Tenancies Act 2004, s. 12(1)(a).

landlord may expressly covenant to keep the premises in a state of good repair. In the case of a long lease (e.g., for a term of 300 years) of an apartment, the lessor will usually expressly covenant to repair damage to the exterior of the property and to maintain the common areas. This function is frequently delegated to a management company, or transferred to such a company along with ownership of the common areas, and the lease will include a covenant by the lessee to pay a service charge to cover such expenses. If the landlord covenants to carry out repairs, it is often accompanied by a related covenant giving the landlord or his agent the right to enter or view the premises at reasonable notice, in order to carry out such repairs.

156. If the lease or tenancy agreement is silent on the issue of repairs, traditionally there was no implied covenant on the part of the landlord in this respect. The principle of *caveat emptor* applied which meant that the tenant had to take the property as he found it.[399] The tenant was also obliged under the law of waste[400] to keep the premises 'wind and watertight' or in a 'tenant-like manner' depending on the type of tenancy. Over the years, the common law[401] and legislation have modified this position in respect of residential tenancies let by public authorities or private landlords. In the case of the letting of a *furnished* house, the common law implied a covenant on the part of the lessor that the premises are fit for human habitation at the commencement of the tenancy.[402] The Housing (Miscellaneous Provisions) Act 1992 facilitated the introduction of regulations governing standards for lettings of rented dwelling houses.[403] Subject to certain exceptions, landlords are obliged to ensure that houses meet certain minimum standards which relate *inter alia* to the structural condition, sanitary facilities, heating, food preparation/storage, laundry; ventilation, lighting, fire safety, refuse facilities and electricity/gas. Enforcement is the responsibility of the local authorities, and their powers have recently been extended to include the possibility of serving improvement

---

399. *Scales v. Vandeleur* (1913) 48 ILTR.

400. As amended by ss 25–39 of Deasy's Act, *see* Wylie, *Landlord and Tenant Law,* 3rd edn (Dublin: Bloomsbury Publishing, 2014), paras 15.22–15.24. The Law Reform Commission has recommended that the law of waste should no longer apply between landlord and tenants and that ss 25–39 of Deasy's Act should be repealed without replacement, *see Consultation Paper on General Law of Landlord and Tenant* (LRC CP 28–2003), paras 10.3–10.5; Draft General Scheme of the Landlord and Tenant Law Reform Bill 2011, Head 45(1).

401. In addition (or as an alternative) to any liability for breach of an implied contractual term, the landlord may be found to be liable for damages for negligence, *see Siney v. Dublin Corporation* [1980] IR 400, 422. Note that the Law Reform Commission has recommended the enactment of a statutory provision imposing an overriding obligation on the landlord on the grant of a tenancy of premises for immediate occupation or use in its existing state to take reasonable care to see that all persons who might reasonably be expected to be affected by defects in the state of the premises at the date of the grant (whether or not those defects have been created by the landlord) are reasonably safe from personal injuries or from damage to their property caused by such defects, *see* s. 29 of the draft Bill attached to the Law Reform Commission, *Report on the Law of Landlord and Tenant* (LRC 85–2007); Draft General Scheme of the Landlord and Tenant Law Reform Bill 2011, Head 29.

402. *Wilson v. Finch Hatton* (1877) 2 Ex D 336.

403. Housing (Standards for Rented Dwellings) Regulations 1993 (SI 147/1993); Housing (Standards for Rented Dwellings) Regulations 2008 (SI 534/2008); *see* Ryall, 'Great Expectations: Standards for Rented Housing', *Conveyancing and Property Law Journal* 15, no. 1 (2010): 15.

and prohibition notices on the landlord.[404] These statutory obligations are supplemented by section 12 of the Residential Tenancy Act 2004 which requires the landlord to carry out certain structural and internal repairs, to insure the dwelling, to reimburse tenants for expenditure on repairs that were appropriate to the landlord and to refund deposits unless there is damage beyond normal wear and tear.

157. Section 42 of Deasy's Act implies a covenant in every lease that the tenant shall keep[405] the demised premises and give peaceable possession of it in good and substantial repair and condition on the determination of the lease. Section 16 of the Residential Tenancies Act 2004 imposes certain obligations on residential tenants, including a duty to inform the landlord of any defect which it is the landlord's responsibility to repair,[406] to allow the landlord access to carry out repairs, to refrain from actions which would result in the condition of the premises deteriorating below its condition at the commencement of the tenancy (fair wear and tear excepted), or which results in the premises failing to meet the minimum standards imposed by the regulations made under the Housing (Miscellaneous Provisions) Act 1992. The tenant is also obliged to refrain from anti-social behaviour in the vicinity of the premises and actions which would invalidate the landlord's insurance policy. In addition, the tenant is obliged to pay any increase in the landlord's insurance premium attributable to the tenant's actions. The Law Reform Commission has recommended the introduction of certain statutory obligations on landlords and tenants in relation to repairs, maintenance and insurance to govern other tenancies[407] which would mirror to a large extent those set out in the 2004 Act. These obligations would, however, only apply as the default position, in the absence of relevant legislation or an express provision in the tenancy agreement or lease.

V. Covenants Relating to Rent and Outgoings

158. The primary covenant undertaken by the tenant is to pay a specified rent at appointed, regular intervals often in advance. The tenant will usually be responsible for paying rates and other overheads, such as gas and electricity, although in short-term residential tenancies, landlords sometimes undertake to pay certain outgoings. Section 42 of Deasy's Act implies a covenant into all leases that the tenant will pay the rent reserved, when due, and section 16 of the Residential Tenancies Act 2004 imposes a similar obligation to pay the rent and any other charges or taxes expressly imposed

404. *See* the amendments to s. 18 of the Housing (Miscellaneous Provisions) Act 1992 introduced by the Housing (Miscellaneous Provisions) Act 2009.

405. The obligation to keep the premises in repair has been held to imply an obligation to put the premises into repair if it is in a state of disrepair at the commencement of the tenancy, *see Groome v. Fodhla Printing Co Ltd* [1943] IR 380.

406. Note that the landlord is under an obligation to provide the tenant with details of any agent with authority to act on his behalf and how the tenant may contact the landlord or his agent.

407. Law Reform Commission, *Consultation Paper on General Law of Landlord and Tenant* (LRC CP 28–2003), paras 6.18 and 10.1–10.10, and Ch. 11. *See also* ss 28, 30, 45 and 46 of the draft Bill attached to the Law Reform Commission, *Report on the Law of Landlord and Tenant* (LRC 85–2007). Draft General Scheme of the Landlord and Tenant Law Reform Bill 2011, Heads 28, 30, 45 and 46.

by the lease or tenancy agreement.[408] This is subject to an important limitation imposed by section 19 of the Residential Tenancies Act 2004 that the initial rent or any subsequent rent set by way of a rent review shall not exceed the market rent for the tenancy at the time. A rent review clause has traditionally been a valuable feature of a lease from the landlord's perspective,[409] although the more onerous aspects of such clauses have been substantially modified by recent legislation. Section 20 of the Residential Tenancies Act 2004, as amended, provides that a rent review cannot take place more than once every twenty-four months[410] unless there is a substantial change in the nature of the accommodation which would influence the market rent. The landlord must also follow certain procedures when carrying out a rent review, designed to ensure that a residential tenant has sufficient notice and protection.[411] In the commercial sector, a last-minute provision[412] was included in the Land and Conveyancing Law Reform Act 2009 which imposes a prohibition on 'upwards only' rent review clauses in leases of land to be used wholly or partly for the purpose of carrying on a business entered into after the commencement date.[413] Such a clause shall instead be construed as allowing for a downwards as well as an upwards review. Recently, more forthright measures of rent control were introduced in the residential rental sector. The Planning and Development (Housing) and Residential Tenancies Act 2016 facilitated the introduction of a cap on rent increases at 4% per annum for the next three years in designated Rent Pressure Zones.[414]

---

408. The Law Reform Commission has recommended the introduction of a similar default statutory obligation on tenants of other tenancies to pay rent and outgoings, *see Consultation Paper on General Law of Landlord and Tenant* (LRC CP 28–2003), Ch. 8; ss 38 and 44 of the draft Bill attached to the Law Reform Commission, *Report on the Law of Landlord and Tenant* (LRC 85–2007); Draft General Scheme of the Landlord and Tenant Law Reform Bill 2011, Heads 38–44.
409. Where the lease does not include a rent review clause, the landlord has a statutory right to require a rent review pursuant to the Residential Tenancies Act 2004, s. 21.
410. As originally enacted, s. 20 restricted the frequency of rent reviews to once every twelve months, but the frequency was restricted to once every twenty-four months for a four-year period by the Residential Tenancies (Amendment) Act 2015, s. 25. Note, however, that landlords of new tenancies (and existing tenancies following a transitional period) in Rent Pressure Zones are entitled to a rent review every twelve months pursuant to the Planning and Development (Housing) and Residential Tenancies Act 1916, s. 36.
411. For example, landlords must serve the tenant with a written notice in the prescribed form ninety days before the revised rent is due to take effect, *see* Residential Tenancies Act 2004, s. 22 (as substituted by Residential Tenancies (Amendment) Act 2015, s. 26).
412. Land and Conveyancing Law Reform Act 2009, s. 132. *See* Bennett, 'Section 132 of the Land and Conveyancing Law Reform Act 2009', *Conveyancing and Property Law Journal* 15, no. 1 (2010): 12.
413. 28 Feb. 2010.
414. The Planning and Development (Housing) and Residential Tenancies Act 2016, Part 3. At the date of writing, Dublin and Cork city and certain Local Electoral Areas in Co Cork, Galway, Kildare, Wicklow and Meath have been designated Rent Pressure Zones.

VI. Enforcement of Obligations

159. Where one party is in breach of his obligations under the lease, a number of remedies may be provided by the agreement or by the general law. As the agreement is usually drawn up on behalf of the landlord, until recently, these remedies tended to favour the landlord. Either party may sue the other for damages for breach of contract for any losses incurred as a result of a breach of covenant. Alternatively, an order for specific performance of the agreement or an injunction to prevent certain behaviour from continuing may be sought. Section 87 of the Landlord and Tenant Amendment Act 1980, which applies only to tenements, entitles a tenant to execute repairs and then to set off the expenditure against the rent, provided the landlord refuses or fails to carry out repairing obligations despite being called upon by the tenant to do so.[415]

160. If the tenant is in breach of his obligation to pay rent, the remedies available under contract law are supplemented by section 45 of Deasy's Act, which confers the landlord with a statutory right to sue for rent in arrears. In addition, the landlord may, at least in theory, avail of the common law remedy of distress which allows the landlord the right to enter the premises and seize the chattels of the tenant and hold them as a pledge until the tenant pays the rent. This remedy is no longer available in respect of certain tenancies and in other cases stringent restrictions have been imposed on its exercise by legislation.[416] It is argued that the remedy may be inconsistent with the protection afforded to property rights by the Irish Constitution[417] and the Law Reform Commission has proposed its abolition in so far as it continues to survive.[418] Landlords have a special right of ejectment[419] for non-payment of rent under section 52 of Deasy's Act right, a remedy which is rarely invoked as at least one-year's rent must be in arrears.[420]

415. Section 49 of the draft Bill attached to the Law Reform Commission, *Report on the Law of Landlord and Tenant* (LRC 85–2007) extends and tightens up the remedy provided by s. 87 of the 1980 Act. *See also* Draft General Scheme of the Landlord and Tenant Law Reform Bill 2011, Head 49. In England, a landlord's failure to perform covenants in a lease has, in certain circumstances, been held to amount to a repudiatory breach of contract, *see Chartered Trust plc v. Davies* [1997] 2 EGLR 83; Wylie, 'The Great Escape', *Law Society Gazette* (April 1999), 28. Draft General Scheme of the Landlord and Tenant Law Reform Bill 2011, Head 61, clarifies that the doctrine of repudiatory breach of contract may be invoked by a tenant against a landlord.

416. It was abolished in relation to tenancies of dwellings by the Housing (Miscellaneous Provisions) Act 1992, s. 19. In other cases, it is highly restricted; for example, under section 7 of the Sunday Observance Act (Ir.), 1695 distress cannot be made on a Sunday and under the Law of Distress and Small Debts (Ir.) Act, 1888, various goods are protected or exempt from distress. If a wrongful distress is made, then the tenant may seek damages or an injunction to prevent against the loss of the goods.

417. *See* Wylie, *Irish Land Law,* 5th edn (Dublin: Bloomsbury Publishing, 2013), para. 19.73.

418. *See* s. 41 of draft Bill attached to the Law Reform Commission, *Report on the Law of Landlord and Tenant* (LRC 85–2007); Draft General Scheme of the Landlord and Tenant Law Reform Bill 2011, Head 41.

419. It has been noted that the term 'ejectment' is a misnomer in this context as the primary aim is not to recover possession but to enforce payment of the rent, *see* Law Reform Commission, *Consultation Paper on General Law of Landlord and Tenant* (LRC CP 28–2003), para. 8.19.

420. The Law Reform Commission has recommended that this action should be abolished, *Ibid.*, para. 8.20.

161. At common law, the landlord can re-enter the property or treat the lease as forfeited if the tenant is in breach of a condition (a vital term) of the agreement. However, an express re-entry or forfeiture clause to govern any breach of covenant by the tenant is commonly included in a lease. These remedies shall be further discussed in the next section.

§6. Determination of the Relationship

162. There are a number of ways in which the relationship of landlord and tenant may come to an end. It is important to bear in mind, however, that this area is subject to statutory control and the tenant in question may have a right to a new tenancy.[421]

I. Expiry and Notice

163. In the case of a lease for a fixed term, the tenancy will determine on the expiry of that term. Sometimes, such a lease may include a clause permitting either or both parties to determine the tenancy before completion of the term by serving a notice to quit. It is also common for landlords to include a proviso for re-entry or forfeiture in the event of a breach of a covenant by the tenant. If the tenancy is periodic, for example from week to week or month to month, then a notice to quit must be served to bring it to an end. Unless protection is conferred by legislation, the landlord is entitled to determine a periodic tenancy simply because he wants to; his motive is irrelevant and the tenant does not have to be in breach of any of the covenants. In the case of agricultural or pastoral holdings,[422] houses[423] and residential tenancies,[424] the notice must be in writing and, even if written notice is not required, it may be important for the purposes of proof. If a period of notice is not specified in the agreement, the common law requires reasonable notice to be given. In the case of a weekly tenancy, one week's notice is required, in the case of a monthly tenancy, one month's notice is required and in the case of a yearly tenancy, six month's notice is required.[425] Section 16 of the Housing (Miscellaneous Provisions) Act 1992 introduced a statutory minimum period of four week's notice for tenants of houses. In many cases, this requirement is now be superseded by the notice periods set out in Part 5 of the Residential Tenancies Act 2004.[426] A residential tenancy may only be terminated by a notice of termination served in accordance with the requirements set out under the 2004 Act. Such a tenancy may be terminated by the landlord for any reason during the first six months (unless

421. *See* paras 168, 169 and 173 below.
422. *See* Landlord and Tenant (Ir) Act 1870, ss 58 and 71; Notices to Quit (Ir) Act 1876.
423. Housing (Miscellaneous Provisions) Act 1992, s. 16.
424. Residential Tenancies Act 2004, s. 62(1)(a).
425. The common law requirements in relation to notice shall be replaced by certain default provisions set out by the Draft General Scheme of the Landlord and Tenant Law Reform Bill 2011, Part 7, Ch. 4.
426. New notice periods were recently inserted by the Residential Tenancies (Amendment) Act 2015, ss 31 and 32.

it is a fixed term tenancy) and, thereafter, by the tenant provided the specified notice periods are complied with. After the first six months, the tenant becomes entitled to a 'Part 4 Tenancy' for a further period of three and a half years (i.e., four years in total) or five and a half years (i.e., six years in total), depending on when the tenancy was created).[427] During a Part 4 Tenancy the landlord may only terminate the tenancy in specified circumstances set out in section 34 of the Residential Tenancies Act 2004: for example, if the tenant fails to comply with his obligations after being notified of a breach and given a chance to remedy it, if the landlord is selling the property or requires it for his own occupation or occupation by a member of his family or if he intends to substantially refurbish, renovate or change the use of the dwelling and planning permission, if necessary, has been obtained. Certain evidential requirements must be complied with by landlords relying on section 34 reasons for termination.[428] In addition, restrictions were recently imposed on a landlord wishing to terminate a Part 4 Tenancy on the basis that they are selling the property if it forms part of a development of ten units or more owned by the same landlord and they intend to sell the other units.[429]

II. Surrender

164. A tenant does not have a right to surrender the tenancy unless it is expressly conferred by lease or statute. Section 40 of Deasy's Act permits a tenant, who is not subject to an express covenant to repair, to surrender the tenancy on the destruction of demised premises by accidental fire or other inevitable accident not due to the default or neglect of the tenant.[430] Under section 7 of Deasy's Act, a tenant can surrender the tenancy to the landlord by a deed or note in writing or by act and operation of law. This facilitates an oral surrender accompanied by other actions, such as handing over the keys and vacating the premises.

III. Forfeiture and Re-entry

165. As has already been mentioned, if a tenant does not comply with a condition of the tenancy, the tenancy may be forfeited by the landlord and the lease itself may

427. *See* Residential Tenancies Act 2004, s. 28. The term of a Part 4 tenancy was extended from four years to six years by the Planning and Development (Housing) and Residential Tenancies Act 2016, s. 37, in respect of new tenancies created on or after 24 Dec. 2016.
428. As inserted by the Residential Tenancies (Amendment) Act 2015, ss 28 and 29.
429. Residential Tenancies Act 2004, s. 35A, as inserted by the Planning and Development (Housing) and Residential Tenancies Act 2016, s, 40.
430. The Law Reform Commission has recommended the introduction of statutory clarification that an agreement excepting an obligation to do repairs relating to insured risks operates to exclude the tenant's right of surrender under s. 40 of Deasy's Act, *see Consultation Paper on General Law of Landlord and Tenant* (LRC CP 28–2003), para. 11.04. It also recommended that tenants should have the right to insist that any insurance proceeds are used to reinstate the premises as an alternative to the right of surrender, *see* para. 11.07; Draft General Scheme of the Landlord and Tenant Law Reform Bill 2011, Head 30.

contain a forfeiture clause for any breach of covenant.[431] This method of termination is not available in respect of residential tenancies.[432] The right of the landlord to validly forfeit is dependent on certain conditions being satisfied. He must show that he followed certain procedures designed to give the tenant a reasonable opportunity to remedy the breach. Section 14(1) of the Conveyancing Act 1881 Act requires the lessor to serve a notice on the lessee before he enforces any right of forfeiture which specifies the breach complained of and requires it to be remedied or else compensation to be paid to the landlord. In addition, for an effective forfeiture to occur the landlord must either get an order for possession from the court or must actually and physically enter the property and retake possession of same.[433] A landlord who attempts to effect a forfeiture by re-entry must be wary of the dangers of violating section 2 of the Forcible Entry and Occupation Act 1971 which makes it a criminal offence to use force to enter the land. It is often safer to seek a court order for possession by bringing an action for Ejectment on Title based on Forfeiture of the Lease, which is the most common type of ejectment proceedings. It should be noted that the tenant and any sub-tenant has the right to apply to court for relief against forfeiture. The court has a general discretion to grant whatever relief it thinks is fit in light of the parties' conduct and all the other circumstances of the case.[434] The Draft General Scheme of the Landlord and Tenant Law Reform Bill 2011 sets out various provisions designed to simplify the law in this area.[435]

§7. Statutory Rights under the Landlord and Tenant (Amendment) Act 1980

166. The Landlord and Tenant (Amendment) Act 1980 applies only to 'tenements' as defined by section 5,[436] although the Law Reform Commission has recommended that this restriction and the requirement for buildings on the land should be removed.[437] In addition, it has proposed the repeal and replacement of substantial segments of this Act, although it has also recommended that any reforms should only apply to tenancies granted after the commencement of the implementing legislation.[438]

431. *See* para. 159 above.
432. Residential Tenancies Act 2004, s. 58(1).
433. O. Hanlon J emphasized this point in *Bank of Ireland v. Lady Lisa Ireland Ltd.* [1992] 1 IR 404.
434. *See Ennis v. Rafferty* (1838) 72 ILTR 56; *Blake v. Hogan* (1933) 67 ILTR 237.
435. Part 7, Chapters 6 and 7.
436. To qualify as a 'tenement', the premises must comprise land wholly or partly covered by buildings and any land uncovered by buildings must be subsidiary and ancillary to those buildings.
437. Law Reform Commission, *Consultation Paper on Business Tenancies* (LRC CP 21–2003), paras 3.15–3.16. Draft General Scheme of the Landlord and Tenant Law Reform Bill 2011, Head 80(a). 3.
438. Part 8 of the draft Bill attached to the Law Reform Commission, *Report on the Law of Landlord and Tenant* (LRC 85–2007), Draft General Scheme of the Landlord and Tenant Law Reform Bill 2011, Part 8.

I. The Right to Compensation for Improvements

167. Under Part IV of the 1980 Act, a tenant of a tenement is entitled to compensation from his landlord where the tenant quits the tenement for every improvement[439] made by him or his predecessors in title which adds to the letting value and is suitable to the character of the tenancy. It is available to both residential and business tenants unless the tenant terminated the tenancy by notice of surrender or otherwise or it was terminated by the landlord for non-payment of rent.[440] The amount of compensation is usually agreed between the landlord and the tenant but if there is a failure to reach agreement, the Circuit Court fixes the amount of compensation payable as the capitalized value of the addition to the letting value of the tenement.[441] To be able to take advantage of this right, the tenant must serve a notice of intention to execute the improvement in question, giving details of the work and estimates of its cost and a copy of the planning permission if it is required.[442] If the landlord does not object within one month, he is deemed to have consented to the changes. During this one-month period the landlord has three options: he can simply consent to the improvement; serve an 'improvement undertaking' agreeing to do the work himself and asking for an increased rent in the future; or object to the improvement by serving an 'improvement objection'. Where consent has been forthcoming, the tenant must execute the improvement within one year.[443] Where an improvement undertaking has been served by the landlord, the tenant can object to the increased rent and bring an application to the Circuit Court to determine the new rent or to deal with the matter as an improvement objection.[444] In the case of an outright objection by the landlord, the tenant can simply resign himself to withdrawing the notice for improvement or apply to the Circuit Court for an order authorizing the improvement.[445] The court may reject the tenant's application if satisfied that the tenancy has less than five years to run and the tenant is not entitled to a new tenancy[446] because the landlord can establish one of the grounds specified in section 17(2)(a) of the Act.[447] The rationale behind this restriction is that the tenant's interest is too slight to justify an improvement. While the service of an improvement notice is not obligatory, if the tenant fails to do so, he runs a risk of losing his entitlement to compensation if the landlord can establish that he was prejudiced by the failure to serve notice, that the improvement was in contravention

439. Defined by s. 45 of the 1980 Act as 'any addition or alternation of the buildings comprised in the tenement and includes any structure erected on the tenement which is ancillary or subsidiary to those buildings and also includes the installation in the tenement of conduits for the supply of water, gas or electricity but does not include work consisting only of repairing, painting and decorating, or any of them'.

440. Landlord and Tenant (Amendment) Act 1980, s. 46.

441. It is a mathematical calculation made in accordance with s. 47 of the 1980 Act which takes into account benefits received by the tenant by way of deduction of rent.

442. Landlord and Tenant (Amendment) Act 1980, s. 48.

443. Landlord and Tenant (Amendment) Act 1980, s. 50.

444. Landlord and Tenant (Amendment) Act 1980, s. 51.

445. Landlord and Tenant (Amendment) Act 1980, s. 55.

446. Landlord and Tenant (Amendment) Act 1980, s. 52.

447. Discussed in para. 167 below.

of a clause in the lease or that it injured the amenity or convenience of the neighbourhood.[448] Finally, where an improvement is carried out by the tenant, the landlord must issue, if asked, an improvement certificate certifying that the improvement has been made in accordance with the notice or order.[449] This certificate is conclusive evidence against a landlord or his successors in title who challenges the improvement at a later time. The Law Reform Commission has recommended the abolition of compensation for improvements on the basis that tenants should be expected to take a more commercial view of such matters; improvements should be regarded as an investment in the business which should not be entered into unless the tenant is satisfied that there will be an adequate return. The Commission was of the opinion that the scheme as it currently operates was open to abuse by tenants.[450]

II. The Right to a New Tenancy

168. Part II of the 1980 Act conferred a right to a new tenancy on tenants of tenements on the basis of a 'long occupation' equity, a 'business' equity, or an 'improvement' equity. The right to a new tenancy on the basis of long occupation required the continuous occupation of the property by the tenant or his predecessors in title for at least twenty years.[451] Since 1 September 2009, this right is no longer available in the case of tenancies governed by the Residential Tenancies Act 2004. Both a business and residential tenant may rely on section 13(1)(c) of the 1980 Act which confers tenants with right to a new tenancy where improvements have been carried out to the tenement and one-half of the letting value is attributable to those improvements.[452]

169. A business tenant may have a right to a new tenancy under section 13(1)(a) of the 1980 Act. This right is conferred on all tenants who have occupied and made total or partial use of the premises for the purposes of carrying on a business for a continuous period of five years.[453] In calculating this continuous period, a 'temporary break in the use' of a business tenement can be disregarded if the court considers it reasonable to do so.[454] Section 17 of the 1980 Act sets out various circumstances which will prevent a tenant from claiming an entitlement to a new tenancy. The right to a new tenancy does not arise if the existing tenancy was terminated for non-payment of

448. Section 54(2) of the 1980 Act.
449. Landlord and Tenant (Amendment) Act 1980, s. 55.
450. *Consultation Paper on Business Tenancies* (CP 21–2003), paras 3.38–3.40.
451. Landlord and Tenant (Amendment) Act 1980, s. 13(1)(b).
452. The tenant must also be in a position to prove that he would be entitled to claim compensation for those improvements under Part IV of the Act if he was quitting the premises. This prerequisite is not set out in relation to the right to a new tenancy on the basis of improvements set out in the draft Bill attached to the Law Reform Commission, *Report on the Law of Landlord and Tenant* (LRC 85–2007), although s. 4(1)(b) specifies that the improvements must not have been made in breach of a term of the tenancy. *See also* Draft General Scheme of the Landlord and Tenant Law Reform Bill 2011, Head 84(1)(b).
453. The period of occupation was extended from three to five years by s. 3(1) of the Landlord and Tenant (Amendment) Act 1994.
454. Landlord and Tenant (Amendment) Act 1980, s. 13(2).

rent, for a breach of covenant by the tenant, by the tenant's surrender of the tenancy or if the landlord gave notice to quit to the tenant for a good and sufficient reason. In addition, there is no entitlement to a new tenancy if the court is satisfied that the landlord intends or has agreed to execute a demolition, rebuilding or reconstruction scheme, requires vacant possession to redevelop the property or if a new tenancy would be inconsistent with good estate management. In these latter circumstances, the tenant may be entitled to compensation for disturbance on quitting the premises.[455]

170. While originally it was not possible to contract out of the rights conferred by the 1980 Act,[456] there has been a gradual legislative retreat from this position. Section 4 of the Landlord and Tenant Amendment Act 1994 permitted a tenant to execute a renunciation of his right to a new tenancy prior to the commencement of the original tenancy provided he had received independent legal advice and the tenancy related to a premises to be used wholly and exclusively as an office. The restrictive nature of this facility to contract out was subsequently criticized and the Law Reform Commission recommended the introduction of a general right to renunciate.[457] This proposal was implemented by sections 47 and 48 of the Civil Law (Miscellaneous Provisions) Act 2008.

171. To claim a new tenancy, a notice of intention to claim relief must be served on the landlord.[458] The court has power to extend the time limit within which such a notice must be served[459] and the tenant may remain in occupation until the application has been dealt with. The terms of the new tenancy are usually agreed between the tenant and the landlord, but if agreement cannot be reached, they may be fixed by the Circuit Court. Where the terms are fixed by the court, certain limits and criteria are taken into account in fixing the duration of the lease[460] and the rent payable.[461]

§8. The Residential Tenancies Act 2004

172. The Residential Tenancies Act 2004 does not apply to a dwelling which is used wholly or partly as a business by an occupant who would be entitled to a new tenancy pursuant the Landlord and Tenant (Amendment) Act 1980, a dwelling occupied by a tenant who would be entitled to purchase the ground rent pursuant to the Landlord and Tenant (Ground Rents)(No. 2) Act 1978, a dwelling governed by Part 2 of the

455. Landlord and Tenant (Amendment) Act 1980, s. 58(1)(a).
456. Landlord and Tenant Amendment Act 1980, s. 85.
457. *Consultation Paper on Business Tenancies* (CP 21–2003), paras 3.5–3.11.
458. Landlord and Tenant (Amendment) Act 1980, s. 20.
459. Landlord and Tenant (Amendment) Act 1980, s. 83.
460. Currently, a minimum term of five years and a maximum term of twenty years is fixed by the Landlord and Tenant (Amendment Act) 1994 Act, although the Law Reform Commission has proposed a reduction in the maximum term to ten years, *see* s. 90(1) of the draft Bill attached to the Law Reform Commission, *Report on the Law of Landlord and Tenant* (LRC 85–2007). Draft General Scheme of the Landlord and Tenant Law Reform Bill 2011, Head 90(1).
461. For example, in deciding the rent to be payable, the court may make an allowance for any improvements carried out by the tenant, *see* Landlord and Tenant (Amendment) Act 1980, s. 23(4).

Housing (Private Rented Dwellings) Act 1982,[462] a dwelling held under a shared ownership lease, a dwelling let for the purpose of a holiday or a dwelling occupied by the landlord or certain members of his family.[463] Although the 2004 Act originally excluded all public authority lettings, the Residential Tenancies (Amendment) Act 2015 extended the remit of the 2004 Act and lettings by approved housing bodies to a household which qualifies for social housing[464] that are now subject to a modified version of the obligations and protections conferred by the Act.

173. . Many of the rights conferred by the Residential Tenancies Act have already been mentioned. It imposes certain implied obligations on landlords and tenants which cannot be varied, modified or restricted by any provision of a lease or a tenancy agreement.[465] It also restricts to a certain extent the rent which can be demanded and the frequency of rent reviews.[466] However, the primary goal of this piece of legislation is to ensure security of tenure for residential tenants, by conferring an entitlement to a Part 4 tenancy. Once a person has occupied the dwelling under a tenancy for six months, the tenancy shall continue for a further three and a half years or five and a half years (depending on when the tenancy was created)[467] and may only be terminated by the landlord by the service of a notice of termination on the expiry of that period or provided one of the specified grounds are satisfied.[468] The Act makes provision for additional Part 4 tenancies to arise on the expiry of the previous one, provided a valid notice to terminate has not been served.

174. The Act also established the Residential Tenancies Board,[469] which in addition to its other functions[470] performs a dispute resolution role[471] in relation to disputes which arise between landlord and tenants regarding such matters as the

---

462. These dwellings were formerly known as 'controlled dwellings' under the Rent Restrictions Acts 1960 to 1981. 'Controlled' status was removed by the Housing (Private Rented Dwellings) Act 1982 and the terms of tenancies governing former controlled dwellings, including the rent payable, were set by the Rent Tribunal established under the Housing (Private Rented Dwellings) Amendment Act 1983. The Rent Tribunal was dissolved on 8 Jan. 2016 by the Residential Tenancies (Amendment) Act 2015 and its functions were transferred to the Residential Tenancies Board.
463. Residential Tenancies Act 2004, s. 3(2).
464. Residential Tenancies Act 2004, s. 3(2)A.
465. Residential Tenancies Act 2004, s. 18.
466. Residential Tenancies Act 2004, Part 3. Note the recent reforms which have been introduced in this respect, discussed at para. 158, above.
467. Residential Tenancies Act 2004, s. 28. The term of a Part 4 tenancy was extended from four years to six years by the Planning and Development (Housing) and Residential Tenancies Act 2016, s. 37, in respect of new tenancies created on or after 24 Dec. 2016.
468. These grounds are set out in the table to s. 34 of the 2004 Act and are listed in para. 161 above.
469. The name of the Board was recently changed from the Private Residential Tenancies Board to the Residential Tenancies Board to reflect its extended remit, *see* Residential Tenancies (Amendment) Act 2015, s. 13.
470. Residential Tenancies Act 2004, s. 151.
471. Residential Tenancies Act 2004, Part 6.

retention or refund of deposits,[472] rental and other obligations, disputes in relation to the termination of tenancies and the failure by tenants to vacate the premises following a termination, claims for costs or damages relating to breaches of obligations and disputes in relation to compliance with determinations made by the Board.[473]

§9. The Right to Purchase the Ground Rent

175. During the nineteenth century, it became common for landowners to enter into an arrangement with a builder to grant a lease conditional on a house being constructed on the land. After the house was built, a lease would be granted to a nominee of the builder, or a sub-lease or assignment of the original lease would be granted to a purchaser who would pay a large capital sum or fine (reflecting the value of the house). These leases were typically granted for long terms of ninety-nine years or more and the rent reserved under such leases was typically low, reflecting only the value of the ground. The difficulty, from the perspective of the occupant under the lease, was that on the expiry of the lease, the lessor became the owner of the house under the law of fixtures and as the term drew to an end, the lease became an unmarketable wasting asset. In an effort to improve the position of such lessees, legislation was introduced which conferred them with an entitlement to a reversionary lease which would commence on the expiry of the original lease.[474] A more forthright attempt to resolve the problems of such lessees was adopted by the Landlord and Tenant (Ground Rents) Act 1967 which conferred on lessees who satisfied certain conditions a right to purchase the ground rent (i.e., the fee simple) and any other intermediate interests in the property. The test for determining the right to buy out the freehold is now governed by the Landlord and Tenant (Ground Rents) No. 2 Act 1978[475] which also prohibited the creation of new ground rents in relation to dwelling houses. In addition, the 1978 Act introduced a new simplified procedure for acquiring the ground rent of dwelling houses which is operated by the Property Registration Authority. The purchase price is currently calculated in accordance with a formula which is set out in section 7 of the Landlord and Tenant (Amendment) Act 1984.[476]

472. Residential Tenancies Act 2004, s. 135A, as inserted by the Residential Tenancies (Amendment) Act 2015, s. 61, imposes an obligation on the landlord to transfer the tenant's deposit to the Board for its protection during the tenancy. Note, however, that at the date of writing, the relevant provisions have yet to be commenced.

473. Residential Tenancies Act 2004, s. 78.

474. *See* the Landlord and Tenant Act 1931 and the Landlord and Tenant (Reversionary Leases) Act 1958.

475. As amended by the Landlord and Tenant Amendment Acts 1980 and 1984. *See* , in particular, ss 9, 10, 15 and 16 of the Landlord and Tenant (Ground Rents) (No. 2) Act 1978.

476. *See* further Brennan, *Ground Rents: A Practitioner's Guide* (Dublin: Roundhall, 2005); Wylie, *Landlord and Tenant Law,* 3rd edn (Dublin: Bloomsbury Professional, 2014), Ch. 31.

Chapter 7. Security Interests in Land

§1. General

176. If an unsecured loan is made, the lender runs the risk of not being repaid the sum owed. If the borrower simply refuses to pay, the lender will have to bring legal proceedings and obtain a judgment against him. If the borrower refuses to comply with the judgment, the lender will have to bring more proceedings to enforce the judgment. In the meantime, if the borrower is declared bankrupt, the lender may fail to recover any of the debt or may only succeed in recovering a fraction of it, as secured creditors will have priority in terms of recovering their debts. Lenders of money typically seek to reduce this risk by making the loan conditional on the debtor providing personal or proprietary security. A guarantee by a third party is an example of personal security, while a mortgage is an example of proprietary security. A lender with a mortgage over land owned by the borrower will be able to enforce that security against the secured property to discharge the debt in priority to any general creditors if the debtor is declared bankrupt.

§2. The Creation of a Mortgage

177. Until recently, legal mortgages of unregistered land were created by a conveyance of the fee simple, an assignment of the leasehold interest, or a demise (lease) or sub-demise (sub-lease) of a term in favour of the mortgagee, subject to a proviso for redemption (a covenant to re-convey or re-assign the interest) or cesser of the term if all monies due under the mortgage are repaid. The interest retained by the mortgagor in the property is referred to as his 'equity of redemption' and can be valued as the current market value of the property less the amount required to redeem the mortgage. In the case of a mortgage by a conveyance of the fee simple, the entire of the legal estate is vested in the mortgagee, so any subsequent mortgages over the property could only be carved out of the equity of redemption. Such equitable mortgages are referred to as puisne mortgages. An advantage of a mortgage by sub-demise was that it facilitated subsequent legal mortgages by sub-demise, with the term granted for each successive mortgage being for a slightly longer period.

178. Since the commencement of the Land and Conveyancing Law Reform Act 2009,[477] it is no longer possible to create a legal mortgage by these methods. The Law Reform Commission was of the opinion that the traditional method of transferring ownership of the land to the mortgagee was inconsistent with the true nature of a mortgage transaction which is to provide security for a loan.[478] It recommended the simplification of the law on this issue and concluded that the obvious solution was to

477. 1 Dec. 2009.

478. *Consultation Paper on Reform and Modernization of Land Law and Conveyancing Law* (LRC CP 34–2004), para. 9.04.

apply the method of mortgaging registered land, by way of charge, to unregistered land.[479] Under this approach, the registered owner retains ownership but the legislation makes it clear that the owner of the charge has all the rights and powers of a mortgagee under a mortgage by deed for the purpose of enforcing his charge.[480] An advantage of this method of creation is that any number of legal charges may be created in relation to the land, although the holders of subsequent legal charges will obviously need to be wary of the dangers of lending on the basis of inadequate security.

179. Section 89(1) of the Land and Conveyancing Law Reform Act 2009 provides that from the commencement date, a legal mortgage of land may only be created by a charge by deed, thereby aligning the law in this area for both unregistered and registered land. It also abolishes the welsh mortgage,[481] a method of security which is unheard of in modern times. It is likely that any attempt to create a legal mortgage by the old methods will result in the creation of an equitable mortgage. Section 89(6) of the 2009 Act expressly preserves the law relating to the creation of equitable mortgages.

180. Traditionally, the most common type of equitable mortgage was one created by a deposit of title deeds with the lender. This gives the mortgagee a lien on the land to which the deeds relate. It is only necessary to deposit the deeds which provide material evidence of title and in the case of registered land, until recently, this required the deposit of the land certificate. A deposit of title deeds is regarded as prima facie evidence of an equitable mortgage unless it can be proved that the deeds were lodged with the bank for safe keeping. Any ambiguity in relation to the reason for the deposit could, of course, be removed by recording the intention of the parties in writing. However, as was illustrated by the decision in *Fullerton v. Provincial Bank of Ireland*,[482] there is a danger that such a document could be construed as a deed which must be registered in the Registry of Deeds in order to secure priority. Although the theoretical basis for such a mortgage has sometimes been disputed,[483] it is a well-established method of creating a mortgage. However, the mortgage by deposit of title deeds has become less popular in recent times. Its dwindling popularity can probably be attributed to the current banking crisis which renders such informality in the creation of mortgages highly unlikely in the future and also to the abolition of land certificates and charge certificates by section 73 of the Registration of Deeds and Title Act 2006. These certificates had to be lodged in the Land Registry in order to register any disposition involving registered land to ensure that an equitable mortgagee was not defrauded. However, the system was criticized as being completely incompatible with the

---

479. *Ibid.*, paras 9.05–9.06.

480. Registration of Title Act 1964, s. 62. Since the Land and Conveyancing Law Reform Act 2009(Sch. 1), a prescribed form must be used to create a charge, *see* rule 105, Land Registration Rules 2012 (SI 483/2012. The charge must be registered as a burden affecting the land, Registration of Title Act 1964, s. 69(1)(b). Until recently, a charge certificate would be issued by the Land Registry to the owner of the registered charge. However, these certificates are no longer issued and have ceased to have effect pursuant to s. 73 of the Registration of Deeds and Title Act 2006, *see* para. 180 below.

481. Defined by s. 89(8) of the 2009 Act as a transaction under which the mortgagee is entitled to hold possession, and take rents and profits in lieu of interest on a loan, of land without the mortgagor being under a personal obligation to repay the loan, but being entitled to redeem.

482. [1903] AC 309, on appeal from [1902] 1 IR 483.

483. Wylie, *Irish Land Law*, 5th edn (Dublin: Bloomsbury Professional, 2013), para. 12.45.

introduction of an eConveyancing system[484] and giving rise to a huge administrative burden for the Land Registry in terms of the storage and replacement of lost land and charge certificates. Their abolition means that it will no longer be possible to create an equitable mortgage by a deposit of title deeds over registered land in the future. However, existing equitable mortgagees were given the opportunity to protect their security by the registration of a lien on the folio before 1 January 2010.[485]

181. It is also possible to create an equitable mortgage by an assignment of an equitable interest in land as security for the monies advanced. This is usually created by deed, although section 6 of the Statute of Frauds (Ireland) Act 1695 only requires it to be in writing and signed by the assignor. Finally, an agreement for a legal mortgage which complies with the statutory formalities for contracts in relation to land[486] or which can be enforced pursuant to the doctrine of part performance also creates an equitable mortgage.

§3. The Position of the Parties under a Mortgage

182. The mortgagee and the mortgagor have a number of rights and powers in relation to the property. In relation to mortgages created prior to the Land and Conveyancing Law Reform Act 2009, it was the legislature's intention that their positions would continue to be governed by the old law: a combination of the express terms of the mortgage and the provisions of the Conveyancing Acts 1881–1911 as modified by those express terms. However, as shall be discussed below,[487] a legislative lacuna appears to have been temporarily created by the repeal of certain provisions. Mortgages created after the commencement of the 2009 Act are governed by Part 10 of that Act, which has incorporated certain consumer protectionist elements which can no longer be avoided by the express terms of a mortgage created in respect of a housing loan. However, where a commercial mortgage is created, the provisions set out in Part 10 remain (for the most part) default terms which may be varied or excluded by the terms of the mortgage.

I. The Mortgagee: Title Documents

183. Where a mortgage was created by a conveyance of the fee simple prior to the 2009 Act, the mortgagee, as the owner of the fee simple, is automatically entitled to possession of the title deeds. However, where the mortgage was created by an assignment of a leasehold interest or the demise or sub-demise of a term, the mortgagee has no rights to the freehold title deeds, unless the mortgagor surrendered his rights by the mortgage deed. As has already been mentioned, in the case of registered land,

484. *See* 183 Seanad Debates Col. 783.
485. Registration of Deeds and Title Act 2006, s. 73(3).
486. Such an agreement must be evidenced in writing and signed by the person against whom the action is brought or his authorized agent, *see* Land and Conveyancing Law Reform Act 2009, s. 51.
487. *See* paras 185–186 below.

the land certificate and the certificate of charge are no longer effective as title documents and the owner of a registered charge must now rely solely on the register as evidence of its security. In relation to mortgages created after the commencement of the 2009 Act, section 90(2) provides that the first mortgagee has the same right to possession of documents of title as such a mortgagee would have had if the security had been created by a conveyance before the commencement of the Act. This right to possession of the title deeds is qualified by the mortgagor's entitlement to inspect and make copies of them at reasonable times[488] and to have them restored to his possession on the redemption of the mortgage. Section 90(3) of the 2009 Act imposes a statutory duty on the mortgagee to ensure their safe custody.[489]

II. The Mortgagee: Insurance

184. In the case of a mortgage created by deed prior to the 2009 Act and a legal mortgage created under Part 10 of the 2009 Act, the mortgagee has a statutory power to insure the mortgaged property.[490] In the absence of an express term to the contrary in a mortgage deed created prior to the 2009 Act, the amount of insurance cover is limited to two-thirds of the reinstatement value. No such restriction is imposed by the statutory power to insure conferred by the 2009 Act.

III. The Mortgagee: Enforcement of Security

185. The most important powers of the mortgagee concern the enforcement of its security for the loan in the event of a default by the mortgagor. First, it should be mentioned that the remedy of foreclosure which is commonly relied on in England and consists of the extinguishment of the mortgagor's equity of redemption has never proved popular in Ireland. The mortgagee's right of foreclosure is abolished by section 96(2) of the Land and Conveyancing Law Reform Act 2009. Second, it should be noted that although the legislature intended the old law to continue to govern mortgages created before the commencement of the 2009 Act, the 2009 Act repealed certain important statutory provisions relating to the enforcement of security. It repealed section 19 of the Conveyancing Act 1881 which conferred a statutory power on a mortgagee in a mortgage made by deed to sell the property and to appoint a receiver and section 62(7) of the Registration of Title Act 1961 which allowed the owner of a charge of registered land to apply to court for an order for possession. Some have argued that section 27(1)(c) of the Interpretation Act 2005 applied to these older mortgages to preserve any rights 'acquired' or 'accrued' under any enactment before

488. Land and Conveyancing Law Reform Act 2009, s. 91, which re-enacts Conveyancing Act 1881, s. 16.
489. This reverses the common law position that a mortgagee was not responsible for their safe custody, see *Gilligan v. National Bank Ltd* [1901] 2 IR 513.
490. Conveyancing Act 1881, s. 19; Land and Conveyancing Law Reform Act 2009, s. 110.

its repeal.[491] However, in a very controversial decision, *Start Mortgages v Gunn,*[492] Dunne J ruled that unless the principal sum had become due before the commencement of the 2009 Act, the right of the owners of the charges before him to seek possession under section 62(7) of the 1964 Act had not 'accrued' or been 'acquired' and, therefore, was not saved by the Interpretation Act. In that particular case, the principal sum did not become due under the terms of the mortgage until a demand for payment had been made. This decision created significant doubts about the enforceability of the security created by certain mortgages and the situation was exacerbated by its timing. Many mortgages were created before 1 December 2009 and the financial crises led to a very substantial rise in defaults on mortgages. It should also be remembered that many mortgages had been acquired by the National Asset Management Agency[493] which would, in many cases, be relying on the usual mortgagee remedies for the enforcement of its security. Subsequent case law introduced more uncertainty. For example, in *Kavanagh and Lowe v Lynch*[494] Laffoy J held that mortgagees of such older mortgages could still rely on the express terms of their mortgage deeds which created independent contractual rights of enforcement. This would be the case, even if the deed incorporated the repealed statutory provisions by way of cross-reference but varied them. However, the limits to such an approach became obvious in *Irish Life and Permanent Plc v Duff*[495] where Hogan J held that in the case of a charge of registered land, a contractual right to possession could not be relied on and, therefore, the repeal of s. 62(7) of the 1964 Act was critical.

186. The uncertainty created by this case law imposed a substantial burden on legal professionals advising lenders. Whether you could enforce a mortgage created before the 2009 Act would depend on: whether the mortgage related to unregistered land or registered land; whether a legal date for redemption was included in the deed or whether a demand for payment had to be made before the money became due and this condition had been satisfied before 1 December 2009; and whether or not any contractual powers were conferred by the deed.[496] Although originally the government intended to wait for a Supreme Court ruling on appeal clarifying that the repealed provisions continued to apply to these older mortgages, eventually it had to succumb to pressure to introduce legislative clarification. The situation has since been remedied by section 1 of the Land and Conveyancing Law Reform Act 2013 which reverses the repeal of the relevant statutory provisions. Therefore, although mortgagees may now enforce their security by relying on the old law, it may be necessary to institute new enforcement proceedings as the reversal only operates from the commencement date.[497]

---

491. *See* Wylie, *Irish Land Law,* 5th edn (Dublin: Bloomsbury Professional, 2013), paras 14.23–14.27; *McEnery v Sheahan* [2012] IEHC 331.
492. [2011] IEHC 275.
493. This Agency (known as 'NAMA') was established by the National Asset Management Agency Act 2009 to rescue insolvent banks through the acquisition of 'toxic' debts. For a discussion of the impact of the repeal on the remedies available to NAMA, *see* Wylie, *Irish Land Law,* 5th edn (Dublin: Bloomsbury Professional, 2013), para. 14.40.
494. [2011] IEHC 348.
495. [2013] IEHC 235. *See* also *Irish Life and Permanent Plc v Dunphy*]2013] IEHC 43 where Hogan J stated a case for the opinion of the Supreme Court on this issue.
496. *See* Wylie, *Irish Land Law,* 5th edn (Dublin: Bloomsbury Professional, 2013), para. 14.39.
497. 24 Jul. 2013.

A. Court Order for Possession Followed by a Sale by the Mortgagee

187. A sale of the property with vacant possession by the mortgagee is likely to realize the best price. In the case of a mortgage created prior to the 2009 Act, the mortgagee as the owner of a legal fee simple or leasehold interest has an automatic right to possession by virtue of that ownership, although most mortgagees will be content to allow the mortgagor to retain possession unless he defaults on his repayments. In the case of legal mortgages created by charge executed post-2009, this automatic right to possession is preserved.[498] Where the mortgagee seeks an order for possession it will typically be a precursor to exercising an express or statutory power of sale. However, the mortgagee may seek possession or appoint a receiver to take possession in order to take over the management of the business with a view to salvaging it and ensuring the ongoing repayment of the mortgage. In such circumstances, it may still eventually become necessary to realize the security by a sale of the property. The courts have an inherent jurisdiction to make an order to put a legal or an equitable mortgagee into possession[499] and the 1962 Rules of Superior Court 1986 facilitate an application for such a remedy by special summons.[500]

188. The 2009 Act has imposed a number of limitations on the mortgagee's right to possession where the mortgage is to secure a housing loan. A mortgagee who wishes to take possession must obtain a court order unless the mortgagor consents in writing to the mortgagee taking possession within seven days of such action. The court order for possession may be granted to the applicant on such terms and conditions as the court thinks fit.[501] A summary procedure is available to obtain possession if the mortgagor has abandoned the property and urgent steps are necessary to protect it.[502] Once possession has been taken, the mortgagee is under a duty to take steps within a reasonable time to exercise the power to sell the property or, if this is not appropriate, to lease the property and use the rent to reduce the mortgage debt.[503]

189. Most mortgages contain an express term permitting the mortgagee to sell the property freed from the equity of redemption. In the absence of such a term, section 19 of the Conveyancing Act 1881 confers such a power of sale on mortgagees in respect of all mortgages created by deed. Once the power of sale has 'arisen' under this section, the interest of the mortgagor is overreached on a sale by the mortgagee to the purchaser. This statutory power of sale does not arise until the mortgage money has become due. In the case of a mortgage by instalments, it arises once the mortgagor fails to meet an instalment, but in the case of most mortgages, it arises once the legal date for redemption has passed (usually three or six months into the mortgage). However, the mortgagee's power of sale is only exercisable if one of the following three conditions set out in section 20 of the Conveyancing Act 1881 is met: a notice

---

498. Land and Conveyancing Law Reform Act 2009, s. 90(1)(b).
499. *See Re O'Neill* [1967] NI 129.
500. Order 54, rule 3. Note that the Registration of Title Act 1964, s. 62(7), permits the registered owner of a charge to apply to court for an order for possession when repayment of the principal money secured by the charge has become due.
501. Land and Conveyancing Law Reform Act 2009, s. 97.
502. Land and Conveyancing Law Reform Act 2009, s. 98.
503. Land and Conveyancing Law Reform Act 2009, s. 99.

requiring payment of the money has been served on the mortgagor and a failure to make payment has continued for three months after the service of the notice; some of the interest payable under the mortgage has been in arrears and unpaid for two months after becoming due; or the mortgagor has been in breach of a covenant in the deed other than the covenant to repay the money.[504]

190. If the mortgage money is not due, the power of sale has not 'arisen' and the sale to the purchaser will be subject to the mortgagor's equity of redemption. If the power has arisen but is not exercisable, the rights of the mortgagor will be overreached by the sale[505] but the mortgagee may have to compensate someone who suffers damage as a result of the improper use or irregular use of the statutory power of sale. The mortgagee, when exercising his power of sale under this section, has a broad discretion as to how he may sell the property, e.g., he may sell it in lots and by private treaty or public auction.[506] The proceeds of sale are then applied to discharge all prior encumbrances, to pay the costs of the sale, to discharge the mortgage debt, interest and costs due under the mortgage, and the balance is paid to subsequent mortgagees or the mortgagor.[507]

191. In accordance with the Law Reform Commission's recommendation in this regard,[508] the distinction between a power of sale arising and becoming exercisable has been eliminated in respect of mortgages executed post-2009. Section 96(1)(b) of the 2009 Act provides that the statutory powers and rights of the mortgagee under a mortgage created by deed vest as soon as the mortgage is created. However, in recognition of the security nature of the transaction,[509] these powers do not become exercisable unless their exercise is for the purpose of protecting the mortgaged property or realizing the mortgagee's security.[510] In addition, where a housing loan is involved, the power of sale does not become exercisable unless one of the three conditions mentioned above[511] has been satisfied and a twenty-eight days' notice served on the mortgagor, warning of the possibility of such a sale, has expired.[512] As is the case with taking possession, such a power of sale shall no longer be exercisable without a court order unless the mortgagor consents to the sale within seven days of the power being exercised.[513] An application for an order for possession and an order for sale may be

504. Conveyancing Act, s. 20, is re-enacted by Land and Conveyancing Law Reform Act 2009, s. 100(1).
505. *See* the protections for the purchaser imposed by the Conveyancing Act 1881, ss 21(2) and 22(1) and the Conveyancing Act 1911, s. 5(1). Similar protections are imposed by the Land and Conveyancing Law Reform Act 2009, ss 105 and 106(1).
506. Conveyancing Act 1881, s. 19(1)(i); Conveyancing Act 1911, s. 4. Similar powers are imposed by the Land and Conveyancing Law Reform Act 2009, s. 102.
507. Conveyancing Act 1881, s. 21(3). The Land and Conveyancing Law Reform Act 2009, s. 107, re-enacts this order of payment.
508. *Consultation Paper on Reform and Modernization of Land Law and Conveyancing Law* (LRC CP 34–2004), paras 9.13–9.14.
509. *Ibid.*, paras 9.13–9.15.
510. Land and Conveyancing Law Reform Act 2009, s. 96(1)(c).
511. *See* end of para. 186 above which sets out the conditions provided by the Conveyancing Act 1881, s. 20, and re-enacted by the Land and Conveyancing Law Reform Act 2009, s. 100(1).
512. Land and Conveyancing Law Reform Act 2009, s. 100(3).
513. Land and Conveyancing Law Reform Act 2009, s. 100(2).

heard together[514] and the Circuit Court is deemed to have exclusive jurisdiction in such matters where a housing loan is involved.[515] The court has jurisdiction, in considering such applications, to adjourn them or to stay the enforcement or implementation of an order for such period as it thinks reasonable where it appears to the court that the mortgagor is likely to be able within a reasonable period to pay any arrears, including interest, due or to remedy any other breach of obligation arising under the mortgage.[516] This jurisdiction is in addition to the power of the court to stay proceedings for possession or a sale of the family home if it appears that the spouse of the mortgagor is desirous and capable of paying the arrears within a reasonable time and future repayments.[517] In any proceedings by a mortgagee seeking an order for possession of land comprising the mortgagor's principal private residence, the court now also has the power to adjourn possession proceedings for up to two months to facilitate the making of a proposal for a Personal Insolvency Arrangement.[518] Finally, in a number of recent cases[519] the court has considered whether there was compliance with certain codes of practice regulating mortgage lenders in exercising its discretion on whether to grant an order for possession. The Consumer Protection Code 2012 and the Code of Conduct on Mortgage Arrears 2013 require a lender to take certain steps to resolve the consumer's difficulties before enforcement action is taken in relation to mortgage arrears and, where the arrears relate a mortgage on a borrower's primary residence, the lender is required to operate procedures designed to explore alternatives to enforcement action.

192. When the mortgagee exercises a power of sale, it is in the interest of the mortgagor and any subsequent mortgagees that the best price possible is obtained. However, it has been held that the mortgagee is not a trustee of his power of sale, although he must act in good faith when exercising this power. The implications of this good faith requirement were examined by the Supreme Court in *Holohan v. Friends Provident and Century Life Office*[520] which held that it involved an examination of what a reasonable man would do in the mortgagee's position. A reasonable man was required to bear in mind the interests of the mortgagor and subsequent mortgagees and to take care to see that a fair market price is obtained for the property. In the case of a mortgage by a building society, the building society is under a statutory obligation to ensure, as far as is reasonably practicable, that the property is sold at the best price reasonably obtainable.[521] Section 103(1) of the Land and Conveyancing Law Reform Act extends a similar statutory obligation to all mortgagees or receivers exercising an

514. Land and Conveyancing Law Reform Act 2009, s. 100(4).
515. Land and Conveyancing Law Reform Act 2009, s. 101(5).
516. Land and Conveyancing Law Reform Act 2009, s. 101(1).
517. Family Home Protection Act 1976, s. 7.
518. Land and Conveyancing Law Reform Act 2013, s. 2. A Personal Insolvency Arrangement is one of the debt resolution mechanisms introduced by the Personal Insolvency Act 2012 designed to enable debtors to discharge their debts without having to become bankrupt. It can be applied to secured debts, such as a mortgage, provided the debt does not exceed €3 million.
519. *See Stepstone Mortgage Funding Ltd v Fitzell* [2012] IEHC 142; *Irish Life and Permanent Plc v Duff* [2013] IEHC 43.
520. [1966] IR 1.
521. Building Societies Act 1989, s. 26(1).

express or statutory power of sale which cannot be varied or excluded, even by the terms of a commercial mortgage.

B. Court Order for Sale

193. If the mortgagee cannot sell the property without the intervention of the court, he may bring proceedings to have the property sold by the court. A court sale is generally less lucrative than a sale conducted by the mortgagee and always takes place by auction. The court will determine if the mortgage is well charged on the mortgagor's property (i.e., was it validly created) and then make an order directing the sale of the property if the amount due is not paid within three months. The order directing the sale will also direct that the priority of the mortgages affecting the property be determined.

C. Priority Disputes

194. Priority disputes between successive mortgagees are generally resolved in accordance with registration principles[522] or the doctrine of notice[523] which were discussed in an earlier chapter.[524] However, a number of doctrines have operated to modify these principles. If the mortgage was created before the 2009 Act and the right was expressly reserved, a mortgagee may have the right to consolidate certain mortgages. This right arose if the same mortgagor created two mortgages affecting two different properties in favour of the same mortgagee. It protected the mortgagee if the mortgagor sought to redeem one of his mortgages leaving the other mortgage inadequately secured. This right has been criticized and has been abolished in respect of the redemption of any housing loan mortgage by section 92 of the 2009 Act. However, it may still be exercised by commercial mortgagees, even if the right is not expressly reserved. Another modification to the general rules governing priorities is referred to as 'tacking' and it applies if a mortgage is expressed to be created for the purpose of securing future advances and is followed by subsequent mortgages. The original mortgagee is entitled, in priority to any subsequent mortgage, to the payment of any sum due in respect of such future advances unless the subsequent mortgagee gave express notice in writing of the creation of the subsequent mortgage to the original mortgagee.[525]

---

522. Charges of registered land must be registered as burdens and will take effect in accordance with the order of registration. Although a mortgage/charge of unregistered land need not be registered in the Registry of Deeds, registration will ensure priority against an earlier unregistered deed (unless there was actual knowledge of that earlier unregistered deed.
523. Where a mortgage is unregistrable e.g., an equitable mortgage created by a deposit of title deeds, the priority of such a mortgage over a subsequent registered mortgage will depend on whether the latter mortgagee had notice of the earlier mortgage.
524. *See* paras 70–75.
525. *See* Registration of Title Act 1964, s. 75; Land and Conveyancing Law Reform Act 2009, s. 111(1). Note that s. 111(3) of the 2009 Act abolishes all other forms of tacking from the commencement date, *see* Wylie, *Irish Land Law,* 5th edn (Dublin: Bloomsbury Publishing, 2013), para. 13.120.

D. *The Position of the Mortgagee in Possession*

195. As was mentioned earlier,[526] the mortgagee will generally seek possession of the property as a precursor to realizing his security by sale. However, a mortgagee may also go into possession to secure the regular payment of the interest charged on the capital sum by intercepting the rents and profits issuing out the land. A mortgagee in possession is entitled to lease the property pursuant to section 18 of the Conveyancing Act 1881 subject to certain limitations and the satisfaction of certain conditions.[527] Such a mortgagee also has the power to cut or sell timber where the trees are not of an ornamental nature.[528] The main disadvantage of his position is that a mortgagee in possession is strictly liable to account to the mortgagor for the income which he actually receives but also the income which could have been generated from the land but for his mismanagement.[529] In addition, he is generally not entitled to charge remuneration for the work he does in this respect. As a result, the practice developed of appointing a receiver to manage the property. The receiver is deemed to be an agent of the mortgagor and so the mortgagee would not be liable to account for the receiver's acts or defaults.[530] The restrictions on taking possession and the obligations imposed on mortgagees in possession pursuant to housing loans have already been outlined.[531] In making an order for possession, the court may impose whatever terms and conditions it thinks fit. In addition, sections 112 and 113 of the 2009 Act substantially re-enact the powers of leasing conferred by section 18 of the 1881 Act, but with certain modifications.[532]

E. *The Appointment of a Receiver*

196. The power to appoint a receiver may be expressly set out in the mortgage or it may arise under section 19 of the Conveyancing Act 1881 Act in respect of mortgages created prior to the 2009 Act or under section 108 of the 2009 in relation to more recent mortgages. This power is only exercisable if one of the three conditions discussed earlier in the context of the power of sale is satisfied.[533] A receiver is often appointed where the property comprises a business and its value as a security is largely dependent on the efficient running of that business (e.g., a hotel). The receiver manages the property, receiving any rents and profits, and ensuring that the income does not go directly to the mortgagor but is applied in accordance with a statutory order of priority.[534]

526. *See* para. 187 above.
527. Note that this power to lease the property is also available to the mortgagor.
528. Conveyancing Act 1881, s. 19(1)(iv).
529. *Metcalf v. Campion* (1828) 1 Mol 238.
530. Conveyancing Act 1881, s. 24; Land and Conveyancing Law Reform Act 2009, s. 108(2).
531. *See* para. 188 above.
532. For a discussion of the old and the new rules governing the power to lease and accept a surrender of a lease which may be exercised by both the mortgagor and the mortgagee, *see* Wylie, *Irish Land Law,* 5th edn (Dublin: Bloomsbury Professional, 2013), paras 13.65–13.78.
533. *See* end of para. 186 above which sets out the conditions provided by the Conveyancing Act 1881, s. 20, and re-enacted by the Land and Conveyancing Law Reform Act 2009, s. 100(1).
534. Conveyancing Act 1881, s. 24(8); Land and Conveyancing Law Reform Act 2009, s. 109.

IV. The Mortgagor: The Right to Redeem

197. The most important right of the mortgagor is his right to redeem the mortgage, which is his right to get the property back freed from the mortgage or charge, on the repayment of the loan. At common law, the rule was that unless the loan was repaid on an agreed day, known as the legal date of redemption, the mortgagor's right to redeem the mortgage was extinguished and the mortgagee became the absolute owner of the land. This strict approach to the date of redemption was exacerbated by the fact that the debt owed to the mortgagee remained in existence and the mortgagor could be sued for it notwithstanding the fact that his land had been forfeited. The courts of chancery gradually intervened and mitigated the harsh approach of the common law courts in this respect. Equity 'looked to the substance and not the form of the transaction' and viewed the main purpose of the transaction as the provision of security for the repayment of a debt. Time was not the essence of the transaction[535] and a failure to make the payment on the day fixed by the contract was not a sufficient reason to permanently deprive the mortgagor of what, in reality, was his property. The mortgagor, therefore, possesses an equitable right to redeem after the contractual or legal date of redemption. This position is preserved by section 90(1) of the Land and Conveyancing Law Reform Act 2009 in relation to mortgages created after the 2009 Act which provides that the mortgagor has the same powers and rights and the same protection at law and in equity as the mortgagor would have been entitled to if the mortgage had been created by a conveyance of the legal estate.

198. It is a basic principle, therefore, that once the loan has been repaid, the mortgagor must be able to redeem the mortgage and get it back freed from all the conditions and incidents of the mortgage. . Any clause which attempts to exclude the mortgagor's right to redeem will be void as being inconsistent with the nature of a mortgage. Equity's approach is encapsulated in a variety of maxims, such as 'a mortgage cannot be made irredeemable' and 'clogs or fetters may not be placed upon the equity of redemption'. However, the application of this principle to various clauses included in mortgages has not always been straightforward or free from controversy. When examining such clauses the courts have been attempting to walk a tightrope and achieve a balance between giving effect to freely negotiated contracts while protecting the equity of redemption. It has been suggested that the courts or the legislature should limit its application in modern times given its propensity to hinder the development of new forms of financial security and restrict the contractual freedom of commercial parties operating at arm's length.[536]

A. Clauses Which Postpone the Right to Redeem

199. A balance has to be achieved in relation to conditions postponing the right to redeem, as an early redemption makes for a less profitable transaction from the mortgagee's point of view. In order for such a condition to be valid, it must not render

535. The mortgagee instead expects that the loan and the interest on it will be paid off in instalments over many years, usually between fifteen and thirty years.

536. Thompson, 'Do We Really Need Clogs?', *Conveyancer and Property Lawyer* 65 no. 6 (2001): 502.

the right to redeem illusory or be an oppressive or unconscionable term. Where the property is held pursuant to a lease, certain conditions may be easily identified as rendering the right to redeem illusory. In *Fairclough v. Swan Brewery Co Ltd*,[537] the tenant of a brewery with only seventeen and half years left to run on his lease entered into a mortgage. The mortgage contained a provision preventing redemption until the lease had only six weeks left to run. The court held that this provision rendered the right to redeem illusory and ruled that redemption could take place before this date. Where a mortgage of a fee simple is concerned, it may be more difficult to determine the acceptability of the condition postponing redemption and it will often be examined on the basis whether it is oppressive or unconscionable. In *Knightsbridge Estates Trust Ltd v. Byrne*,[538] the court upheld a term postponing the right to redeem a mortgage for forty years. The loan was repayable by instalments over a forty-year period as requested by the mortgagors and there was no provision permitting early redemption. The mortgagors sought to redeem because interest rates had fallen and they hoped to negotiate a new loan at a lower rate. The court held that they were not entitled to an early redemption as the mortgage had been freely negotiated between powerful commercial enterprises and there was nothing oppressive or unreasonable in its terms. Note, however, that in the case of housing loans the mortgagor is entitled to redeem at any stage without being liable for a redemption fee except in the case of a loan with a fixed rate of interest.[539]

B. Clauses Which Allow the Mortgagee to Become the Owner

200. Clauses which enable the mortgagee to become the owner of the property or confer an option to purchase on the mortgagee will be declared void if they are considered to be part of the mortgage transaction. If the option to purchase is a condition of granting the mortgage it will be struck down.[540] However, if it is conferred in a later transaction it will be upheld.[541] In *Jones v Morgan*[542] a clause in a document executed three years after the original mortgage under which the lender became entitled to a 50% share in the borrower's land after the borrower had redeemed the mortgage was held void as the later document was treated as a variation of the original mortgage and therefore part of it. This clause was struck down on the basis that it was a clog on the equity of redemption, although it was not considered to be unconscionable. Some have criticized this decision on the basis that the court should have taken the opportunity to revise the extent of the protection conferred by the principle which unnecessary in modern times.[543]

537. [1912] AC 565.
538. [1939] Ch 441.
539. Consumer Credit Act 1995, s. 121.
540. *Samuel v. Jarrah Timber and Wood Paving Corp Ltd* [1904] AC 323.
541. *Reeve v Lisle* [1902] AC 461.
542. *Jones v Morgan* [2001] EWCA Civ 995.
543. *See* Thompson, 'Do We Really Need Clogs?', *Conveyancer and Property Lawyer* 64 no. 6 (2001): 502.

C. *Clauses Which Confer Collateral Advantages on the Mortgagee*

201. A provision which entitles the mortgagee to a collateral advantage will be closely scrutinized by the courts and may be struck down on two grounds: if it operates as a clog on the equity of redemption or if it is unconscionable. A collateral advantage is a benefit due to the mortgagee in addition to the capital and interest due on the loan, such as commission, a share of profits or a 'tied house' arrangement (i.e., where a public house is tied into a supply arrangement with a mortgagee which operates a brewery). A collateral advantage which extends beyond the date of redemption may be struck down as fettering the equity of redemption. In *Noaks and Co Ltd v. Rice*,[544] the mortgage of a public house included a covenant obliging the mortgagor to sell only the malt liquor of the mortgagee, which was to continue after redemption for the entire duration of the lease. This was held void in so far as it applied after redemption. However, in *Biggs v. Hoddinott*,[545] a similar clause in a mortgage of a public house provided that the mortgagor could only take his supplies of liquor from the mortgagee during the term of the mortgage which was due to continue for five years. The court upheld the collateral advantage as it did not constitute a clog on the right to redeem and it was not unconscionable.[546]

202. If the collateral advantage can be construed as independent of the mortgage, it shall be upheld even if it continues after redemption, unless it is unconscionable. In *Kreglinger v. New Patagonia Meat and Cold Storage Co Ltd*,[547] a firm of woolbrokers lent a firm of meat packers the sum of EUR 10,000. It was secured by a floating charge and the lenders agreed not to call in the principal for five years, although the agreement permitted repayment before the expiry of the five-year term. A clause gave the lenders a right of pre-emption for all the meat packers' sheepskins and a commission of 1% on all sheepskins sold to persons other than the lenders for a period of five years. The loan was repaid before the expiry of the five-year term, and the collateral advantage was upheld by the court as it was independent of the mortgage, it did not operate as a clog on the right to redeem and it was not unfair or unconscionable. It has been argued that it was easier for the court to construe the advantage as independent of the security as it was secured by a floating charge rather than a fixed charge.[548] Finally, it should be mentioned that the courts may strike down an interest rate clause if it is so grossly disproportionate with rates generally charged in the market for such a loan that it amounts to a penalty. In examining this issue, the courts will look at the relative bargaining positions of the parties.[549]

544. [1902] AC 24.
545. [1898] 2 Ch 307.
546. Note that a mortgage which contained a solus agreement obliging a garage proprietor to acquire all petrol supplies from the mortgagee under a mortgage agreement which was irredeemable for twenty-one years was held to be void as amounting to an unjustifiable restraint of trade in *Esso Petroleum Ltd v. Harper's Garage* [1968] Ch 269.
547. [1914] AC 25.
548. *See* Maddox, *Mortgages Law and Practice* (Dublin: Thomson Roundhall, 2007), para. 4.13.
549. *Cityland and Property (Holdings) Ltd v. Dabrah* [1968] Ch 166; *Secured Property Loans Ltd v Floyd* [2011] IEHC 189.

§4. Judgment Mortgages

203. Before the commencement of the Land and Conveyancing Law Reform Act 2009, the Judgment Mortgage (Ireland) Acts 1850–1858 provided a mechanism whereby a creditor who had acquired a judgment against a debtor could register that judgment as a mortgage against land owned by his debtor.[550] This would enable the creditor to have the land sold and the proceeds used to discharge the debt if payment on foot of the judgment was not forthcoming. The law governing judgment mortgages is now governed by Part 11 of the Land and Conveyancing Law Reform Act 2009 which substantially re-enacts the relevant provisions of the 1850 and 1858 Acts but with certain clarifications, as recommended by the Law Reform Commission.[551] As the 2009 Act only applies to judgment mortgages created after its commencement, the old law continues to govern the validity of judgment mortgages created before that date.

204. Under the old regime, to obtain a judgment mortgage, the creditor had to follow the procedure set out in sections 6 and 7 of the 1850 Act. The first step was to file an affidavit sworn by the judgment creditor, stating that the judgment debtor owned certain land, in the court where judgment had been entered against the debtor. This affidavit had to contain certain details, such as the title of the action and the court, the date and amount of the judgment, the full names of the parties, their titles, trades or professions, their places of abode and the location of the lands. In the case of unregistered land, the description of the land had to specify the county, barony, town, city or parish in which the lands were located, while registered land could be described by reference to the folio number and county. The section 6 requirements have, on occasion, been strictly construed by the courts, which has led to judgment mortgages being declared invalid on highly technical grounds.[552]

205. The second step involved the registration of a copy of the affidavit in the Registry of Deeds or the Land Registry, as appropriate. Section 7 of the 1850 Act provided that the registration of the affidavit in the Registry of Deeds operated to transfer all of the land which it mentioned to the creditor and vested it in him for the same estate or interest held by the debtor, subject to the debtor's right to redeem on paying the outstanding monies mentioned in the affidavit. The registration of the judgment mortgage thus gave the creditor the status of a mortgagee. In the case of registered land, a judgment mortgage is a registrable burden under section 69(1)(i) of the Registration of Title Act 1964 and section 71(4) of that Act provided that registration of the affidavit operated to charge the interest of the judgment debtor and conferred the judgment creditor with the rights and remedies specified by court order for the enforcement of the charge. To enforce his security, the judgment creditor sought a

550. Note that a judgment mortgage takes effect by operation of law and therefore s. 3 of the Family Home Protection Act 1976 does not apply, *see Containercare (Ireland) Ltd v. Wycherley* [1982] IR 143; *Murray v Diamond* [1982] ILRM 113.

551. *Consultation Paper on Judgment Mortgages* (LRC CP 30–2004).

552. *See Allied Irish Banks plc v. Griffin* [1992] 2 IR 70; *Re Murphy's and McCormack's Contract* [1930] IR 322; *Dovebid Netherlands BV v Phelan* [2007] IEHC 131; de Londras, 'The Technical Defence to a Judgment Mortgage: Time to Say Goodbye?', *Conveyancing and Property Law Journal* 13, no. 1 (2008): 5.

declaration from the court that the judgment mortgage was well charged on the interest of the debtor and an order for the sale of the land.

206. The complicated procedural requirements set out under the 1850 Act have been replaced by a simpler system under the Land and Conveyancing Law Reform Act 2009.[553] Section 116 of the 2009 Act provides that a creditor who has obtained a judgment against a person may apply to the Property Registration Authority, in the prescribed form,[554] to register a judgment mortgage against that person's estate or interest in land and the judgment mortgage shall be registered in the Registry of Deeds or the Land Registry, as appropriate. Section 117 provides that the registration of a judgment mortgage operates to charge the judgment debtor's estate or interest in the land with the judgment debt and entitles the judgment mortgagee to apply to the court for an order for the sale of the land and the distribution of the proceeds, an order determining the priority of any encumbrances affecting the property, or any other order for the enforcement of the judgment mortgage as the court thinks appropriate. Where a judgment mortgage has been registered against the interest of a co-owner of land, the judgment creditor should proceed under section 31 of the Land and Conveyancing Law Reform Act 2009 when seeking to enforce his security.[555] Section 30(3) of the 2009 Act clarifies that from the commencement date, the registration of a judgment mortgage against the interest of a joint tenant does not sever the joint tenancy and so the judgment mortgage will be extinguished on the death of the debtor.[556]

207. For the judgment mortgage to be effective, the debtor must be beneficially entitled to the land. It should also be noted that, in general, a judgment mortgage has the same status as a voluntary deed and therefore takes effect subject to all prior unregistered legal or equitable rights.[557] However, the judgment creditor may be able to 'avoid' a voluntary conveyance that was entered into after the judgment was obtained

553. This system has been extended to registered land by s. 130 of the Land and Conveyancing Law Reform Act 2009 which inserts a new s. 71 into the Registration of Title Act 1964 by way of substitution.

554. *See* Form 16 set out in the Registration of Deeds (No. 2) Rules 2009 (SI 457/2009); Form 60 of the Land Registration Rules 2012 (SI 484/2012).

555. Under the old law, a judgment mortgagee seeking to enforce his security would have to rely on the fact that he was a co-owner by virtue of the judgment mortgage and apply for an order for sale in lieu of partition pursuant to the Partition Acts 1868 and 1876. Such a judgment mortgagee would only have *locus standi* if the judgment mortgage was created over unregistered land. If the land was registered the judgment mortgagee only acquired a charge and would have difficulty realizing his security, *see Irwin v Deasy* [2004] IEHC 104. This arbitrary inconsistency is rectified by the 2009 Act. Note that under the old law the courts have, on occasion, considered whether the co-owned home was a family home in reaching its decision to make or refuse an order for its sale, *see First National Building Society v Ring* [1992] 1 IR 375; *Trinity College v Kenny* [2010] IEHC 20.

556. Before 2009, whether a severance occurred depended on whether the joint tenancy affected registered or unregistered land, *see* para. 67, above.

557. *See Eyre v. McDowell* (1861) 9 HLC 620; *Re Murphy and McCormack* [1930] IR 322, now confirmed by the Land and Conveyancing Law Reform Act, s. 117(3). *See also* Registration of Title Act 1964, s. 71(4), which sets out the same position in relation to judgment mortgages affecting registered land.

but before it was registered as a judgment mortgage by establishing that it was made with the intention of defrauding him.[558]

208. If the judgment debtor discharges his debt, the registration of a certificate of satisfaction issued by the court where the judgment was obtained in the Registry of Deeds operates to extinguish the judgment mortgage.[559] In the case of registered land, it is necessary to make an application to cancel the judgment mortgage as a burden by the submission of a certificate of satisfaction.

558. *See* Land and Conveyancing Law Reform Act 2009, s. 117(5), which re-enacts a similar protection set out in the Judgment Mortgage Act 1850, s. 8.

559. *See* Land and Conveyancing Law Reform Act 2009, s. 118, which re-enacts s. 9 of the Judgment Mortgage Act 1850.

Part II. Irish Law of Personal Property

Chapter 1. Classification and Interests

§1. Classification of Personal Property

209. As has been already mentioned,[560] personal property or chattels represent a residual category of property, comprising everything other than land and fixtures. The law in relation to leases of land, which are sometimes referred to as 'chattels real' (indicating their original status as personal property), now forms part of the law governing real property.[561] 'Chattels personal' can be divided into two classes: tangible moveables, such as goods or money, and intangible moveables. Intangible moveables can be subdivided into documentary intangibles, such as bills of lading, where title can be transferred by the transfer of a document which represents ownership, and pure intangibles, such as goodwill and intellectual property rights.[562] Part II of this monograph examines the main interests which can exist in relation to goods,[563] the rules governing the sale of goods,[564] the acquisition of title by finding[565] and security interests in personal property.[566]

§2. Interests in Personal Property

210. Ownership has been defined 'as the greatest possible interest in a thing which a mature system of law recognizes'.[567] Just as the law distinguishes between legal and equitable ownership in relation to land, it recognizes the same distinction in

560. *See* para. 3 above.
561. *See* Part I., Ch. 6 above.
562. For a discussion of the law governing intellectual property, *see* Clark, Smith & Hall, *Intellectual Property Law in Ireland,* 4th edn (Dublin: Bloomsbury Professional, 2016); White, *Commercial Law,* 2nd edn (Dublin: Thomson Roundhall, 2012), Chs 3437.
563. 'Goods' are defined by the Sale of Goods Act 1893, s. 62, as including all chattels personal other than things in action (i.e., intangible moveables) and money.
564. *See* Ch. 2 below.
565. *See* Ch. 3 below.
566. *See* Ch. 4 below.
567. Honoré, 'Ownership', in *Oxford Essays in Jurisprudence*, ed. Guest (Oxford: Clarendon Press, 1961), 107, at 108.

relation to personal property.[568] Identifying the owner of a good may be crucial in a number of situations. For example, the risk of accidental damage usually rests with the owner[569] and determining if ownership has passed to the buyer may be relevant in establishing whether an unpaid seller can sue for the price of the goods.[570]

This issue is also of vital significance if the possessor of goods is declared bankrupt, as a person who has retained ownership through a retention of title clause, a trust or a bailment arrangement can recover those goods from the assignee in bankruptcy.

211. Possession of goods is also significant in that it amounts to prima facie evidence of ownership and may be relevant if there is a conflict of title.[571] Also, the delivery of possession may be crucial in determining if ownership of goods has passed, for example, in the case of a gift. In addition, certain actions[572] may only be brought by a person in actual possession or with an immediate right to possession. Ownership does not always coincide with possession of goods; for example, a person may be entitled to possession of goods under a bailment, lease or hire arrangement. Under a hire-purchase arrangement, at the end of the hire period, the hirer is granted an option to purchase the goods in return for a final optional payment.

212. Finally, a person may own a security interest in goods, such as a pledge, a lien or a mortgage or charge. While the owner of a pledge or a lien retains possession of the goods until the security is terminated, under a mortgage or a charge the owner of the goods is generally entitled to retain possession unless it becomes necessary to enforce the security.

568. *See* para. 244 below.
569. Sale of Goods Act 1893, s. 20.
570. Sale of Goods Act 1893, s. 49.
571. *See* the rules discussed in para. 219 below which allow a seller or buyer in possession to transfer title to a purchaser even though the seller or buyer is not the owner.
572. Trespass, conversion and detinue.

Chapter 2. Transfer of Ownership

§1. INTRODUCTION

213. Generally, the transfer of ownership of personal property is a simpler process than is the case with land. For example, a gift of most items of personal property can be effected by means of the delivery of the item in question to the donee. Also, such transfers are not generally subject to a registration requirement.[573] However, it is important to note that if a gift of personal property has not been completed, the maxim 'equity will not perfect an imperfect gift' will usually apply. The donee of an imperfect gift will not be able to enforce a promise to transfer property, if the promise is unsupported by consideration. This basic principle is subject to a number of exceptions: the rule in *Strong v. Bird*,[574] the *Donatio Mortis Causa*,[575] and the Doctrine of Proprietary Estoppel.[576] This chapter is not concerned with gifts of personal property but focuses instead on the sale of goods.

§2. TITLE DISPUTES

214. The fundamental principle which governs priority or title disputes in relation to the sale of goods is *nemo dat quod non habet*, which means that no one can transfer a better title than he himself has. This rule is set out in section 21 of the Sale of Goods Act 1893: 'Subject to the provisions of this Act, where goods are sold by a person who is not the owner thereof, … the buyer acquires no better title to the goods than the seller had.'[577] However, a number of exceptions to this principle were recognized by the common law and these exceptions are now re-stated by the Factors Act 1889 and the Sale of Goods Act 1893. These exceptions were designed to protect and encourage commercial transactions[578] and it has been observed that the exceptions render the fundamental rule more commonly honoured in the breach than the observance.[579]

---

573. With the exception of company shares (Companies Act 1963, s. 81) ships (Mercantile Marine Act 1955, s. 45) and aircraft (Irish Aviation Authority (Nationality and Registration of Aircraft) Order, SI 634 of 2005, Art. 15).

574. *See* Biehler, *Equity and the Law of Trusts in Ireland*, 6th edn (Dublin: Thomson Roundhall, 2016), 129–131.

575. *Ibid.*, 131–138.

576. *Ibid.*, 830–888.

577. Note that nothing in the Act affects the validity of any contract of sale under any special common law or statutory power of sale or under a court order, Sale of Goods Act 1893, s. 21(2)(b). Examples include a pledgee's power of sale or the statutory powers of unpaid sellers or pawnbrokers.

578. As noted by Lord Denning in *Bishopsgate Motor Finance Corporation Ltd v. Transport Brakes Ltd* [1949] 1 KB 322 at 336–337.

579. *See* White, *Commercial Law* 2nd edn (Dublin: Thomson Roundhall, 2012), 376.

215. A purchaser may have to rely on one of these exceptions against an owner seeking to recover goods, if the seller (or his predecessor in title) stole the goods, obtained them pursuant to a voidable contract, or possessed them under a hire-purchase contract or a contract containing a reservation of title clause. Although the purchaser may have acquired possession of the goods through a chain of transactions, it is only necessary to prove that one of those transactions qualified as a *nemo dat* exception. In such circumstances, the parties to any subsequent transaction will have a good defence to the owner's claim.[580] If a purchaser cannot rely on one of the *nemo dat* exceptions, he will be required to surrender the goods or pay their value to the owner. However, such a purchaser may be able to sue for breach of the implied term in the contract for sale that the seller had the right to sell the goods and that the purchaser would enjoy quiet possession of them.[581] Such a claim will allow him to recover the full purchase price.[582]

216. The *nemo dat* exceptions may only be availed of by purchasers of goods who acted in good faith and without notice of the seller's defect in title. The burden of proof rests on the buyer seeking to rely on the exception.[583] The requirement of good faith requires the purchaser to act honestly[584] and a subjective test is applied. Notice, although not specifically defined by legislation, is construed more narrowly that in the context of land transactions.[585] For example, notice for the purposes of a commercial transaction is confined to 'actual notice'[586] and does not include constructive notice.[587] However, if it can be shown that if the buyer deliberately turned a blind to certain facts which would be regarded as suspicious by the reasonable man he will be treated as having actual notice of such facts.[588]

I. Market Overt

217. Section 22 of the Sale of Goods Act 1893 renders sales conducted in a 'market overt' an exception to the *nemo dat* rule, provided the sale was conducted 'according to the usage of the market'. A market overt is an open public market constituted by a charter, statute or custom. The goods must also be of the type normally sold in such a market and the sale must have taken place during daylight hours. It has been argued that either this exception should be abolished, as has taken place in England,[589] or it should be extended to all sales from retail premises. Although the extension of the market overt exception would further protect innocent purchasers and

580. Note that the owner may be able to recover against a party to transaction which precedes the transaction which qualifies as *a nemo dat* exception.
581. Sale of Goods Act 1893, s. 12.
582. *Rowland v. Divall* [1923] 2 KB 500.
583. Except in the case of the voidable contract exception, *see* para. 217 below.
584. Sale of Goods Act 1893, s. 62(2).
585. *See* para. 71 above.
586. *See Worcester Works Finance Ltd v. Cooden* [1972] QB 210, per Lord Denning at 218.
587. *See Manchester Trust v. Furness* [1895] 2 QB 539, per Lindley LJ at 545.
588. *See London Joint Stock Bank v. Simmons* [1892] AC 20; *Evans v. Truman* (1830) 1 Mood & R. 10 per Lord Tenderden at 12.
589. Sale of Goods (Amendment) Act 1994.

facilitate commercial transactions generally, such an extension could also be criticized on the basis that it would facilitate the sale of stolen goods and may leave the owner without a remedy.[590]

II. Mercantile Agents

218. Section 21(2)(a) of the Sale of Goods Act 1893[591] makes sales by mercantile agents, who are in possession of the goods or title documents with the consent of the owner, in the ordinary course of their business, an exception to the *nemo dat* rule. A mercantile agent must have a business and must in the course of that business deal with goods belonging to his principal by selling, buying or raising money on them. Many of the modern cases concerning this exception involve the unauthorized sale of motor cars. The exception will not apply where the goods or title documents were stolen from the owner.[592] Also, the owner's consent must be such that the mercantile agent had possession of the goods for one of the mercantile purposes mentioned. For example, if he had possession to carry out repairs, the exception will not apply.

III. Sellers and Buyers in Possession

219. Section 25 of the Sale of Goods Act 1893 is designed to protect persons who deal with sellers in possession of goods which they no longer own or buyers in possession of goods which they do not yet own. Such transactions shall have the same effect as if the person engaged in the transaction had been expressly authorized by the owner of the goods to enter into it.

IV. Agency and Estoppel

220. An owner will be bound by any disposition of his goods by an agent acting with his authority or consent. In a similar vein, an owner will be bound by a disposition if he is, by his conduct, precluded or estopped from denying the seller's authority to sell.[593]

V. Voidable Title

221. Section 23 of the Sale of Goods Act 1893 provides that if the seller of goods has a voidable title (e.g., due to a misrepresentation or undue influence on his part) but the transaction had not been avoided at the time of the sale to the buyer, the buyer shall acquire a good title.

590. *See* White, *Commercial Law* 2nd edn (Dublin: Thomson Roundhall, 2012), 389.
591. In conjunction with the Factors Act 1889, s. 2(1).
592. *National Employers General Insurance Association Ltd v. Jones* [1990] 1 AC 24.
593. Sale of Goods Act 1893, s. 21.

§3. The Sale of Goods

222. A contract for the sale of goods is defined by section 1(1) of the Sale of Goods Act 1893 as 'a contract whereby the seller transfers or agrees to transfer the property in goods to the buyer for a money consideration, called the price'. Unlike the sale of land, which typically involves a contract for sale followed by the execution and registration of a deed of conveyance or transfer, a sale of goods operates as an executed contract and a conveyance in one.

223. A contract for a sale of goods required no formalities at common law and so could be made orally. However, section 4(1) of the 1893 Act provides that a contract for goods now worth EUR 12.70 or more is not enforceable unless one of the following conditions is satisfied: the buyer accepted and received part of the goods sold; the buyer gave something in earnest to bind the contract or made a part payment; or there was a note or memorandum in writing of the contract and signed by the party to be charged.[594]

224. Contracts for the sale of goods are governed by the Sale of Goods Act 1893 as amended by Part II of the Sale of Goods and Supply of Services Act 1980. This legislation sets out the core duties of the parties: the seller's duty to deliver the goods and the buyer's duty to accept and pay for the goods in accordance with the terms of the contract of sale. It also provides certain valuable rights, protections and remedies for both buyers and seller.[595]

225. The point at which ownership is transferred under a contract for the sale of goods is governed by the intention of the parties. In ascertaining this intention, regard is had to the terms of the contract, the conduct of the parties and the circumstances of the case.[596] An express retention of title clause, under which title is retained until the purchase price has been paid in full, is commonly included in such a contract to protect the seller against the possibility of the buyer's bankruptcy or insolvency. Where the intention of the parties is not clear from the contractual terms, their conduct or the circumstances of the case, a series of rules based on the presumed intention of the parties is set out in the 1893 Act. These rules draw a distinction between specific goods, which are fully identified at the time the contract is made,[597] and unascertained goods.

I. Unascertained Goods

226. Section 16 of the 1893 Act, which cannot be excluded or varied by the terms of the contract or the intention of the parties, provides that title to unascertained goods is not transferred to the buyer unless and until the goods are ascertained. Ascertainment occurs when the goods are 'unconditionally appropriated'[598] to the contract, by irrevocably attaching or earmarking the goods for use in its performance.

594. Formalities may also be imposed by other legislation e.g., Consumer Credit Act 1995.

595. For an excellent review of the law in this area, *see* White, *Commercial Law* 2nd edn (Dublin: Thomson Roundhall, 2012), Part III.

596. Sale of Goods Act 1893, s. 17.

597. Sale of Goods Act 1893, s. 62.

598. Sale of Goods Act 1893, s. 18, rule 5(1).

For example, if the seller delivers goods to an independent carrier or bailee for onward transmission to the buyer, he is taken to have satisfied this requirement.[599] This rule can have adverse consequences for a pre-paying buyer of part of a bulk commodity if the seller becomes insolvent.[600] It may appear particularly harsh if the source of the goods is identified at the time of the contract, a category of unascertained goods known as quasi-specific goods. The rule has been modified in England[601] and the United States[602] in relation to quasi-specific goods which have been paid for, so that such a buyer acquires an undivided share in the bulk and becomes a tenant in common with the other owners. It has been argued that a similar reform should be introduced in Ireland.[603]

II. Specific Goods

227. Where an unconditional contract for the sale of specific goods in a deliverable state has been entered into, ownership passes to the buyer when the contract is made, regardless of whether the purchase price has been paid or the goods have been delivered.[604] Goods may be in a deliverable state despite being defective. However, the rule will not apply if the seller has not yet done something to the goods which he had agreed to do before delivery.[605] Where specific goods are not in a deliverable state, property does not pass until they are, and the buyer has notice of the fact.[606] Also, if the goods are in a deliverable state but an act has to be carried out by the seller in order to ascertain the price, ownership does not pass until the act is done and the buyer has notice of the fact.[607] Where goods are delivered on approval or for sale or return, title passes to the buyer if one of the following four conditions is satisfied: if the buyer signifies his approval or acceptance of them to the seller; if the buyer does another act adopting the transaction; if the buyer retains the goods without rejecting them beyond the time limit fixed for their return; or if no time limit for their return is fixed, on the expiry of a reasonable period of time.

599. Sale of Goods Act 1893, s. 18 rule 5(2).
600. *See Re Wait* [1927] 1 Ch 606; *Re London Wine Co (Shippers) Ltd* [1986] PCC 121.
601. Sale of Goods (Amendment) Act 1994.
602. Uniform Commercial Code, s. 2–105(4).
603. White, *Commercial Law* 2nd edn (Dublin: Thomson Roundhall, 2012, 356.
604. Sale of Goods Act 1893, s. 18, rule 1.
605. *Underwood Ltd v. Burgh Castle Brick and Cement Syndicate* [1922] 1 KB 343.
606. Sale of Goods Act 1893, s. 18, rule 2.
607. Sale of Goods Act 1893, s. 18, rule 3.

Chapter 3. Acquisition of Title by Finding

§1. Introduction

228. If an item of personal property is found by a person on someone else's land, a dispute may arise between the finder and the owner or occupier of the land in relation to who has the better title to the find. Naturally, the true owner of the chattel will always have a superior title to the finder or the landowner.[608] However, if the true owner cannot be located or fails to make a claim, the court will have to decide the dispute on the basis of who has a superior possessory title. The phrase 'finders keepers' reflects a common law rule that the finder of an item acquires a good title against all but the true owner. However, this rule is not always applied and, in some circumstances, the courts recognize the freehold owner or the leasehold occupier as having a superior title. The case law appears to draw a clear distinction between chattels which are found below the surface of the land and those which are found above the surface.[609] However, in practice, it will not always be easy to determine whether the item was found 'in' or 'on' the land.[610]

§2. Chattels Found below the Surface of the Land

229. A number of cases illustrate the superior right of the landowner or occupier to any finds below the surface of the land. In *South Staffordshire Water Company v. Sharman*,[611] the freehold owner, who also occupied the land, employed the defendant to remove mud from the bottom of a pond. When the defendant found two gold rings embedded in the mud, the owner-occupier was held to be entitled to the find. Lord Russell CJ[612] quoted from Pollock and Wright's essay on *Possession in the Common Law* stating: 'the possession of the land carries with it ... possession of everything which is attached to or under that land, and, in the absence of a better title elsewhere, the right to possess it also'.[613] The traditional approach to finds 'in' or beneath the surface of the land was recently reiterated by the English Court of Appeal in *Waverly Borough Council v. Fletcher*[614] when a claim was brought by a finder who had unearthed a brooch while metal detecting in a park. Waverly Borough Council, the freehold owner of the park, was found to have a better title. Auld LJ gave three reasons for the landowner's superior title in such circumstances: when an object is embedded in the

608. *Moffatt and Another v. Kazana* [1968] 3 All ER 271.
609. *See* Tooher, 'Jubilant Jamie and the Elephant Egg: Acquisition of Title by Finding', *Australian Property Law Journal* 6 (1998): 29 for a critique of the rules devised by the courts in this area.
610. *See Tamworth Industries Ltd v. Attorney General of New Zealand* [1991] 3 NZLR 616.
611. [1896] 2 QB 44. *See also Webb v. Ireland* [1988] IR 353 at 588–589.
612. [1896] 2 QB 44 at 45–46.
613. Pollock & Wright, *Possession in the Common Law* (Oxford: Clarendon Press, 1888), 41.
614. [1995] 4 All ER 756.

land, it is an integral part of the realty; removal of it would normally involve interference which may damage the land; objects found below the surface are less likely to be reclaimed by the original owner and so the owner of the land in which it is lodged is the substitute owner.[615]

230. In *London City Corporation v. Appleyard*,[616] two workmen were demolishing premises when they found a safe built into a cellar wall. They found bank notes to the value of nearly GBP 6,000 in a box in the safe. The true owner of the money was never traced. The developers held under a lease granted by London City Corporation. The court adopted the rationale applied in the *South Staffordshire Water Company* case and held that the safe formed part of the premises leased to the developers. The court noted that possession of the safe carried with it possession of the box and implied that the lessee developers would have had a better title than the freehold owner, except for a clause which had been included in the lease which reserved to the lessor ownership of anything valuable found in or under any part of the site.

231. The ruling in the *Appleyard* case seems to contradict the approach taken in a much earlier case, *Elwes v. Brigg*[617] which also involved a dispute between a freehold owner and an occupier under a lease. In that case, the freehold owner was held to be entitled to a prehistoric boat found six feet below the surface by the lessee, a gas company, when carrying out excavations. Although the freehold owner was found to have a superior title in both the *Appleyard* and the *Elwes* cases, in the *Appleyard* case, the freehold owner was entitled because of the clause in the lease while in *Elwes* the freehold owner succeeded where there was no such clause. The *ratio* of the *Elwes* case is a little obscure but an academic attempt has been made to reconcile the two decisions.[618] It has been pointed out that although possession of the boat passed to the lessee under the lease in *Elwes*, the lessee's possessory title was subject to the prior possession and superior right of freehold owner. In *Elwes*, the lease had only been granted the year before the boat was discovered and it seems fair to assume that the boat would have been present in the land when Elwes was in possession; therefore, the freehold owner had prior possession. In contrast, in *Appleyard*, the lease had been granted in 1889 but the banknotes had only issued in 1943 or 1944; therefore, the money could not have been present when the freehold owner, London City Corporation, had possession of the land. As the freehold owner had no right by virtue of prior possession, the Corporation had to base its claim on the clause in the lease. This analysis would seem to indicate that where there is a dispute in relation to a find between the freehold owner and the leasehold occupier, the superior claim of the freehold owner is dependent on prior possession.[619]

615. *Ibid.*, at 762. The finder was held to be trespassing in this case which further weakened his claim and strengthened the rights of the landowner.
616. [1963] 2 All ER 834.
617. [1886] 33 Ch D 562.
618. *See* Hoath, 'Some Conveyancing Implications of Finding Disputes', *Conveyancer and Property Lawyer* (1990): 348.
619. According to Hoath, the freehold owner must prove that he previously occupied the property and that on the balance of probabilities the item was present during his period of occupation, *Ibid.*, 52–53.

§3. Treasure Trove

232. The superior title of the landowner to such finds is qualified in the event that the find qualifies as treasure trove.[620] Any archaeological object found in the State after the National Monuments (Amendment) Act 1994 came into force[621] which has no known owner now vests in the State as treasure trove.[622] An Archaeological object is defined as 'any chattel .... which by reason of the archaeological interest attached thereto or of its association with any Irish historical event or person has a value substantially greater than its intrinsic (including artistic) value and the expression includes ancient human, animal or plant remains'.[623] Previously, the doctrine of treasure trove was governed by the common law and if an item with no known owner was discovered, it would only qualify as treasure trove if it was made substantially of gold or silver and had been deliberately buried under the ground with the intention of recovering it. This common law doctrine was originally deemed to be a royal prerogative in England.[624] However, in *Webb v. Ireland*,[625] Finlay CJ, delivering the judgment of the Supreme Court, held that the doctrine also applied in Ireland as an inherent attribute of a sovereign State, recognized and declared by the Constitution.[626] Finlay CJ took the opportunity to encourage the legislature to expand the definition of treasure trove to include items other than gold or silver,[627] a recommendation which was taken on board by the drafters of the 1994 Act.

233. Although ownership of treasure trove vests in the State, section 10 of the 1994 Act permits the State to pay a reward to the finder, the owner of the land and the occupier of the land where the object is retained by the State. In assessing the amount of the award, the Director of the National Museum is directed to take into account the intrinsic value of the object, its general historical and archaeological importance, the circumstances of the finding and the amount of rewards paid by the State in the case of comparable archaeological objects.

620. It should also be noted that most mines and minerals are vested in the State by Art. 43 Constitution and the Minerals Development Act 1940.
621. The Act came into force on 6 Jul. 1994.
622. National Monuments (Amendment) Act 1994, s. 2.
623. National Monuments (Amendment) Act 1994 s. 14.
624. Note that the law governing treasure trove in England is now governed by the Treasure Act 1996.
625. [1988] IR 353. This case concerned the discovery of the Derrynaflan Hoard by Mr Webb and his son on another's land using metal detectors. The State had purchased the landowner's entitlement to the find and was ultimately found to have a superior title to the Webbs for two reasons: the Webbs were trespassing and the items were found 'in' the land. The applicability of the doctrine of treasure trove was only considered by the court as the Webbs had claimed a right to a reward under that doctrine, in the alternative. Although this argument failed, the Webbs did succeed in a claim based on the doctrine of legitimate expectation.
626. *Ibid.*, 594.
627. *Ibid.*, 597.

§4. Chattels Found above the Surface of the Land

234. The common law rule in relation to such finds is that the act of finding a chattel which has been lost and taking control of it gives the finder rights in respect of that chattel. This rule can be explained by the traditional importance ascribed by the law to possession which confers a type of title. As was stated by court in *Armory v. Delamirie*,[628] 'the finder of a jewel, though he does not by such finding acquire an absolute property or ownership, yet he has such a property as will enable him to keep it against all but the rightful owner'.

235. There are two exceptions to this rule: if the finder is trespassing, this will weaken his title and strengthen the claim of the landowner or occupier;[629] or if the freehold owner or the leasehold occupier manifested an intention to exercise control over the building and any articles found in it before the object was found, he will have a superior title. *Parker v. British Airways Board*[630] represents the *locus classicus* on the application of the second exception.[631] In that case, Mr Parker found a bracelet in the executive lounge in Heathrow Airport. He handed it over to a British Airways official with his name and address so that it could be returned to him if it was not claimed by the owner. The owner never came forward and British Airways sold the bracelet for GBP 800. Donaldson LJ in his judgment listed the rights and obligations of the finder. He held that someone who finds an article which is not attached to land or buried under it and who takes it into his care and control has a title to it which is good against all but the true owner. He pointed out that a finder has an obligation to take reasonable measures to locate the true owner and care for the chattel in the meantime. He held that the occupier of the building where it is found will only have a superior title if before the item was found, he manifested an intention to exercise control over the building and articles found in it. Although British Airways had control over who accessed the executive lounge, this was not sufficient in the eyes of Donaldson LJ. The occupier had to be able to demonstrate that he intended to exercise control over all lost items found on the premises. Such an intention could be implied in certain circumstances; Donaldson LJ noted that if a bank manager was showing someone around a bank vault and that person found a gold bracelet on the floor of the vault, the bank would have a better title, as an intention to exercise a very high degree of control would have been manifested.[632] Eveleigh LJ and Cairns LJ mentioned that such an intention might be implied where the item was found in a private house.[633]

628. (1722) 93 ER 664.
629. *See Webb v. Ireland and Attorney General* [1988] IR 353; *Waverly Borough Council v. Fletcher* [1995] 4 All ER 756.
630. [1982] 1 All ER 834.
631. *See also Bridges v. Hawksworth* (1851) 21 LJQB 75 (a finder who found bank notes in the public part of a shop succeeded against the owner of the shop); *Hanna v. Peel* [1945] KB 509 (a soldier who found a brooch in a crevice on top of a window frame succeeded against the owner of the house who had never occupied it).
632. [1982] 1 All ER 834, 845.
633. [1982] 1 All ER 834, 845 and 846.

236. Finally, it should be mentioned that if the finder finds the item in the course of his employment or agency, his employer or principal acquires his finder's rights.[634] However, if the finding is wholly incidental or collateral to the employment (e.g., in the *Parker* case, the finder was on his way to a work meeting), this rule does not apply.

634. *See* the obiter dictum statement of McNair J to this effect in *London City Corporation v. Appleyard* [1963] 2 All ER 834, 838–839.

Chapter 4. Security Interests in Personal Property

§1. Introduction

237. Personal property may be used to secure a debt or a loan in three different ways: by pledge, by lien and by mortgage/charge. Such securities can be classified in accordance with whether they are possessory or non-possessory and consensual or non-consensual. The pledge and the lien require the person receiving the security to retain possession of the goods, while the mortgage/charge is non-possessory as the owner of the goods retains possession. Although a pledge and a mortgage/ charge are created consensually by an agreement between the parties, a lien generally arises by operation of law and so may be described as non-consensual. It should also be noted that certain devices or clauses (e.g., a hire-purchase agreement or a retention of title clause) may perform a quasi-security role, in that they are designed to ensure that the vendor gets paid before ownership of the goods passes to the buyer. Although, such quasi-securities place the supplier in a very strong position, if the buyer fails to pay or becomes insolvent, they should be carefully drafted. It may be wise to insert a term to ensure that the risk of accidental damage passes to the buyer[635] and caution should be exercised to ensure that the arrangement cannot be construed as creating a bill of sale or a charge which would be subject to a registration requirement.[636]

§2. Pledge

238. A pledge involves a debtor delivering goods to a creditor who has the right to retain possession of the goods as security until payment of the debt or some other obligation has been discharged, at which point, the pledgee becomes obliged to restore possession of the goods to the pledgor. The most common type of pledge in a consumer context is a 'pawn'.[637] The formation of a pledge is dependent on actual or constructive possession[638] of the goods being conferred on the pledgee. Therefore, it may not be an appropriate form of security for intangible assets or if the debtor requires access to the property to be used as security. An advantage of this form of security, however, is that its creation requires little formality (just the agreement of the parties), and it is not subject to any registration requirement. If the debt is not paid by the agreed date, the pledge can sell the goods,[639] and if no date was stipulated, a sale may occur once the debt has not been redeemed within a reasonable time. If the sale proceeds exceed

635. Forde, *Commercial Law,* 3rd edn (Haywards Heath: Tottel Publishing, 2005), para. 7.093.
636. Forde, *Commercial Law,* 3rd edn (Haywards Heath: Tottel Publishing, 2005), paras 7.107–7.108.
637. Pawns and pawnbrokers are regulated by the Pawnbrokers Act 1964, as amended by the Consumer Credit Act 1995.
638. Holding a key to a warehouse where the goods are stored or holding a document of title to the goods (e.g., a bill of lading) would constitute constructive possession.
639. *Exp. Hubbard* (1866) 17 QBD 699.

the amount owed and the costs of the sale, the pledgee must account to the pledgor for the balance.[640]

§3. Lien

239. A lien is a form of non-consensual possessory security and may arise at common law in the context of certain trades or professions; for example, a repairer has a lien over goods repaired for the cost of the repair. A lien may also exist over documents; for example, a solicitor is entitled to retain his client's documents or any funds under his control until his costs and expenses have been discharged. The Sale of Goods Act 1893 confers unpaid vendors with a statutory lien over goods in transit in respect of the purchase price.[641] Like the pledge, liens are not required to be registered. However, unlike the pledge, a lien does not confer a power of sale on its holder if the owner of the goods defaults; it is a right of detention only.[642]

§4. Mortgages and Charges

240. It is quite common for a person running a business to mortgage or charge the plant and machinery used to run the business or other personal assets, such as book debts. As non-possessory forms of security, a mortgage or a charge allows the owner of the business to use the assets unless he defaults on the loan and the mortgagee/chargee needs to enforce his security against those assets. As is the case with mortgages and charges affecting land, the security is typically enforced by obtaining possession of the goods and selling them[643] which may require the intervention of the court. A mortgage or a charge may have legal or equitable status which will be significant in determining its priority and the applicability of any registration requirements. While a chattel mortgage involves an outright assignment of ownership to the mortgagee subject to a proviso for re-assignment once the debt has been paid off, a charge does not involve a transfer of ownership. A charge may be created over a specific asset, which is known as a fixed charge, or over a fluctuating group of assets which may be used in the course of business, which is known as a floating charge. It is quite common for a fixed charge to be imposed over plant and machinery, and a floating charge to be put in place in relation to other assets, such as stock in trade, work in progress and book debts. A floating charge will crystallize if the company ceases to carry on business, a winding up commences or on the occurrence of an event stipulated by a term of the agreement. Once crystallization takes place, the floating charge is converted into a fixed charge affecting the assets which make up the security fund at that moment in time. It should be noted that some of the reforms to the law of mortgages introduced

640. *Halliday v. Holgate* (1868) LR 3 Ex 299.
641. Sale of Goods Act 1893, s. 62(3).
642. Although certain statutory liens or contractual liens may confer a power of sale.
643. *See* the powers conferred by the Bills of Sale (Ireland) Act 1883, s. 7.

by the Land and Conveyancing Law Reform Act 2009[644] apply to mortgages (and charges) created by deed after the commencement date[645] over personal property.

241. The main disadvantage of chattel mortgages and charges created by individuals is that they are subject to the registration requirements imposed by the Bills of Sale (Ireland) Act 1879–1883. The document creating the security over the chattels, known as a bill of sale, must be made in the format prescribed by the 1883 Act,[646] attested by a credible witness and registered at the Central Office of the High Court within seven days of its issue.[647] Registration ensures both its validity and also establishes priority in accordance with the order of registration.

242. Charges or mortgages (known as debentures) over company assets are exempt from the requirements of the Bills of Sale (Ireland) Acts[648] and are subject to their own registration requirements.[649] Debentures tend to be a very common form of security relied on by companies as they are not required to take any particular form and the registration requirements are simpler[650] than those which apply to bills of sale. Where two or more charges are created over the same property, priority is determined by the order of creation provided that the charges in question were registered within twenty-one days of their creation. This rule is varied where a fixed charge is created after the creation of a floating charge; the fixed charge will have priority unless the holder of the fixed charge had actual notice that the floating charge contained a negative pledge not to create any mortgages or charges on any of its assets which would rank in priority to or *pari passu* with the floating charge.[651]

243. It has been argued that the current convoluted system of personal property security law, involving numerous registers and different priority rules and methods of enforcement, should be replaced by a single system which would govern all types of consensual securities created over personal property.[652]

644. *See* Land and Conveyancing Law Reform Act 2009, Part 10, Chapters 2 and 3; *see also* Part 1, Ch. 7 above.
645. 1 Dec. 2009.
646. Bills of Sale (Ireland) Act 1883, s. 9 and sch. 1.
647. Bills of Sale (Ireland) Act 1883, s. 8.
648. Bills of Sale (Ireland) Act 1883, s. 17.
649. Note this is also the case with agricultural chattel mortgages which are governed by the Agricultural Credit Act 1978.
650. Certain details of any charge effected by a company over its assets must be registered within twenty-one days of the charge being given, *see* Companies Act 1963, s. 99.
651. *Welch v. Bowmaker (Ireland) Ltd* [1980] IR 251.
652. *See* White, *Commercial Law* 2nd edn (Dublin: Thomson Roundhall, 2012), 510–511.

Part III. The Law of Trusts in Ireland

Chapter 1. General Characteristics and Classification of Trusts

§1. General Characteristics

244. As has already been mentioned, the modern trust evolved from a medieval device known as the use,[653] and results in the division of ownership rights so that the trustee, who administers the trust, is vested with legal ownership while the beneficiary is deemed to be the equitable owner. A trust can be created over any kind of real or personal property which is capable of being owned and transferred. This device is one of the cornerstones of the common law system and has evolved to resolve problems and respond to difficulties in many different areas over the years. It may be relied on to resolve certain family property disputes and to make testamentary provision for minor children. It also forms the basis for many investment or pension schemes and is increasingly relied on for security purposes in the commercial world. In addition, it facilitates gifts to charity and prevents a person in a fiduciary position from deriving advantage from it. As one civilian jurist noted:

> They are like those extraordinary drugs curing at the same time toothache, sprained ankles and baldness sold by peddlers on the Paris boulevards; they solve equally well family troubles, business difficulties, religious and charitable problems.[654]

245. Although it is difficult to precisely define the trust given the variety and flexibility of the different types of trust recognized by law, the following definition has been endorsed by a number of Irish textbooks on the subject:

> A trust is the relationship which arises whenever a person (called a trustee) is compelled in equity to hold property, whether real or personal, and whether by legal or equitable title, for the benefit of some persons (of whom he may be one and who are termed beneficiaries) or for some object permitted by law, in such

653. *See* para. 10 above.
654. Lepaulle, 'Civil Law Substitutes for Trusts', *Yale Law Review* 36, no. 8 (1927): 1126.

a way that the real benefit of the property accrues, not to the trustees, but to the beneficiaries or other objects of the trust.[655]

246. It may also be of benefit to refer to terms which explain the trust in a more system neutral manner, without any reference to equity, a concept which is unfamiliar to many civilian lawyers. A trust creates a 'special patrimony' so that the trust property is kept separate from the trustee's general patrimony and is unavailable to his creditors in the event of bankruptcy or insolvency.[656] The latter 'insolvency effect'[657] is often used to distinguish the trust from other devices such as a Roman *fiducia*.[658] Another important feature is that the trustee is an 'office holder'.[659] This means that trustees may retire and be freed from further responsibility, but they are also subject to the supervisory jurisdiction of the courts and can be removed and replaced if hindering the proper execution of the trust.

247. An additional fundamental characteristic associated with the trust is the 'real' or proprietary nature of the rights of a beneficiary. Although a trustee who misappropriates trust property or parts with it in breach of his trust obligations would be liable to the beneficiary in damages, the beneficiary may alternatively seek to enforce a trust of land against a purchaser for value under the doctrine of notice or as an overriding interest.[660] Similarly, the equitable remedy of tracing may be relied on to follow trust funds, even if they have been converted into a different form or mingled with other funds, into the hands of a person who received them who is not a purchaser for value without notice.[661]

§2. Classification of Trusts

248. Trusts can be classified as a private or a public trust. A private trust is for the benefit of a specific person or class of persons. Trusts to carry out a purpose are generally treated as invalid as they offend the beneficiary principle which insists on the existence of a beneficiary who can enforce the trust.[662] One exception to the

655. Keeton & Sheridan, *The Law of Trusts,* 12th edn (Chichester: B. Rose Law Publishers, 1993), 3.
656. *See* Gretton, 'Trusts Without Equity', *International and Comparative Law Quarterly* 49 (2000): 599, 608–615.
657. *See Ibid.*, 606.
658. Ryan, *An introduction to Civil Law* (Australia: The Law Book Co of Australasia Pty Ltd, 1962), 224–226. The separate legal personality of a company also invites comparisons between this device and the trust and, in the commercial sphere, the use of either brings with it different benefits and constraints, *see* Hansmann & Mattei, 'The Functions of Trust Law: A Comparative Legal and Economic Analysis', *New York University Law Review* 73 (1998): 434.
659. *See* Honoré, 'Obstacles to the Reception of the Trust? The Examples of South Africa and Scotland', in *Aequitas and Equity,* ed. Rabello (Jerusalem: Sacher Institute for Legislative Research and Comparative Law, 1997).
660. *See* para. 71 above.
661. Keogan, Mee & Wylie, *The Law and Taxation of Trusts* (Dublin: Tottel Publishing, 2007), Ch. 21.
662. *See Morice v. Bishop of Durham* (1804) 9 Ves.399 as per Grant MR at 405.

beneficiary principle is the public or charitable trust which is a trust set up for charitable purposes. As shall be discussed in Chapter 5, public or charitable trusts tend to be tightly defined.

249. Trusts can also be classified as express, resulting or constructive trusts. An express trust is expressly created by the settler, often by a deed or will. They are frequently used in a testamentary context to provide for a person who cannot take an absolute gift of the property because he or she suffers from some legal incapacity e.g., minority or mental illness. Such trusts may be fixed or discretionary. Under a fixed trust the beneficiaries have a fixed current entitlement to a specific share in the trust property. In contrast, the beneficiaries of a discretionary trust have no actual entitlement to any part of the trust property. The trustees decide in accordance with their discretion how the income and capital are to be disposed of amongst a number of beneficiaries. The principal advantage of a discretionary trust is that it allows trustees to adapt to changing circumstances but because they are so heavily taxed[663] they are not as widespread as one might expect. An express trust may also form the basis of a pension or investment scheme or a charitable donation.

250. The resulting trust got its name from the fact that the beneficial interest reverts or results to the settlor, or if he is dead, to his estate. Resulting trusts can be further categorized into automatic resulting trusts and presumed resulting trusts.[664] The automatic resulting trust arises where a trust fails or the settlor neglects to dispose of the entire beneficial interest in the property. A presumed resulting trust is implied by the law based on the presumed intention of a person who transfers or purchases property.

251. A constructive trust[665] is said to arise by operation of law to satisfy the demands of justice and good conscience. It is flexible and dynamic and is imposed in a variety of circumstances. For example, a purchaser who has entered into a contract to purchase land acquires a beneficial interest in the land under a constructive trust. A constructive trust may also be relied on to prevent a person in a fiduciary position from gaining an unfair advantage or profit from that position.

663. *See* Keogan, Mee & Wylie, *The Law and Taxation of Trusts* (Dublin: Tottel Publishing, 2007), Ch. 27.
664. *See* Ch. 5 below.
665. *See* Ch. 6 below.

Chapter 2. The Creation of an Express Trust

252. The creation of a valid express trust requires a declaration of trust which complies with the requisite statutory formalities and contains the essential elements of an express trust known as the 'three certainties'. Also, unless the settlor (i.e., the person creating the trust) declares himself to be the trustee, it is essential that the trust is completely constituted. This means that the trust property must be transferred to the trustees in a manner effective at law.[666] As Turner LJ pronounced in *Milroy v. Lord*,[667] 'the settlor must have done everything which, according to the nature of the property comprised in the settlement, was necessary to be done in order to transfer the property'. This requirement is subject to an exception which provides that if the settlor has done everything in his power to transfer the title to the property but cannot ensure compliance with some formality which is outside his control, the trust will nevertheless be regarded as completely constituted.[668]

§1. Statutory Formalities

253. In certain circumstances, a declaration of trust will be ineffective if created orally and must comply with statutory formalities. A declaration of a trust of land must comply with section 4 of the Statute of Frauds (Ireland) 1695 which provides that the trust must be evidenced in writing and signed by some person in a position to declare the trust, or by his will. It is important to note that this requirement does not apply to resulting or constructive trusts.[669] Although, the declaration of the trust does not have to be in the format of a deed, it frequently is. All that is required is written evidence which proves the existence of the trust and sets out its essential terms (i.e., contains the three certainties).[670] If the section 4 formalities have not been complied with, the trust will generally be unenforceable, unless this would result in a fraud[671] and there is some other evidence to establish the existence and nature of the trust. It is long established that equity will not permit a statute to be used as an instrument of fraud.[672]

254. While an oral declaration of trust in relation to personal property is fully effective, provided it takes effect during the settlor's lifetime, it is preferable to put it in writing to avoid future disputes over its creation. All testamentary trusts of land or personal property must comply with the statutory requirements for making a valid will set out in section 78 of the Succession Act 1965. The will must be in writing, signed

666. The Land and Conveyancing Law Reform Act, s. 62, clarifies that a legal estate in land may only be conveyed by deed.

667. (1862) 4 De GF &J.

668. *Re Rose* [1952] Ch 499.

669. Statute of Frauds (Ireland) Act 1695, s. 5.

670. A letter may contain this evidence, *see Childers v. Childers* (1857) 1 De G & J 482 or a telegram, *see McBlain v. Cross* (1871) 25 LT 804.

671. *See Conroy v. Fitzpatrick* (HC) 18 Dec. 2003; *McGillicuddy v. Joy* [1959] IR 189; *Rochefoucauld v. Boustead* [1697] 1 Ch 196.

672. *See McCormick v. Grogan* (1896) LR 4 HL 82 as per Lord Westbury at 97.

at the foot or end thereof by the testator and the testator's signature must be made or acknowledged in the presence of two or more witnesses, present at the same time, each of whom must attest the signature of the testator by his own signature. In this context, also, equity has intervened to prevent a fraud and this was the historical justification for the enforcement of secret trusts.[673] It should also be mentioned at this point, that section 6 of the Statute of Frauds (Ireland) 1695 provides that all subsequent dispositions of a beneficial interest held under a trust must be in writing and signed by the person making the disposition or be by his will.

§2. The Three Certainties

255. All express trusts must contain the three certainties, namely certainty of intention, subject matter and objects. As O'Byrne J set out in *Chambers v. Fahy*:[674]

> It has been established that in order that a trust may be created, the subject matter must be certain, the objects of the trust must be certain, and the words relied upon as creating the trust must have been used in an imperative sense, so as to show that the testator intended to create an obligation.

I. Certainty of Intention

256. Although the settlor does not need to use the word 'trust' in its creation, the court must be certain that settlor intended to impose an obligation on the recipient of the property to hold it on trust. The use of precatory words (i.e., words expressing a hope, desire or a wish that the recipient would deal with property in a certain way), may present a difficulty in this respect. Generally, the use of such words will not create a trust and will result in the recipient taking the property absolutely.[675] However, the use of precatory words does not automatically preclude a finding of certainty of intention; it may still be present by construing the language of the will as a whole.[676]

II. Certainty of Subject Matter

257. The property which is to form the subject matter of the trust must be clearly identified[677] and the beneficial shares to be taken in the subject matter must also be clearly set out,[678] unless a discretionary trust has been created. However, if an objective

673. *See* Ch. 3 below.
674. [1931] IR 17, 21.
675. *See Humphrey's Estate* [1916] 1 IR 21; *Re Coulson* (1953) 87 ILTR 93; *Re Sweeney* [1976–1977] ILRM 88.
676. *See Comiskey v. Bowing-Hanbury* [1905] AC 84.
677. *See Palmer v. Simmonds* (1854) 2 Drew 221; *Re Jones* [1898] 1 Ch 438.
678. A failure to set out the beneficial shares may result in the trust property being held on automatic resulting trust for the settlor or his estate.

criterion is supplied by the settlor to facilitate the identification of the subject matter of the trust, it will not fail due to uncertainty of subject matter.[679] Difficulties have arisen where a settlor seeks to create a trust over a definite portion of assets which have not yet been identified. To create a trust over goods or chattels, they must be ascertained and segregated.[680] However, this approach may not apply to intangible property such as shares in a company.[681]

III. Certainty of Objects

258. The beneficiaries of the trust must be clearly identified or identifiable at the time the trust comes into operation. If a trust fails for lack of certainty of objects, an automatic resulting trust will be triggered so that the trustee holds the trust property on resulting trust for the settlor or, if he is dead, his estate (i.e., his residuary legatees as identified by his will or his intestate successors). It should be noted that a doubt about the whereabouts of a beneficiary or whether he is alive, will not generally defeat a trust. The courts can make a Benjamin order[682] which allows the trustees to distribute the property as if the person was dead. If the person subsequently comes forward, he may be able to avail of a tracing remedy against the other beneficiaries, but the trustees will not be liable in such circumstances. Instead of making such a court application, the trustees could take out missing beneficiary insurance which may prove to be a less costly and practical solution to this problem.[683]

259. Problems in relation to certainty of objects tend to arise where the beneficiaries are not identified by name but, instead, are referred to as a class (e.g., a trust set up for the settlor's friends). The case law tends to make a distinction between two potential difficulties in this context, that of conceptual uncertainty and evidential uncertainty. The concept used to define the class must have a precise meaning so that it is possible to decide, in principle, whether any particular person falls inside or outside the class. As has been noted, 'to insist on complete certainty would defeat most trusts'[684] and therefore the courts have tried to be practical and flexible when it comes to determining if a trust is conceptually certain. For example, the terms 'relatives' and 'dependants' have been held to be sufficiently conceptually certain.[685] In *Parker v. Kilroy*,[686] Budd J stated that the court should make every endeavour to find a meaning for the term because the testator, having made a will, demonstrated that he did not intend to die intestate.[687] In that case, a discretionary trust for the testator's'necessitous' nieces and

679. In *Re Golay's Will Trusts* [1965] 1WLR 969, a trust which was to provide a 'reasonable income' for a beneficiary was upheld on this basis.
680. *Re Goldcorp Exchange Ltd* [1995] 1 AC in relation to whether a beneficial interest had been created in bullion. *See also Re London Wine Co. Ltd* [1986] PCC.
681. *See Hunter v. Moss* [1993] 3 All ER 215. Note that there are no Irish authorities on this point.
682. Named after *Re Benj*amin [1902] 1 Ch 723.
683. *See Re Evans* [1999] 2 All ER 777.
684. Hanbury & Martin, *Modern Equity,* 17th edn (London: Sweet & Maxwell, 2005), 108.
685. *Re Baden's Deed Trusts* (No. 2) [1973] Ch 9.
686. [1966] IR 308.
687. *Ibid.*, at 328.

nephews and their children was upheld. Budd J held that it was possible to judge if a niece or nephew was necessitous by examining their particular circumstances in life. It is also established that any conceptual uncertainty can be cured by phrasing the description of the class of beneficiaries so that the opinion of the trustees on a person's eligibility is to settle the matter.[688]

260. In determining if a trust is sufficiently evidentially certain, the courts endeavour to ascertain whether it is possible to prove as a matter of fact who falls inside or outside the class. Thus, a trust will fail on this basis if it is not possible to draw up an exhaustive list of all the beneficiaries. In Ireland, the courts have, to date, insisted that fixed and discretionary trusts must be both conceptually and evidentially certain. In contrast, the English courts, since the House of Lords decision in *McPhail v. Doulton*,[689] have been prepared to uphold discretionary trusts which can only satisfy the requirement of conceptual certainty.[690] In adopting this approach, the English courts appear to be applying the less stringent test for certainty of objects which is applied to powers of appointment.[691] In the Irish case, *Parker v. Kilroy*,[692] Budd J proceeded on the basis that all the members of the class who could be selected under the terms of the discretionary trust must be ascertained or capable of ascertainment. The requirement for an exhaustive list was satisfied as the testator did not have many nieces and nephews and Budd J was satisfied that sufficient financial data could be collected by the trustees to enable them to identify those who were necessitous.[693] More recently, the approach adopted in *Parker* was approved by Murphy J in *O'Byrne v. Davoren*,[694] although the discretionary trust in question was found to be void because it infringed the rule against perpetuities and perpetual trusts. He noted that, in Ireland, the decision of Budd J in *Parker* was a 'precedent of greater authority' than the House of Lords decision in *McPhail v. Doulton*. He also expressed a clear preference for the reasoning adopted in the former decision.[695]

261. In more recent times, the English courts have suggested that a discretionary trust which is conceptually and, technically, evidentially certain, may also fail if it is administratively unworkable. This ground of uncertainty was put forward by Lord Wilberforce in *McPhail v. Doulton*.[696] He stated that a trust may fail for uncertainty 'where the definition of the beneficiaries is so hopelessly wide as not to form "anything

688. *See Re Leek* [1969] 1 Ch 563 the class of potential beneficiaries included any persons who the trustees considered to have a moral claim on the settlor.
689. [1971] AC 424. This decision over-rules the earlier House of Lords decision in *IRC v. Broadway Cottages Trust* [1955] Ch 20.
690. Note that the English courts require the presence of both conceptual and evidential certainty in order to create a valid fixed trust.
691. *See Re Gulbiankian's Settlements* [1970] AC 508. A power of appointment confers a power on a donee to appoint property in favour of objects. It can be distinguished from a discretionary trust by the fact that a donee of a power cannot be compelled to act whereas a trustee must exercise his discretion and select who is to benefit.
692. [1966] IR 309.
693. *Ibid.*, at 332.
694. [1994] 3 IR 373.
695. *See* Biehler, *Equity and the Law of Trusts in Ireland,* 6th edn (Dublin: Thomson Roundhall, 2016), 96–97 for a critique of both approaches.
696. [1971] AC 424.

like a class" so that the trust is administratively unworkable'.[697] He gave an example of a discretionary trust for all the residents of Greater London. In such circumstances, although it is theoretically possible to draw up a complete list of such residents, the trustees are given no discernable criteria to guide them in making their selection from such a huge number of potential beneficiaries.[698]

697. *Ibid.*, 457.

698. *See R v. District Auditor ex. parte West Yorkshire Metropolitan Count Council* (1986) 26 RVR 24. There are no Irish authorities on this point.

Chapter 3. Secret Trusts

§1. General

262. It is difficult to classify secret trusts and it has been suggested that a half-secret trust is an express trust, while a fully secret trust is a constructive trust.[699] If this is the case, a half-secret trust created over land would be subject to the formalities set out in section 4 of the Statute of Frauds (Ireland) 1695, while a fully secret trust would not.[700] A fully secret trust arises when a testator leaves property in his will to a person and no trust appears on the face of the will; it looks as if the legatee takes an absolute gift. However, the testator privately communicates his direction to the legatee that the property is to be held on trust for a certain beneficiary or beneficiaries. A half-secret trust arises where the will expressly states that the legatee is to take the property as a trustee but the objects of the trust are communicated to the trustee independently of the will. As wills are public documents,[701] the popularity of secret trusts may be attributable, at least historically, to a desire to keep certain dispositions secret (e.g., a legacy for a non-marital child). In more recent times, it has been suggested that the primary motivation of the settlor may be to retain flexibility over how certain property is to be distributed on his death, in a manner which obviates the need to comply with the usual testamentary formalities.[702]

§2. The Justification for Enforcing Secret Trusts

263. The difficulty with enforcing a secret trust is that the declaration of trust fails to comply with the formalities set out in section 78 of the Succession Act 1965[703] necessary to create a valid testamentary trust. However, if the secret trustee pleads that the trust is invalid due to non-compliance with the Succession Act and the court allows the trustee to take the property beneficially, this would be to permit a statute to be used as an instrument of fraud which will not be tolerated by Equity. The prevention of fraud theory was the historical theoretical justification for the enforcement of secret trusts. As Lord Westbury explained in *McCormick v. Grogan*,[704] the disponee in such

699. *See* Biehler, *Equity and the Law of Trusts in Ireland,* 6th edn (Dublin: Thomson Roundhall, 2016), 115–116. Note that Allan argues that both fully and half-secret trust should be classified as constructive trusts in his article, 'The Secret Is Out There: Searching for the Legal Justification for the Doctrine of Secret Trusts through Analysis of the Case Law', *Common Law World Review* 40 (2011): 311.
700. *See Ottaway v. Norman* [1972] Ch 698); *Brown v. Pourau* [1995] 1 NZLR 352.
701. They may be inspected at the probate office.
702. *See* Keogan, Mee & Wylie, *The Law and Taxation of Trusts* (Dublin: Tottel Publishing, 2007), para. 4.023.
703. *See* para. 250 above.
704. (1869) LR 4 HL 82.

circumstances is converted into a trustee simply on the principle that an individual shall not be benefited by his own personal fraud.[705]

264. Although the fraud argument explains why the legatee should not be allowed to take beneficially, it does not explain why the courts went a step further and actually enforced the secret trust in favour of the secret beneficiary. A fraud would be prevented by a court ruling which required the legatee to hold the property on resulting trust for the residuary legatee. The prevention of fraud theory was even more inadequate when it came to explaining why half-secret trusts should be enforced; the legatee in such circumstances is described as a trustee on the face of the will, thereby preventing any possibility of him taking beneficially.[706] It was necessary to come up with a more satisfactory justification and the modern justification for enforcing secret trusts is that the declaration of trust operates *dehors* (i.e., outside) the will.[707] Therefore, the declaration of trust is not required to comply with section 78 of the Succession Act 1965.

265. The will has an impact on the validity of the trust; however, as it operates to vest the trust property in the trustee and, until that happens, the trust will not be fully constituted. The operation of the 'dehors the will' theory may give rise to some surprising consequences and the case law illustrates that while the rules set out in the Succession Act 1965 may be inapplicable in certain circumstances, they may have a role to play in matters which concern the vesting of the trust property in the trustee. For example, the courts have ruled that section 82 of the Succession Act 1965, which prevents a legatee who witnesses the will from taking the legacy, does not apply to a secret beneficiary who witnesses the will, as the secret beneficiary takes under the trust which arises outside the will.[708] However, if a fully secret trustee witnesses the will, this may lead to the invalidity of the gift.[709] Also, section 91 of the Succession Act provides that the legacy of a beneficiary under a will who predeceases the testator will lapse and fall into the residue. Although the trust will fail due to the operation of the doctrine of lapse if a fully secret trustee predeceases the testator,[710] it has been suggested that if the secret beneficiary predeceases the testator, the estate of the secret beneficiary may take under the trust.[711]

705. *Ibid.*, 97.

706. For a discussion of the continuing relevance of the prevention of fraud justification for the enforcement of secret trusts, *see* Allan, 'The Secret Is Out There: Searching for the Legal Justification for the Doctrine of Secret Trusts through Analysis of the Case Law', *Common Law World Review* 40 (2011): 311.

707. *See Blackwell v. Blackwell* [1929] AC 318.

708. *See O'Brien v. Condon* [1905] 1 IR 51.

709. *See* Oakley, *Constructive Trusts,* 2nd edn (London: Sweet & Maxwell, 1987), 120.

710. *Re Maddock* [1902] 2 Ch 220.

711. *Re Gardner* (No. 2) [1923] 2 Ch 30. Note that this ruling has been widely criticized, *see* Keogan, Mee & Wylie, *Law and Taxation of Trusts* (Dublin: Tottel Publishing, 2007), para. 4.033.

§3. Essential Elements of a Secret Trust

266. To enforce a secret trust, it must be possible to prove three elements: intention, communication and acceptance,[712] on the balance of possibilities.[713] The testator must have intended to impose a trust and that intention must have been communicated to the trustee. Once communication has been established,[714] the courts may infer acceptance from the trustee's silence.[715] In England, a crucial distinction has been drawn in the application of the communication requirement to fully secret and half-secret trusts. In the case of a fully secret trust, it is only necessary to prove that communication took place before the death of the testator. However, in the case of half-secret trusts, the courts have insisted that communication must take place at or before the execution of the will.[716] In Ireland, although the matter has yet to be considered at Supreme Court level, the courts have not made the same distinction and both half and fully secret trusts will be enforced, regardless of when communication took place, provided it was during the testator's lifetime.[717] One implication of the Irish approach is that it appears to allow the testator sometime to make up his mind about who is to take the beneficial interest or to change his mind on the matter, provided he communicates the name of the beneficiary to the trustee before his death.[718]

712. *Riordan v. Banon* (1869) IR 10 Eq 469, per Chatterton VC at 478; *Blackwell v. Blackwell* [1929] AC 318 per Viscount Sumner at 334.
713. *Re Snowden* [1979] Ch 528.
714. Note that in *Re Keen* [1937] Ch 236, the courts ruled that giving the legatee a sealed envelope containing details of the trust which was not to be opened until after the testator's death constituted sufficient communication.
715. *See French v. French* [1902] 1 IR 172 per Lord Davey at 230.
716. *See Re Keen* [1937] Ch 236; *Re Bateman's Will Trusts* [1970] 3 All ER 817; *Re Freud* [2014] EWCH 2577 (Ch), [16].
717. *Re Prendiville* [1995] ILRM 578. Note that certain aspects of Barron J's ruling in this High Court decision have been criticized, *see* Biehler, *Equity and the Law of Trusts in Ireland,* 6th edn (Dublin: Thomson Roundhall, 2016), 113–114; Mee, 'Half-Secret Trusts in England and Ireland', *Conveyancer and Property Lawyer* (2002): 202. However, other jurisdictions have followed the Irish approach on this issue, see the decision of Young J in the New South Wales case, *Ledgerwood v. Perpetual Trustee Co Ltd* (1997) 41 NSWLR 532.
718. *See Re Cooper* [1939] Ch 811 which suggests that the terms of a secret trust may be altered provided the alteration is communicated to the trustee.

Chapter 4. Purpose Trusts

§1. Non-charitable Purpose Trusts

I. Objections to Purpose Trusts

267. Non-charitable purpose trusts are generally regarded as invalid and therefore unenforceable. Three objections tend to be raised to enforcing such trusts. The principal objection is that purpose trusts offend against the beneficiary principle, which requires the presence of someone to enforce the trust.[719] The courts will occasionally surmount this requirement by construing the trust as conferring a direct or indirect benefit on an individual or individuals sufficient to give them *locus standi* to apply to the court to enforce the trust.[720] A second concern is that purpose trusts often offend the rule against perpetual trusts (also known as the rule against inalienability), which is designed to prevent property being tied up in a trust for too long a period.[721] This rule requires property to be freely transferable and not subject to a trust for longer than the perpetuity period (which is twenty-one years, in the absence of a life in being). A final difficulty which may arise in the context of purpose trusts, is the court's unwillingness to enforce trusts phrased in terms which are too uncertain or lack sufficient direction[722] or which are capricious or absurd.[723]

268. Although purpose trusts are regarded as invalid, a number of common law exceptions have been recognized which have been described by Roxburgh J in *Re Astor's Settlement Trusts*[724] as 'concessions to human weakness or sentiment'.[725] It has also been intimated that these exceptional categories ought not to be increased or developed.[726] It should be noted that while the courts have been prepared to waive the beneficiary principle in considering the validity of the following exceptions, the trusts must still be structured so as not to offend the rule against perpetual trusts and they

719. Note that some academics have suggested that purpose trusts should be valid unless clearly unlawful or contrary to public policy and that it should be possible for the trust deed to appoint an 'enforcer' to oversee its enforcement, *see* Hayton, 'Developing the Obligation Characteristic of the Trust', *Law Quarterly Review* 117 (2001) 96; Pawlowski and Summers 'Private Purpose Trusts – A Reform Proposal', *Conveyancer and Property Lawyer* 71 no. 5 (2007): 440.

720. *See Re Denley's Trust Deed* [1969] 1 Ch 373.

721. Unlike the rule against perpetuities, this rule has not been abolished by the Land and Conveyancing Law Reform Act 2009.

722. *See Re Astor's Settlement Trusts* [1952] Ch 534.

723. *See McCaig v. University of Glasgow* 1907 SC 231; *Brown v. Burdett* (1882) 2 Ch D 667.

724. [1952] Ch 534.

725. *Ibid.*, 547.

726. *Re Endacott* [1960] Ch 232, per Harman LJ at 251. It has been questioned whether the Irish courts endorse this general principle that purpose trusts are invalid, *see* Keogan, Mee & Wylie, *Law and Taxation of Trusts* (Dublin: Tottel Publishing, 2007), para.7.001.

must be stated in sufficiently clear and certain terms to enable the court to oversee their performance.

II. Trusts to Erect or Maintain Tombs and Gravestones

269. These trusts were not regarded as charitable by the common law but a line of case law developed in which they were regarded as valid purpose trusts. This common law exception has since been supplemented by section 50 of the Charities Act 1961 which provides that gifts for the provision, maintenance or improvement of a tomb, vault, grave, tombstone or any other memorial to a deceased person are charitable so long as they do not exceed a capital sum of IEP 1,000 (now EUR 1,270) or IEP 60 (now EUR 77) a year in application of income. This figure has not been linked to inflation and the Law Reform Commission recommended in 2000 that this figure should be increased to a capital sum of IEP 16,000 (EUR 20,316) or IEP 1,000 (EUR 1,270) in the application of income.[727] Unfortunately, this recommendation has yet to be implemented and, in the many situations where the financial limits are exceeded, the trust must be saved under the common law exception, which requires compliance with the rule against perpetual trusts[728] and sufficiently clear terms. The ruling in *Mussett v. Bingle*[729] illustrates that a flexible approach may be taken in relation to compliance with the perpetuity period where the gift involves the erection of a monument but a strict approach shall be taken in relation to its maintenance. In that case, the court upheld a gift of GBP 300 to be applied in the erection of a monument, presumably on the assumption that it would be erected within the perpetuity period, but where the interest on a further sum of GBP 200 was to be used for its maintenance, this gift was held to be void as it was of a perpetual nature. The courts have been prepared to uphold such trusts for a period of twenty-one years where a qualification is included which expressly limits its operation to such period as the law permits.[730] In *Re Endacott*,[731] the testator bequeathed his residuary estate to a specified parish council for the purpose of providing some useful memorial to himself. This trust failed, however, as the memorial was to be built outside of church property and the court considered it to be insufficiently clear in its terms.

---

727. *See Report on the Rule Against Perpetuities and Cognate Rules* (LRC 62–2000), para. 5.15.
728. One way around this rule is to bring the trust within the category of a charitable trust by dedicating it to the maintenance of an entire churchyard. Another device used is to bequeath the money to a cemetery company for the purposes of maintaining the particular grave, *see* Biehler, *Equity and the Law of Trusts in Ireland,* 6th edn (Dublin: Thomson Roundhall, 2016), 346.
729. [1876] WN 170.
730. *See Re Hooper* [1932] 1 Ch 38.
731. [1960] Ch 232.

III. Trusts for the Maintenance of Specific Animals

270. A trust to provide for the welfare of animals generally or for a particular class of animals will qualify as a charitable trust[732] but where it is designed to care for and maintain specific animal(s), typically the pets of a testator, it must be saved by relying the common law exception which has evolved to cater for this particular instance of human sentiment.[733] Again, however, such trusts must be limited in duration to the perpetuity period. In *Re Kelly*,[734] Meredith J noted that in calculating this period, animals cannot constitute lives in being. He also noted that while he would not imply a clause limiting the trust's operation to a period of twenty-one years, he could analyse the gift to determine if it included a severable part which amounted to expenditure for a period of twenty-one years and therefore did not infringe the rule against perpetual trusts. Nevertheless, it is probably safer to specifically confine the gift to the perpetuity period. Strictly speaking, these trusts are unenforceable (as there is no human beneficiary to enforce them) and they are sometimes referred to as trusts of imperfect obligation. The court may, however, make a 'Pettingal order' which requires the trustees to give an undertaking not to apply the fund for other purposes and grants *locus standi* to the person entitled to the fund after the animal dies to ensure that the trustees do not breach that undertaking.

IV. Trusts for the Purposes of Unincorporated Associations

271. An unincorporated association will generally involve a group of people coming together for a mutual purpose (e.g., a club). Unlike a company, such an association has no legal personality of its own. Where property is left on trust for the purposes of such an association, it may offend against the beneficiary principle as it is not possible to identify future members and it may also offend the rule against perpetual trusts as it may be construed as having a perpetual nature.[735] However, two approaches have been devised by the courts to uphold at least some of these trusts. First, if it can be construed as a trust for the current members of the association, it will be upheld. The beneficiary principle is satisfied as you can identify the current members and the rule against perpetual trusts is not violated, provided the rules of the association provide that its property may be disposed of at any time. This approach was often used to save gifts to religious orders which did not qualify as charitable or whose purposes were not exclusively charitable[736] until the enactment the Charities Act 1961 rendered such an approach unnecessary.[737] One difficulty with this approach is that if a current

732. *See* para. 286 below.

733. *See Pettingall v. Pettingall* (1842) 11 LJ; *Re Dean* [1889] 41 Ch D 552.

734. [1932] IR 255.

735. *See Leahy v. Attorney-General for New South Wales* [1959] AC 457, although this gift was ultimately saved due to legislation which enabled the gift to be construed so as to prevent its application to non-charitable purposes.

736. *Re Delany's Estate* (1882) 9 LR Ir 226; *Re Byrne* [1935] IR 782; *Re Keogh's Estate* [1945] IR 13.

737. Charities Act 1961, ss 45 and 49.

member of such as an association leaves, he would technically be able to take his share of the trust property with him. In England, the courts have overcome this difficulty by applying the 'contract holding theory'. Under this second approach, the property is deemed to be held in accordance with the contract between the members as set out by the rules of the association, which prevent a member from severing his share, but permit the association to be wound up and its property to be divided between the members at any time.[738]

§2. Charitable Trusts

I. General

272. Charitable Trusts do not have to comply with a number of requirements which are imposed in relation to other express trusts. For example, the rule against perpetual trusts or the beneficiary principle is not applied to such trusts. This more lenient approach is justified on the basis that charitable trusts are considered to be of such value and importance to the community. Previously, they were enforced by the Attorney General and the Commissioners of Charitable Donations and Bequests assisted in the day-to-day administration of charitable trusts. The powers of the Commissioners were conferred by the Charities Acts 1961 and 1973 and, in addition to performing an advisory role to trustees in relation to the administration of trusts, their powers included the power to appoint new trustees to a charity and to frame a *cy-près* scheme. This *cy-prés* jurisdiction, which is now exercised by the Charities Regulator Authority,[739] continues to be exercisable if a charitable purpose becomes impossible or impracticable to carry out[740] and allows the funds to be applied to an alternative charitable purpose as near as possible to that intended by the donor.[741] This is one of the main benefits of charitable status, as the failure of a private trust triggers an automatic resulting trust, the impact of which may be very far removed from the charitable intentions of the settlor.

---

738. *See Neville Estates Ltd v. Madden* [1972] Ch 526; *Hunt v McLaren* [2006] EWHC 2586 (Ch); *Hanchett-Stamford v Attorney-General* [2009] CH 173.
739. This jurisdiction was transferred to the Charities Regulatory Authority by the Charities Act 2009, s. 82.
740. The circumstances in which this jurisdiction is exercisable are set out in the Charities Act 1961, s. 47(1), and include where the original purposes in whole or in part have been fulfilled, or have ceased to be charitable in law, or cannot be carried out according to the directions given and the spirit of the gift, or where more effective use might be made of the property by distributing the trust in another manner.
741. A distinction is made between where the gift fails *ab initio*, in which case the property can only be applied *cy- près* where the donor has manifested a general charitable intention, and a case of subsequent failure where it is not necessary to show a general charitable intention, *see Cheshire Foundation in Ireland v Attorney General* [2012] 1 ILRM 369; Biehler, *Equity and the Law of Trusts in Ireland,* 6th edn (Dublin: Thomson Roundhall, 2016), 442–448.

273. Although the Charities Act 2009 was enacted on 28 February 2009, until 16 October, 2014[742] most of the Act had yet to be brought into force by statutory instrument. The aim of this legislation is to enhance public trust and confidence in charities and to increase accountability and transparency in the sector. As the relevant provisions have finally been commenced, a new Charities Regulatory Authority has been established to take over the functions currently performed by the Commissioners and the Attorney General. Its statutory functions also include the maintenance of a register of charities and the investigation and punishment of abuses of charitable status. The Charities Act 2009 requires charitable organizations to keep proper books of accounts and to comply with certain annual reporting and auditing requirements.[743] The Act also sets out the circumstances which will disqualify a person from the position of charity trustee and makes it an offence to act, or purport to act, as a charity trustee while not qualified to do so. Although many charitable organizations operate through a trust, others operate through an unincorporated association or a company limited by guarantee. None of the existing legal structures is ideally suited to the nature of charitable entities and the Law Reform Commission has recommended the introduction of a new alternative form of legal structure for charities to be called the Charitable Incorporated Organization.[744] The Charities Act 2009 has not implemented this proposal or certain other reforms which were proposed by the Law Reform Commission in relation to charitable trustees but it is hoped that these issues will be dealt with by future legislation.

274. The definition of a charitable trust has traditionally been very restrictive. To date, charitable status has conferred extensive exemptions from income tax, capital acquisitions tax and capital gains tax. The prospect of undeserved fiscal immunity may have led the courts to adopting an unduly restrictive approach in relation to whether a trust qualifies as charitable. Although section 3 of the Charities Act 2009 provides a statutory definition of a charitable purpose for the first time, section 7 provides that nothing in the Act shall affect the law which determines eligibility for tax exemptions. This radical step thus envisages charitable status and the issue of tax exemptions being dealt with separately. It has also been suggested that the restrictive approach to charitable status may have been influenced by a reluctance on the part of the judiciary to over-burden the office of the Attorney General which was required to enforce such trusts, a concern which has been removed since the Charities Regulatory Authority took over this function.

II. The Definition of a Charitable Trust

275. A statutory definition of a charitable trust has only recently been introduced in this jurisdiction. Section 2 of the Charities Act 2009 defines it as a trust 'established for a charitable purpose only' and section 3 of the 2009 Act provides a definition of a

742. The Charities Act 2009 (Commencement) Order 2014 (SI 457/2014) brought most of the Act into force on 16 Oct. 2014.
743. The level of reporting and auditing required depends on the level of resources of the organization.
744. *Report on Charitable Trusts and Legal Structures for Charities* (LRC 80 2006).

'charitable purpose'[745] which mirrors to a large extent the modern judicial test set out by Lord Macnaghten in *Commissioners for Special Purposes of Income Tax v. Pemsel*.[746] To qualify as a charitable trust under the judicial test it had to be either for the relief of poverty, the advancement of education or religion or for any other purpose that is of benefit to the community. Once a trust satisfied this requirement, it had to overcome a second hurdle; it had to satisfy what has become known as the 'public benefit requirement'. The trust had to benefit a section of the public whose size is not numerically negligible and whose distinguishing features from the rest of the public does not depend on the members' relationship to a particular individual or membership of an organization.[747] To complicate matters, the requirement for public benefit was not applied consistently across the different categories of charitable trust, traditionally being interpreted less strictly in relation to trusts for the relief of poverty and trusts for the advancement of religion. Although the statutory definition of a charitable purpose set out in section 3 of the Charities Act 2009 substantially reflects the definition set out in the *Pemsel case*, it also clarifies certain ambiguities which had arisen and sets out a non-exhaustive list of purposes which will be considered to be of benefit to the community. The requirement to prove an element of public benefit is also specified, although guidance is given on the circumstances which will negate or impact on such a determination.[748] A significant feature of this new statutory public benefit requirement is its more even application across the various categories of charitable purpose.[749]

276. Originally, a trust had to be exclusively charitable before it could be awarded charitable status.[750] The situation was improved in Ireland by section 49 of the Charities Act 1961 which provides that where any of the purposes of a gift include both charitable and non-charitable objects its terms shall be construed so as to exclude non-charitable objects. It is unclear what the impact of the Charities Act 2009 will have on mixed trusts. The definition of a charitable trust specifies that it must be established for charitable purposes *only*[751] although section 49 of the Charities Act 1961 is not expressly repealed.

III. Trusts for the Relief of Poverty

277. Trusts for the relief of the poor generally or the poor of a particular area or religious denomination have traditionally been upheld.[752] Section 3 of the Charities

745. Note that a list of charitable purposes was set out in the preamble to the Irish Statute of Charitable Uses 1634 which was repealed in 1878. Although it was never intended to amount to an exhaustive legal definition, this list proved useful over the years, in that trusts which were considered to be within the 'spirit and intendment' of the preamble were regarded as charitable.
746. [1891] AC 531.
747. *See Re McEnery's Estate* [1941] IR 323; *Oppenheim v. Tobacco Securities Trust Co Ltd* [1951] AC 297.
748. *See* Charities Act 2009, ss 3(3)(4)(7) and (8), *see* para. 278 below.
749. Although trusts for the advancement of religion are presumed to be of public benefit.
750. *Chichester Diocesan Fund v. Simpson* [1944] AC 341.
751. *See* Charities Act 2009, s. 2.
752. *See Attorney General v. Mathews* (1677) 2 Lev 167; Attorney *General v. Exeter Corporation* (1862) 2 Russ 45; *Attorney General v. Wansay* (1808) 15 Ves 231.

Act 2009 clarifies that a 'charitable purpose' includes 'the prevention or relief of poverty or economic hardship'. It has been argued that the existing case law on the meaning of the term 'poverty' or 'poor' shall remain a useful guide.[753] As Evershed MR noted in *Re Coulthurst*[754] 'it is quite clearly established that poverty does not mean destitution'. Poverty is treated as a relative term and therefore the class designed to benefit need not be in 'grinding need or utter destitution'.[755] However, where the trust is not adequately related to the relief of poverty, it will not qualify[756] (e.g., a gift to amuse the poor would not be considered charitable[757]). Although the public benefit requirement was traditionally very easily satisfied under this heading, the reforms introduced by the Charities Act 2009 in this respect will result in a stricter application of this requirement in the future. The previously generous approach developed based on the 'poor relations' cases, where trusts to relieve the poverty of a testator's poor relations were upheld, despite the personal nexus between the testator and the class of persons to benefit.[758] This exception to the public benefit requirement was also extended to poor employees of a particular organization[759] and poor members of a particular society.[760]

278. It should be noted that pursuant to the Charities Act 2009 'poor relations' and 'poor employees' trusts shall cease to be charitable. Section 3(7) provides that in determining whether a gift is of public benefit, account shall be taken of any limitation imposed by the donor on the class of persons who may benefit from the gift and whether it is justified and reasonable. More significantly, section 3(8) provides that a limitation shall not be justified and reasonable if all of the intended beneficiaries of the gift or a significant number of them have a personal connection with the donor of the gift. Section 2(a) of the Act defines a 'personal connection' as including a family or employment relationship.

753. Biehler, *Equity and the Law of Trusts in Ireland,* 6th edn (Dublin: Thomson Roundhall, 2016), 373.
754. [1951] Ch 661 at 665–666.
755. *IRC v. Baddeley* [1955] AC 572, per Viscount Simonds at 585.
756. In *Re Sanders Will Trust* [1954] Ch 265.
757. *Baddeley v. IRC* [1953] 1 WLR 84, 88.
758. *Mahon v. Savage* (1803) 1 Sch & Lef 111; *Re Scarisbrick* [1951] Ch 622; *Re Segelman deceased* [1996] Ch 171.
759. *Dingle v. Turner* [1972] AC 601.
760. *Re Denison* (1974) 42 DLR (3d) 652.

IV. Trusts for the Advancement of Education

279. Although gifts to schools,[761] universities[762] or to found a scholarship[763] will qualify under this heading, the concept of education, in this context, has broadened in recent times and does not necessarily involve a teaching element. It was accepted, for example, that this category of charitable trust included gifts for cultural advancement such as gifts for the establishment of theatres or art galleries or the promotion of literature and music.[764] However, while section 3(1)(b) of the Charities Act 2009 reflects the *Pemsel case* definition by setting out 'the advancement of education' as the second category of charitable purpose, section 3(11)(k) of the Charities 2009 Act lists the advancement of the arts, culture, heritage or sciences under the fourth category of 'other purposes of benefit to the community'. Where young people are involved, the courts have treated education as including their physical education as well as the education of their minds. On this basis, trusts to promote sport or certain games, which traditionally have not qualified as charitable where directed at the general public,[765] have been upheld as charitable when targeted at young people.[766]

280. The public benefit requirement was traditionally very strictly applied to this category of charitable trust.[767] However, settlors were able to get around this strict approach if the trust could be formulated to come within the scope of the 'founder's kin exception', which operates where a gift made to an educational institution includes a direction that preference is to be given to the settlor's relations.[768] It was emphasized, however, that to come within the scope of this exception, the primary object must have been to endow the institution for educational purposes.[769] It would seem that the founder's kin exception may survive the re-formulation of the public benefit requirement set out in section 3(8) of the 2009 Act.

V. Trusts for the Advancement of Religion

281. The advancement of religion has been described as the promotion of the spiritual teachings or doctrines of that religion.[770] In addition, section 3 (6) of the

761. *See Governors of Erasmus Smith's Schools v. Attorney General for Saorstat Eireann* (1932) 66 ILTR 57. Note that a private fee-paying school which applies profits for private purposes will not qualify as charitable, *see Wesley College v. Commissioner of Valuation* [1984] ILRM 117; *see also* the Charities Act 2009, s 3(7)(b), which may prevent fee-paying schools from satisfying the public benefit requirement.
762. *McCormack v. Queens University Belfast* [1958] NI 1.
763. *Queens University Belfast v. Attorney General for Northern Ireland* [1966] NI 115.
764. *See Re Worth Library* [1995] 2 IR 301, per Keane J at 336.
765. *See Re Nottage* [1865] Ch 649.
766. *IRC v. McMullen* [1981] AC 1; *Re Dupree's Deed Trusts* [1945] Ch 16.
767. *Re McEnery's Estate* [1941] IR 323; *Re Worth Library* [1995] 2 IR 301; *Re Crompton* [1945] Ch 123; *Oppenheim v. Tobacco Securities Trust Co Ltd* [1951] AC 297.
768. *See Spencer v. All Souls College* (1762) Wilm 163; *Laverty v. Laverty* [1907] 1 IR 9, per Barton J at 13.
769. *Re Crompton* [1945] Ch 123 per Lord Greene at 132.
770. *Keren Kyrmeth Le Jisroel Ltd v. IRC* [1931].

Charities Act 2009 provides that a charitable gift for the purpose of the advancement of religion shall have effect and shall be construed 'in accordance with the laws, canons, ordinances and tenets of the religion concerned'. The fact that the religion has only a very limited following would not seem to preclude qualification.[771] Gifts to support clergy[772] and missionaries[773] or to decorate churches[774] qualify as charitable under this heading. While a gift to an ecclesiastical office holder will be upheld as charitable,[775] a gift for that particular individual in their personal capacity would not qualify as charitable.[776]

282. For the most part, common law jurisdictions have been adopting an increasingly flexible attitude to what qualifies as a religion. However, section 3(10) of the Charities Act 2009 provides that a gift is not for the advancement of religion if it is made for the benefit of an organization or cult which has as its principal object the making of a profit or if it engages in oppressive psychological manipulation of its followers or for the purposes of gaining new followers. One controversial issue which has emerged is whether the definition is restricted to religions which involve a belief in a Supreme Being or God. This issue was considered in the English case, *Re South Place Ethical Society*,[777] where a trust was set up to promote a society which was based on studying and disseminating ethical principles. The court held that it was not a trust to advance religion as the two essential elements of religion are faith in a God and worship of that God. The trust was, however, upheld as an educational trust. Although this restrictive approach was adopted in England in *R v. Registrar General; Ex p Segerdal*[778] where it was held that the Church of Scientology did not qualify as a religion for the purposes of the Places of Religious Worship Registration Act 1855, this decision was overruled by the UK Supreme Court in *R (on the Application of Hodkin) v Registrar General of Births, Deaths and Marriages*.[779] In Australia, a belief in a Supreme Being is not considered essential, and a body which claims to be religious and offers a way to find meaning and purpose in life would qualify as charitable.[780] The Law Reform Committee of the Law Society of Ireland has recommended that statutory clarification should be provided on whether the legal definition of religion extends to embrace a belief in principles or ethics not involving the worship of a Supreme Being.[781] No clarity is provided on this issue by the Charities Act 2009.

283. In contrast with the strict approach adopted in England on this issue, the Irish courts apply a more lenient approach to the satisfaction of the public benefit requirement where religious trusts are concerned. This issue proved particularly

771. *Re Watson* [1973] 1 WLR 1472.
772. *Re Foster* [1939] 1 Ch 22.
773. *Dunne v. Duignan* [1908] 1 IR 228.
774. *Re Greene* [1914] 1 IR 305.
775. *Gibson v. Representative Church Body* (1881) 9 LR Ir 1.
776. *Donnellan v. O'Neil* (1870) IR 5 Eq 525.
777. [1980] 3 All ER 918.
778. [1970] 3 All ER.
779. [2013] UKSC 77.
780. *Church of the New Faith v. Commissioner of Pay-Roll Tax (Vict.)* (1983) 154 CLR 120.
781. *Charity Law: The Case for Reform* (July 2002), 75.

contentious in the context of gifts to contemplative religious orders[782] or gifts for the saying of private masses.[783] The matter was put beyond doubt by section 45(1) of the Charities Act 1961 which provided that once it was established that a trust advances a religion, it could be conclusively presumed that there was a public benefit. Section 45(2) confirmed that gifts for the celebration of masses, whether in public or in private, were valid charitable gifts. Section 45 of the 1961 Act was repealed and replaced by section 3(4) of the Charities Act 2009 which provides that it shall be presumed, unless the contrary is proved, that a gift for the advancement of religion is of public benefit. In creating a rebuttable as opposed to a conclusive presumption, the new wording is not as strong. However, section 3(5) provides that the Charities Regulatory Authority shall not make a determination that a gift for the advancement of religion is not of public benefit without the consent of the Attorney General. It seems unlikely that the common law position in relation to private masses or contemplative religious orders will be reversed.

VI. Trusts for Other Purposes Beneficial to the Community

284. The trusts which qualified under this vague catch-all heading were traditionally the most difficult to predict of the *Pemsel* categories. Whether a trust qualified was sometimes resolved by asking if the purpose under consideration is within the 'spirit and intendment' of the preamble to the Statute of Charitable Uses (Ireland) 1634. For example, by analogy with the preamble's reference to 'the relief or maintenance of any manner of poor, succourless, distressed or impotent persons', trusts which made provision for the relief of the elderly, sick or disabled people were traditionally upheld.[784] Gifts to hospitals or nursing homes were also be upheld as charitable under this heading.[785] As has already been mentioned, section 3(11) of the Charities Act 2009 provides a non-exhaustive list of purposes which are deemed to be of benefit to the community, such as the advancement of community welfare, including the relief of those in need by reason of youth, age, ill-health or disability[786] and the promotion of health, including the prevention or relief of sickness, disease or human suffering.[787]

285. While trusts to promote sport will generally not be upheld as charitable,[788] if the trust can be construed as being for another purpose beneficial to the community, for example, by making provision for recreational grounds or leisure facilities in a

782. *See* the English cases, *Cocks v. Manners* (1871) LR 12 Eq 574; *Gilmour v. Coats* [1949] AC 426 and the Irish cases, *Maguire v. Attorney General* [1943] IR 238; *Bank of Ireland Trustee Co. Ltd v. Attorney General* [1957] IR 257.
783. *See* the English case, *Re Hetherington* [1990] Ch 1, and the Irish cases, *Attorney General v. Delaney* (1875)IR 10 CL 104; *O'Hanlon v. Logue* [1906] 1 IR 247.
784. *See Re Robinson* [1951] Ch 198; *Re Lewis* [1955] Ch 104.
785. *Barrington's Hospital v. Commissioner of Valuation* [1957] IR 299.
786. Charities Act 2009, s. 3(11)(a).
787. Charities Act 2009, s. 3(11)(d).
788. *See Re Nottage* [1865] Ch 649; *National Tourism Development Authority v Coughlan* [2009] 3 IR 549.

particular area, it will be upheld as charitable under this heading.[789] As has already been mentioned, if the trust is targeted at the physical or mental education of the youth, it may be upheld as a trust for the advancement of education. The Law Reform Committee of the Law Society of Ireland did not recommend that sport per se should be charitable but stated that it should continue to be viewed as charitable where the purpose of the sport in question is to further another charitable purpose. In addition, it recommended that sport for the promotion of health and fitness should qualify as charitable provided it is of sufficient public benefit.[790] It is possible that such a trust would qualify under section 3(11)(d) of the Charities Act 2009 which deems the promotion of health and the prevention of disease to be of benefit to the community.

286. Gifts to promote the welfare of animals generally or a particular class of animals[791] have traditionally qualified as charitable under this fourth heading. Such trusts are deemed to protect public morality by discouraging cruelty to animals thereby benefiting the community.[792] Section 3(11)(j) of the Charities Act 2009 specifically includes 'the prevention or relief of suffering of animals' as a charitable purpose under this fourth category. Trusts and organizations designed to abolish vivisection have proved particularly controversial and have occasionally been awarded charitable status on the basis that prevent cruelty to animals.[793] However, they have also been denied such status on the grounds that the benefits to humanity in allowing vivisection could not be outweighed by the incidental suffering of the animals and because they are designed to bring about a change in the law, which is deemed to be a political purpose.[794]

287. Trusts for political purposes are not charitable and therefore gifts to political parties will not qualify as charitable. In recent times, it has been argued that the opposition to political trusts has been taken too far, particularly where the purposes of a trust involve advocating for a change in domestic or foreign laws or government policy.[795] This approach means that organizations campaigning for improvements in

789. *See Re Morgan* [1955] 1 WLR 738. In *Re Gray* [1925] Ch 262, a gift to a regiment for the promotion of sport was upheld as it would encourage the physical efficiency of the armed forces.

790. *Charity Law: The Case for Reform* (July 2002), 65. The English Charities Act 2006 provides that a trust for the advancement of amateur sport qualifies as charitable. In Ireland, although such trusts do not qualify as charitable, tax relief may be available for certain amateur non-profit making sporting bodies. Note, however, that a body which qualifies for such tax relief is an 'excluded body' and cannot qualify as a 'charitable organization' as defined by the Charities Act 2009, s 2(1), effectively ruling out any incremental change in the law in this area, *see* Biehler, *Equity and the Law of Trusts in Ireland,* 6th edn (Dublin: Thomson Roundhall, 2016), 431.

791. *Swifte v. Attorney General* [1912] 1 IR 133 (a gift to the Dublin home for Starving and Forsaken Cats).

792. *Re Wedgewood* [1915] 1 Ch 113. Occasionally, the courts have struggled to identify a benefit to the community where the trust is to set up a refuge for birds and animals, *see Re Grove-Grady* [1929] 1 Ch 557. However, other cases have noted the value to humanity in preserving wildlife, *see Attorney General of New South Wales v. Sawtell* [1978] 2 NSWLR 200.

793. *Armstrong v. Reeves* (1890) 25 LR Ir 325.

794. *National Anti-Vivisection Society v. IRC* [1948] AC 31.

795. The rationale behind the traditional approach was set out by Lord Parker in *Bowman v. Secular Society Ltd* [1917] AC 406 at 442. He said that the court has no means of judging whether a proposed change in the law will or will not be for the public benefit.

the law cannot be registered as charities and any trusts which involve such an element may fail to qualify as charitable.[796] This seems particularly harsh where a trust for the relief of poverty confers a power to campaign for changes in the law and government policy to further this aim. As Archbishop Helder Camara of Brazil noted, 'If I feed the poor they call me a saint, if I ask why the poor have no food they call me a Communist.'[797] Similarly, trusts aiming to secure peace or conflict resolution have failed to qualify as charitable on this basis.[798] The Law Reform Committee of the Law Society has noted that to be effective a charity must not only provide relief but must question why the system failed the donees in the first place. It recommended that this area of law be reviewed so that charities are able to advocate a change in the law or public policy where this will help it achieve its charitable purposes.[799] The relief of poverty category set out in *Pemsel's case* is slightly modified by the language used by section 3(1)(a) of the Charities Act 2009 which refers to 'the prevention or relief of poverty or economic hardship'. This may facilitate a more flexible approach in this respect, particularly in light of the distinctly political flavour of some of the purposes listed in section 3(11) of the Charities Act 2009, such as the advancement of conflict resolution or reconciliation,[800] the promotion of religious or racial harmony and harmonious community relations,[801] the protection of the natural environment,[802] the advancement of environmental sustainability[803] and the integration of those who are disadvantaged, and the promotion of their full participation, in society.[804] Note, however, that the omission of any specific reference to the advancement of human rights in this list of purposes has been criticized.[805]

288. Whether the public benefit requirement is met may depend on the purpose of the trust and some decisions indicate that it may be more difficult to satisfy the public benefit requirement where the trust falls into the fourth category.[806] As Carswell J noted in *Re Dunlop* ' … a bridge to be used only by Methodists should fail to qualify where a gift for the education of the children of members of that church might be a valid charity'.[807] However, in *Re Worth Library*,[808] Keane J adopted a very lenient approach to a gift of a library to a hospital which could only be accessed by three

796. *See McGovern v. Attorney General* [1982] Ch 321 (a trust created by Amnesty International for the relief of needy persons who were or had been prisoners of conscience, to attempt to secure the release of prisoners of conscience and to procure of the abolition of torture or inhuman or degrading treatment was denied charitable status).
797. Cited in the submission of Senator John Woodley to the Charities Definition Inquiry.
798. *See Re Collier* [1998] 1 NZLR 81; *Re Greenpeace of New Zealand Inc* [2015] 1 NZLR 169.
799. *Charity Law: The Case for Reform* (July 2002), 85–86.
800. Charities Act 2009, s. 3(11)(e).
801. Charities Act 2009, s. 3(11)(f).
802. Charities Act 2009, s. 3(11)(g).
803. Charities Act 2009, s. 3(11)(h).
804. Charities Act 2009, s. 3(11)(l).
805. *See* Breen, 'Too Political to Be Charitable? The Charities Act 2009 and the Future of Human Rights Organizations in Ireland', *Public Law* 2 (2012): 268.
806. *See IRC v. Baddeley* [1955] AC 572 (a trust to provide recreational facilities for Methodists resident in a particular area was not upheld because it failed to satisfy the public benefit requirement).
807. *See Re Dunlop* [1984] NI 408 at 426.
808. [1995] 2 IR 301.

office holders. Although he was satisfied that it did not qualify as a gift to advance education due to the absence of a public benefit, it was held to qualify under the fourth category due to the role it played in the advancement of the charity represented by the hospital. Although the books would not have been of significant practical benefit to the three office holders, the library itself would have provided a haven of quiet relaxation for the beneficiaries. It has been suggested that Keane J's relaxation of the public benefit requirement in this case may have been motivated by a desire to ensure access to the *cy-près* jurisdiction.[809] As has already been mentioned, the application of section 3 of the Charities Act 2009 should result in a more consistent application of the public benefit requirement across the different charitable purposes and, arguably, a return to a more stringent approach to its satisfaction where the trust falls into the fourth category.

809. Biehler, *Equity and the Law of Trusts in Ireland,* 6th edn (Dublin: Thomson Roundhall, 2016), 413.

Chapter 5. Resulting Trusts

§1. General

289. Resulting trusts, so-called because the beneficial interest in the property reverts or results back to the settlor or to his estate if he is dead, are not created expressly, but implied by the law in certain circumstances. As Megarry J noted in *Re Vandervell's Trusts (No. 2)*[810] that there are two types of resulting trust, the automatic resulting trust and the presumed resulting trust. The automatic resulting trust is imposed where there is a failure to effectively dispose of trust property, while the presumed resulting trust arises where there is an apparent gift of property. While the presumed resulting trust is clearly based on a presumption made by the law in relation to the donor's intention, the automatic resulting trust may also be described as being based on a legal presumption that the settlor would wish the beneficial interest to come back to him or his estate in the event of a failure of the trust. However, while the presumption of a resulting trust can be rebutted by the presumption of advancement or evidence demonstrating that the donor intended the donee to take a gift of the beneficial interest in the property, 'an automatic resulting trust cannot be rebutted by evidence of an intention to give'.[811] It is sometimes suggested that this is the essence of the distinction between the two. It should be noted that in recent times, some judges and academics have attempted to develop unifying theories to explain the operation of both types of resulting trust.[812] There are a number of situations where the law will impose an automatic resulting trust.

§2. Automatic Resulting Trusts

I. Failure to Exhaust the Beneficial Interest

290. If the settlor transfers the property to trustees in fee simple to hold on trust for X for life and neglects to set out who is to take the beneficial fee simple remainder,

810. [1974] Ch 269 at 294–295.

811. Swadling, 'A New Role for Resulting Trusts', *Legal Studies* 16 (1996): 110 at 113.

812. Lord Browne-Wilkinson has argued in *Westdeutche Landesbank Girozentrale v. Islington Borough Council* [1996] AC 669 that both types of resulting trust give effect to the presumed intention of the transferor. Chambers has argued that all resulting trusts come into effect because the provider of the property did not intend to benefit the recipient, *see Resulting Trusts* (Oxford: Oxford University Press, 1997), 2. Mee has argued that both types of resulting trust arise where the transferor/settlor intends to make the transferee/recipient of the property a trustee, *see* 'Presumed Resulting Trusts, Intention and Declaration', *Cambridge Law Journal* 73(1)(2014): 86; 'Automatic Resulting Trusts: Retention, Restitution, or Reposing Trust?' in *Constructive and Resulting Trusts* ed. Mitchell (Oxford: Hart Publishing, 2010): 207.

equity imposes an automatic resulting trust for the benefit of the settlor. A slightly different, but related difficulty, can arise where a trust fund is set up to benefit a person by a particular means (e.g., by providing them with a college education) and there is money left over after the objective has been fulfilled. In certain circumstances, the court will allow the beneficiary to take the money absolutely, to be used for whatever purpose he likes. However, in other cases the court has directed the property to be held on automatic resulting trust for the settlor or, if he is dead, his estate. The difference in approach seems to be based, to a large extent, on whether the beneficiary is still alive when the original purpose of the trust has been fulfilled. In such circumstances, the courts tend to construe the gift as being for the general benefit of the person, not limited by the purpose which was suggested, and therefore no automatic trust arises.[813] However, if the beneficiary has died, the courts tend to direct that the surplus funds should be held on resulting trust.[814]

II. Failure of the Trust

291. If the settlor fails to cater for a particular contingency or event in the settlement deed,[815] if the objects of the deed are uncertain[816] or if there is an attempt to create a charitable trust which fails,[817] an automatic resulting trust will arise in favour of the settlor. If the contributors to a failed charity were anonymous, the implications of an automatic resulting trust could be extremely impractical and the English courts have ruled that, in such circumstances, the property vests in the Crown as *bona vacantia*.[818] In Ireland, the situation has been remedied by section 48 of the Charities Act 1961 which allows donations to be applied to a *cy-près* scheme if donations are made for purposes which fail to qualify as charitable and reasonable enquires fail to identify or locate the donors.[819]

292. A comprehensive declaration of trust is an essential prerequisite to the creation of valid express trusts. The *Vandervell* litigation[820] is an extreme example of how a failure in this regard can lead to the imposition of an automatic resulting trust, but also unfavourable tax implications for the settlor. Vandervell wished to provide the College of Surgeons with money to found a chair of pharmacology. For tax reasons, he also wished to get rid of some shares he had in a products company, so he decided to transfer a block of shares to the college and declare enough dividends on the shares to establish the chair. The plan was that Vandervell would not be liable for surtax on the dividends as he no longer owned the shares. The block of shares was transferred subject to an option to purchase the shares vested in a trust company which Vandervell

813. *Re Andrew's Trust* [1905] 2 Ch 48; *Re Osoba* [1978] 1 WLR.
814. *Re Trusts of the Abbott Fund* [1900] 2 Ch 326.
815. *Re Cochrane* [1955] Ch 309.
816. *See* para. 258 above.
817. *Re Gillingham Bus Disaster Fund* [1959] Ch 300.
818. *Re West Sussex Constabulary's Widows, Children & Benevolent (1930) Fund Trusts* [1971] Ch 1.
819. This power has not been effected by the Charities Act 2009.
820. *Vandervell v. IRC* [1967] 2 AC 291; *Re Vandervell's Trusts (No. 2)* [1974] Ch 269.

had set up with the very general intention that it would look after his family's interests. The provisions of the option did not make it clear who the trust company held the option on trust for. The Revenue claimed that the option was held on automatic resulting trust for Vandervell. Therefore, he was liable for the surtax on the dividends as he had not divested himself of his entire interest in the shares. The House of Lords agreed with the Revenue's argument in *Vandervell v. IRC.*[821] Lord Wilberforce commented that the option was vested in the trustee company on trusts not defined at the time, possibly to be defined later. However, the equitable interest cannot remain in the air. The consequence in law must be that it remains in the settlor.

293. In 1961 the option was exercised and in 1965 Vandervell executed a deed transferring any interest which he had in the shares to the children's trust fund. In 1967, he died. *Re Vandervell's Trusts (No. 2)*[822] concerned the beneficial ownership of the shares between 1961 and 1965. Vandervell's executors claimed that the dividends for that period formed part of his estate. If they succeeded, the estate would also be liable for surtax on the dividends for that period. The option had been exercised by the Trust Company using money from the trust fund for Vandervell's children. The dividends declared on these shares were paid into the children's trust fund. Megarry J, at first instance, was of the opinion that because the trustee company held the option on resulting trust for Vandervell, once the option was exercised, it also held the shares on resulting trust for Vandervell. The Court of Appeal disagreed and held that the resulting trust of the option ended once the option was exercised and then a new trust arose in relation to the shares. No formalities had to be complied with in order to create this trust as it was created over personality. The court was satisfied that three issues pointed to the effective creation of a new trust in favour of the children's trust fund: the money used to buy the shares was provided from the children's trust fund; the dividends were paid into the children's trust fund; and the trustees wrote a letter to the revenue stating that the dividends were held on trust for the children. Although a number of criticisms have been made of this judgment,[823] it indicates that an automatic resulting trust can come to an end once a new trust is declared and this may be established from evidence illustrating the intention of the settlor. This suggests that the intention of the settlor may play a more important role in refuting the existence of an automatic resulting trust than was previously thought to be the case.

III. The Dissolution of Unincorporated Associations

294. An automatic resulting trust may also arise on the dissolution of an unincorporated association, in relation to surplus funds held by the association.[824] However, the application of strict resulting trust principles may be difficult as the original members who contributed funds or property may be dead and it may be difficult to know the exact contributions made. Therefore, more recent case law has rejected

821. [1967] 2 AC 291.
822. [1974] Ch 269.
823. *See* Hanbury & Martin, *Modern Equity,* 18th edn (London: Sweet & Maxwell, 2009), paras 3.010 and 4.015.
824. *Re Printers and Transferrers Amalgamated Trades Protection Society* [1899] 2Ch 184.

the resulting trust approach in favour of a contractual approach to this issue. Typically, the rules of the club will expressly provide that, on dissolution, the property is to be divided amongst the current members in equal shares. However, if no such rule exists, it will be implied by the courts.[825]

IV. Quistclose Trusts

295. An automatic resulting trust may also arise in the context of a Quistclose trust. A Quistclose trust may arise where someone lends money to another for a particular purpose, often the purpose is to pay another debt.[826] Generally, an unsecured loan only has the quality of a contractual obligation, so that if the borrower becomes bankrupt, the lender ranks amongst the borrower's ordinary creditors. However, if the loan can be construed as the subject matter of a trust, it would mean that the beneficiary under the trust has a proprietary interest in the money and would be entitled to it in priority to other creditors, in such circumstances. It had been accepted for many years that a loan for a specific purpose gave rise to a fiduciary obligation on the part of the borrower which the court would enforce and which prevented the borrower from acquiring a beneficial interest in the money if he became bankrupt.[827]

296. Barclays Bank Ltd. v. Quistclose Investments Ltd[828] was the first case in which an attempt was made to explain the types of trusts which arise in such circumstances. A company was in financial difficulties and had declared a dividend which it was now unable to pay. If the dividend was not paid, there would be a loss of confidence which could spark off a liquidation. Quistclose Investments Ltd lent the company money for the specific purpose of paying the dividend and the loan was paid into a separate bank account with Barclays Bank, which was owed money by the same company. Before the dividends were paid, the company went into liquidation and both Barclays Bank and Quistclose Investments claimed the money. Lord Wilberforce held that Quistclose Investments was entitled to recover the money. He explained that a loan for a specific purpose gave rise 'to a relationship of a fiduciary character or trust, in favour, as a primary trust, of the creditors, and secondarily, if the primary trust fail[ed], of the third person' (that third person being the lender).[829] Later in the judgment, Lord Wilberforce stated that when the money is advanced, the lender acquires an equitable right to see that it is applied for the primary designated purpose.[830]

297. Sometimes, the primary trust is referred to as a purpose trust. In the *Quistclose case*, the primary purpose trust was held to have failed and the secondary

825. *See Feeney v. Mac Manus* [1937] IR 23; *Re Bucks Constabulary Widows' and Orphans' Fund Friendly Society (No. 2)* [1979] 1 WLR 936.

826. Note that to date there have been no reported Irish cases giving rise to a Quistclose trust, although Biehler argues that such trusts are likely to assume increasing significance in the future, *see Equity and the Law of Trusts in Ireland*, 6th edn (Dublin: Thomson Roundhall, 2016), 155.

827. *Toovey v. Milne* (1819) 2 B. & A. 683; *Moore v. Barthrop* (1822) 1 B. & C. 5.

828. [1970] AC 567.

829. *Ibid.*, 580.

830. *Ibid.*, 581.

trust, an automatic resulting trust, was triggered in favour of the lender.[831] Similarly, in *Re EVTR Ltd*[832] when a company went into receivership, an automatic resulting trust was held to arise in favour of a lender which had advanced GBP 60,000 to the company to purchase new equipment, most of which was unspent at the time of the proceedings.

298. The situation becomes more complicated where the primary purpose is still capable of being fulfilled as it becomes necessary to identify the beneficiary of the primary trust. The first comment of Wilberforce J in *Quistclose* would seem to indicate that the creditors are the beneficiaries of the primary trust. However, his second comment seems to indicate that the lender is the beneficiary. If the lender is the beneficiary of this primary trust, a related question may arise; can he revoke the arrangement and demand the money back? The courts will often be prepared to allow the creditors to enforce the primary trust if they were aware of the arrangement[833] or if the arrangement with the lender was irrevocable.[834] Although the theoretical basis for Quistclose trusts has given rise to much debate,[835] they are designed to protect lenders who make emergency loans with the purpose of saving corporations on the brink of insolvency. They are clearly desirable as a rescued company is a rescued employer and a rescued trader (thereby also benefiting the lender).

§3. Presumed Resulting Trusts

299. As has already been mentioned, the presumed resulting trust may arise in two different situations: where there is a gratuitous transfer of property or someone purchases property in the name of another.

I. Voluntary Transfer of Property

300. If the owner of property makes a voluntary transfer (i.e., without consideration) of it to the grantee, it gives rise to a presumed resulting trust, so that the grantee holds the property on resulting trust for the grantor. This is a presumption which may be rebutted by evidence that a gift of the beneficial interest was intended or by the presumption of advancement (i.e., a presumption that a gift was intended which arises in the context of certain established relationships[836]). Until recently, conveyancers had

831. Note that Millet in 'The Quistclose Trust – Who Can Enforce It?', *Law Quarterly Review* 101 (1985): 269 argues that it was still possible to pay the dividends in the *Quistclose case* and so the real purpose of the primary trust must have been to prevent the company from going into liquidation, a purpose which had failed.
832. [1987] BCLC 646.
833. *Re Northern Developments Holdings Ltd* Chancery Division, 6 Oct. 1978.
834. *Carreras Rothmans Limited v. Freeman Matthews Treasure Limited* [1984] 3 WLR 1016.
835. *See*, for example, Millet, 'The Quistclose Trust – Who Can Enforce It?', *Law Quarterly Review* 101 (1985): 269; Chambers, *Resulting Trusts* (Oxford: Oxford University Press, 1997), Ch. 3; Swadling (ed.), *The Quistclose Trust – Critical Essays* (Oxford: Hart Publishing, 2004). *See also* Lord Millet's dissenting judgment in *Twinsectra Ltd v. Yardley* [2002] 2 AC 164, 192–193.
836. *See* para. 303 below.

to be particularly careful of the potential impact of the Statute of Uses (Ireland) 1634[837] in the context of a voluntary conveyance of land. The statute would execute any resulting use which arose in such circumstances, so that the grantor became vested with both the legal and beneficial ownership of the land, rendering the conveyance completely ineffective. Conveyancers had to ensure that a 'conveyance to uses' was inserted into such a voluntary deed which would rebut the presumption of a resulting use and eliminate the danger of triggering the Statute of Uses. This danger has been completely eliminated by the Land and Conveyancing Law Reform Act 2009 which repeals the Statute of Uses. In addition, section 62(3) of the 2009 Act provides that a resulting use for the grantor is not implied in a voluntary conveyance executed after commencement, merely because the land is not expressed to be for the use of the grantee.[838] Note that it is unclear if this provision prevents a presumption of a resulting trust arising in such circumstances.[839]

301. It is very common for a person to put personal property into the joint names of himself and another party. In such circumstances, the donee will be required to hold his share on resulting trust for the transferor unless an intention to make a gift to the donee can be proved or the presumption of advancement applies.[840] This is a situation which has given rise to some controversy in the past in relation to joint deposit bank accounts. If both parties are contributing to the account and withdrawing from it, there is no problem as this gives rise to a presumption of a beneficial joint tenancy, which means that when one dies, the other will become entitled to the money in the account under the right of survivorship. Complications arise in this area if one party, A, opens a joint account in the name of A and B but only A contributes to the account, and during A's lifetime B is not permitted to make withdrawals. The intention behind the arrangement is that the fund would pass to B after A's death under the right of survivorship.[841] The difficulty was that the arrangement involved a voluntary transfer of property giving

---

837. *See* para. 10 above.

838. A similar reform was enacted in England by of the Law of Property Act 1925 s. 60(3) and in Ireland a similar provision has been in force for sometime in relation to registered land, *see* Registration of Title Act 1964, s. 123(3).

839. Wylie argues that a presumption of a resulting trust will continue to arise where a voluntary conveyance of land is executed after 1 Dec. 2009, *see The Land and Conveyancing Law Reform Act 2009: Annotations and Commentary* (Dublin: Bloomsbury Professional, 2009), 209. Biehler suggests that the term 'resulting use' was probably intended to equate to a 'resulting trust' in the context of a repeal of the Statute of Uses, *see Equity and the Law of Trusts in Ireland,* 6th edn (Dublin: Thomson Roundhall, 2016), 161. Mee argues in relation to the equivalent English provision: 'the presumption of resulting trust in this context is an anachronism which should not be tolerated in the modern law', *see* 'Resulting Trusts and Voluntary Conveyances of Land', *Conveyancer and Property Lawyer* 76 no. 4 (2012) 307: 325.

840. *Vinogradoff* [1935] WM 68; *Standing v. Bowring* (1883) 31 Ch D.

841. The arrangement was commonly used to avoid the payment of probate tax which was only payable on the deceased's estate. The money in the account would not be liable for probate tax as it passed under the right of survivorship and did not form part of A's estate. Note that probate tax was abolished by the Finance Act 2001, although people may continue to use these arrangements if they do not wish to make a will or if they want to keep the name of the beneficiary secret.

rise to a presumed resulting trust, so that following A's death, B would be obliged to hold the money in the account on resulting trust for A's estate.[842]

302. In *Owens v. Greene*,[843] the Supreme Court held that an intention on the part of the depositor to benefit the recipient after the deposit's death could not be relied on to rebut the presumption of a resulting trust, as the grant of such a right of survivorship was invalid; it amounted to a testamentary disposition which had not complied with the formalities set out in the Succession Act 1965. To rebut the presumption of a resulting trust, it was necessary to demonstrate that when the deceased set up the account, he intended to grant an immediate interest in the monies to the recipient by, for example, permitting him immediate access to the funds. This decision was criticized,[844] primarily because the intentions of the deceased were ignored; his estate took the monies in the account and not the surviving joint account holder. However, it represented the law in this jurisdiction until it was overturned by Supreme Court decision in *Lynch v. Burke*.[845] O'Flaherty J, delivering the decision of the Supreme Court in that case, held that the presumption of a resulting trust was rebutted by the donor's intention that the surviving joint account holder was to take the money after her death.[846] He noted:

> Since historically the concept of an implied or resulting trust was an invention of equity to defeat the misappropriation of property as a consequence of potentially fraudulent or improvident transactions it would surely be paradoxical, if the doctrine is allowed to be invoked to defeat the clear intention of the donor as found by the trial judge.[847]

Although a number of doctrinal issues are left unresolved by the decision,[848] it is to be praised for its practical impact which facilitates the use of this device to make provision for someone after death without the danger that equity will rise up to defeat the clearly expressed intention of the donor.

---

842. *Doyle v. Byrne* (1922) 56 ILTR.
843. [1932] IR 225.
844. *See AIB Finance Ltd v. Sligo County Council* [1995] 1ILRM 81.
845. [1995] 2 IR 159.
846. He found support in an Australian case, *Russell v. Scott* (1936) 55 CLR 440.
847. [1995] 2 IR 159, 166. The decision has since been followed in *Gilvarry v Maher* [2014] IEHC 694.
848. *See* Capper, 'Survivorship Rights in Joint Deposit Accounts', *Northern Ireland Legal Quarterly* 47 (1996): 281; Woods, 'Joint Deposit Bank Accounts and the Conditional Gift Theory', *Irish Jurist* 37 (2002): 281. Note that if the surviving joint account holder failed to sign the application form to open the joint account and therefore was not a party to the contract with the bank, this may prevent them from relying on *Lynch v Burke* [1992] 2 IR 159 to claim the balance in the account on the death of the depositor, *see* the obiter comments of Laffoy J in *O'Meara v Bank of Scotland plc* [2011] IEHC 402, paras 5.7 and 17.1.

II. The Presumption of Advancement

303. As has already been mentioned, the presumption of a resulting trust can be rebutted where the presumption of advancement applies.[849] This presumption, that a gift was intended, arises only in the context of certain established relationships. Equity recognizes that where these relationships exist, the donor is under an obligation to support or provide for the person advanced. However, unfortunately this presumption appears to offend against modern notions of equality and generally only recognizes men as being under a duty to provide. It applies where a man makes a voluntary transfer of property to a child or purchases it in the name of his child[850] but not where a mother engages in a similar transaction, unless it can be proved that she is in *loco parentis*.[851] The presumption of advancement also applies when a husband makes a voluntary transfer of property into the name of his wife or purchases it in her name[852] but not when a wife makes the transfer or purchase.[853] The presumption of advancement can be rebutted by evidence of a contrary intention (i.e., evidence that a gift was not intended), in which case a resulting trust in favour of the donor is triggered.[854]

III. Effect of Fraud or Illegality

304. The presumption of advancement cannot be rebutted by evidence that demonstrates that the transfer was made for a fraudulent or illegal purpose where this purpose has been carried out.[855] This rule is derived from the maxim that he who comes to equity must come with clean hands. However, where the illegal purpose has not been carried out, the courts have allowed evidence to be adduced to rebut the presumption of advancement.[856] In contrast, in order to claim a beneficial interest under the presumption of a resulting trust it is only necessary to prove that the contribution to the purchase price was made. If the underlying purpose of the transaction was to perpetuate a fraud, this will not prevent the operation of the presumption of a resulting trust.[857]

849. *See* para.300 above.
850. *Hepworth v. Hepworth* (1870) LR 11 Eq 10.
851. *See Bennet v. Bennet* (1879) 10 Ch D 474; *McCabe v. Ulster Bank* [1939] IR 1. A voluntary transfer by a person in *loco parentis* is another situation, giving rise to the presumption of advancement.
852. *Re Eykyn's Trusts* (1877) 6 Ch D 115; *J.C. v. J.H.C.* (HC) 4 Aug. 1982; *Malone v. McQuaid* [1998] IEHC 86.
853. *Mercier v. Mercier* [1903]2 Ch 98.
854. *R.F. v. M.F.* [1995] 2 ILRM 572; *Warren v. Guerney* [1994] 2 All ER 472.
855. *Re Emery's Investment Trusts* [1959] Ch 410; *Parkes v. Parkes* [1980] ILRM 137.
856. *Tribe v. Tribe* [1996] Ch 107.
857. *Tinsley v. Milligan* [1994] 1 AC 340.

IV. Purchase of Property in Another's Name

305. The purchase money resulting trust is a type of presumed resulting trust which arises where someone provides some or all the purchase price of a property which is put into the name of another party. The legal owner is presumed to hold the property on resulting trust for the person who advanced the purchase price[858] unless the presumption can be rebutted by evidence that a gift was intended or by the presumption of advancement. This presumed resulting trust may also arise if the property is purchased by two or more parties as joint tenants who contributed to the purchase price in unequal shares and in such circumstances the beneficial ownership is held by them as tenants in common in proportion to their actual contributions.[859]

306. The purchase money resulting trust has been applied in many Irish cases, although most of the case law was generated in the 1970s and 1980s when the device was relied on to resolve property disputes between married couples. These disputes were generated as a result of the separate property regime which governs married couples in Ireland. Unlike civilian jurisdictions where a community property regime governs most marital relationships, in Ireland any property acquired individually by either spouse belongs to that person and the other spouse generally acquires no interest in it. The separate property system operates well if both parties are in a financially equivalent position and can acquire roughly the same amount of separate property. However, this not usually the case and one party, typically the wife, may sacrifice her earning potential and ability to acquire her own separate property in order to care for the family. The system could produce harsh results if the family home was purchased in the name of the husband, which was very common in the 1960s and 1970s, although the wife might be able to demonstrate that she had a beneficial interest in it if she could prove that she had contributed to its purchase price.[860]

307. Although the role played by this remedy in marital property disputes has been reduced due to the introduction of a series of legislative measures designed to protect the family home[861] and resolve such disputes on marital breakdown,[862] the purchase money resulting trust remains an important remedy for cohabiting couples[863]

858. In the words of Eyre CB in *Dyer v. Dyer* (1788) 2 Cox 92, 93 'the trust of a legal estate … results to the man who advances the purchase money'.

859. *See* para. 66 above.

860. The court utilized the purchase money resulting trust when considering applications under the Married Women's Status Act 1957, s. 12, which conferred jurisdiction on the courts to resolve disputes between spouses concerning ownership of property.

861. The Family Home Protection Act 1976 prevents the sale or mortgage of the family home without the prior written consent of the non-owning spouse.

862. Where the relationship breaks down and a judicial separation or divorce is obtained, the non-owning spouse can apply for a property adjustment order under the Family Law Act 1995 or the Family Law Divorce Act 1996. The court is permitted to take a broad range of factors into account in deciding whether to grant such ancillary relief, such as the extent to which each spouse contributed to the welfare of the family or sacrificed his or her earning capacity to look after the family.

863. The principles governing the purchase money resulting trust are not dependent on a marital relationship between the parties, *see McGill v. S* [1979] IR 238; *Power v. Conway* [1980] ILRM 31.

who have, to date, been denied access to such family law remedies. Although Part 15 of the Civil Partnership and Certain Rights and Obligations of Cohabitants Act 2010 will permit, for the first time, an application for a property adjustment order by a qualifying cohabitant who can prove financial dependence on the respondent as a result of the relationship or its breakdown, the restrictive terms of this scheme[864] renders it possible that the purchase money resulting trust may continue to play a role in resolving such disputes in the future.

A. Direct Contributions and the Proportionate Interest Principle

308. It is long established that direct contributions to the purchase price[865] will generate a beneficial interest in the property proportionate to the size of the contributions. In addition, contributions towards the costs of the purchase are generally treated as contributions to the purchase price.[866] Although the rationale has occasionally been criticized,[867] contributions towards mortgage repayments are treated as equivalent to contributions to the purchase price or alternatively the buying back of the equity of redemption. As Finlay P explained in *W v. W*:[868]

> The redemption of any form of charge or mortgage on property in truth consists of the acquisition by the owner or mortgagor of an estate in the property with which he parted at the time of the creation of the mortgage or charge ... there can be no distinction in principle between a contribution made to the acquisition of that interest and a contribution made to the acquisition of an interest in property by an original purchase.

309. The proportionate interest principle is applied in order to assess the extent of the beneficial interest to be awarded. This principle can be easily applied if the house is purchased outright without a mortgage and all the contributions are made at the same time. However, the calculations can become more complicated when a mortgage is obtained and contributions are made over time.[869] The main difficulty is that couples will very rarely keep accurate accounts of who paid for what, making it very difficult, years later, to unravel the history of their financial contributions. Also, on occasion, the courts appear to give themselves a certain amount of flexibility in assessing the beneficial shares,[870] which may make the result difficult to predict.

---

864. *See* Mee, 'A Critique of the Cohabitation Provisions of the Civil Partnership Bill 2009', *Irish Journal of Family Law* 12, no. 4 (2009): 83.
865. *See Heavey v. Heavey* (1974) 111 ILTR 1; *C v. C* [1976] IR 254.
866. *See C v. C* [1976] IR 254.
867. Mee argues that this reasoning leads to the result that a person who contributes to the mortgage repayments gains a share, not in what was purchased with the help of the loan, but in the security for the loan, *see* 'Trusts of the Family Home – The Irish Experience', *Conveyancer and Property Lawyer* (1993): 359, 363.
868. [1986] ILRM 202, 204–205. *See also N v. N* [1992] 2 IR 116, 123.
869. *See K v. K* (1978) 114 ILTR 50.
870. *See GNR v. KAR* (HC) 25 Mar. 1981 (the husband's beneficial share was reduced because of his extravagant lifestyle).

B. *Indirect Contributions*

310. Initially, the courts were unwilling to recognize that an indirect contribution, such as the payment of household expenses freeing up the other party to repay the mortgage, could generate a beneficial interest, in the absence of an agreement in this regard.[871] However, in *W v. W*[872] Finlay P held that where a wife contributes to a general family fund, thus releasing her husband from his obligations to pay the household expenses and permitting him to make the mortgage repayments, in the absence of an agreement to the contrary, she is entitled to a beneficial share proportionate to the amount of her indirect contribution. This approach to indirect contributions was confirmed by the Supreme Court in *McC v. McC*,[873] although a beneficial interest in the family home did not arise on the facts of that case. It is important to note that paying household expenses will only generate a beneficial interest if a mortgage is being repaid. If the payments are made after a property has been purchased outright or the mortgage has been redeemed, they amount to post-acquisition contributions and cannot generate an interest.[874]

C. *Unpaid Work*

311. In *N v. N*[875] part of the home, which was in the husband's name, had been converted into bedsitter flats. The wife claimed and was granted a beneficial share in the home on the basis that she had managed bedsitter flats, and the rental income from those flats went directly or indirectly towards repayment of the mortgage. While unpaid work in the legal owner's business will generate a beneficial interest, unpaid work in the home, such as housework or caring for children, will not generate such an interest. In the High Court decision of *L v. L*, the woman in question was described as a devoted homemaker and mother and Barr J awarded her a 50% beneficial share in the family home on the basis that she had played the constitutionally preferred role of wife and mother.[876] The case was appealed to the Supreme Court which overruled Barr J's decision and held that the claimant must make a 'monied' contribution to the purchase price to generate a beneficial interest and work in the home would not suffice.[877]

871. *MG v. RD* (HC) 28 Apr. 1981.
872. [1981] ILRM 202.
873. [1986] ILRM 1, 2 per Henchy J.
874. *McGill v. S* [1979] IR 238.
875. [1992] 2 IR 116.
876. *See* Art. 41 of the Constitution, where the State recognizes the special role played by the women in the home and guarantees to ensure that mothers shall not be obliged by economic necessity to engage in labour to the neglect of their duties in the home.
877. [1992] 2 IR 77. This decision generated a lot of controversy at the time, which provided the impetus for the introduction of the Matrimonial Home Bill 1993, although this Bill was never enacted.

D. Improvements

312. Carrying out improvements to a property, such as decorating, repairing or building an extension, will not generate a beneficial share in the home. Neither will paying for such improvements in cash.[878] This can lead to unjust results, as demonstrated by *NAD v. TD*.[879] In that case, the husband bought a site in his own name and both the husband and wife contributed towards the cost of building the house. However, she was refused a beneficial interest as the building of the house was regarded as an improvement. Although paying for improvements in cash will not generate a beneficial interest, Mee notes that if the property was mortgaged in order to pay for improvements and a person contributes towards the mortgage repayments, they will be awarded a beneficial interest. He is highly critical of this anomaly.[880]

313. The various inadequacies which have been identified with the purchase money resulting trust are likely to impact mainly on unmarried cohabitees,[881] even following the introduction of the restrictive ancillary relief scheme provided by Part 15 of the Civil Partnership and Certain Rights and Obligations of Cohabitants Act 2010. It is interesting to note that the purchase money resulting trust has not played the same central role in the resolution of family property disputes in England and Wales, where the courts rely instead on the common intention constructive trust.[882] This institution also suffers from inadequacies and inconsistencies. Although the Law Commission for England and Wales has recommended the introduction of a legislative scheme to deal with the financial consequences of relationship breakdown between unmarried couples[883] these proposals for reform have yet to be implemented.

878. *W v. W* [1981] ILRM 202.
879. [1985] ILRM 153.
880. Mee, 'Trusts of the Family Home – The Irish Experience', *Conveyancer and Property Lawyer* (1993): 359, 363.
881. Note that cohabitees may alternatively be able to avail of a remedy pursuant to the doctrine of proprietary estoppel, *see Pascoe v. Turner* [1979] 2 All ER 945; *Greasley v. Cooke* [1980] 1WLR 1306. *See also* Mee, *The Property Rights of Cohabitees* (Oxford: Hart Publishing, 1999), 93.
882. *See Gissing v. Gissing* [1970] AC 886; *Burns v. Burns* [1984] Ch 317; *Grant v. Edwards* [1986] Ch 638; *Lloyds Bank plc. v. Rosset* [1991] 1 AC 107; *Le Foe v. Le Foe* [2001] 2 FLR 970; *Oxley v. Hiscock* [2004] 3 WLR 715; *Stack v. Dowden* [2007] UKHL 17; *Jones v Kernott* [2012] 1 AC 776.; *See also* Biehler, *Equity and the Law of Trusts in Ireland,* 6th edn (Dublin: Thomson Roundhall, 2016), pp 210–223; Mee, 'Jones v Kernott: Inferring and Imputing in Essex', *Conveyancer and Property Lawyer* 76 no. 2 (2012): 167.
883. Law Commission of England and Wales, Cohabitation – The Financial Consequences of Relationship Breakdown (LC307–2007).

Chapter 6. Constructive Trusts

§1. General

314. Instead of being created expressly or implied by the law, constructive trusts are said to arise by operation of law. Their imposition has nothing to do with the intention of the parties and in the words of Denning MR, they are imposed whenever 'justice and good conscience' require it.[884] As is the case with resulting trusts, they need not comply with the formalities necessary to create a valid private express trust.[885] Although it is not possible to exhaustively define the circumstances which give rise to a constructive trust, certain categories of constructive trust are long established and they are traditionally considered under two headings: those which arise in the context of a pre-existing fiduciary relationship and those which do not involve such a relationship.[886]

§2. A Pre-existing Fiduciary Relationship

I. Advantages Received by a Trustee or Fiduciary

315. A constructive trust will be imposed to prevent a trustee or a person in a fiduciary position from making use of his position to derive a personal benefit or utilizing opportunities arising in the context of his trusteeship. Any benefit he derives must be held on constructive trust for the beneficiary or beneficiaries, pursuant to a process sometimes referred to in this jurisdiction as the doctrine of graft.[887] This approach may occasionally appear harsh but, on the whole, it tends to be strictly applied, regardless of the subjective motives of the fiduciary.[888]

316. In *Keech v. Sandford*,[889] a trustee failed to obtain a renewal of a lease for the benefit of an infant beneficiary, although the landlord was prepared to grant the renewal of the lease to the trustee in his personal capacity. The trustee was required to hold the benefit of the lease on constructive trust for the infant. Lord King LC noted:

884. *Hussey v. Palmer* [1972 1 WLR 1286, 1290.
885. Statute of Frauds (Ireland) 1695, s. 4; Succession Act 1965, s. 78.
886. *See* Keogan, Mee & Wylie, *Law and Taxation of Trusts* (Dublin: Tottel Publishing, 2007), Chs 10–12.
887. *See* the discussion by Fitzgibbon LJ in *Dempsey v. Ward* [1899] 1IR 463, 474–475.
888. Note that certain English authorities suggest that a more lenient approach can be taken in relation to certain fiduciaries, other than trustees, if the fiduciary had not abused his position, *see Re Bliss* [1903] 2 Ch 430. The Irish case law does not appear to make such a distinction, *see* Keogan, Mee & Wylie, *Law and Taxation of Trusts* (Dublin: Tottel Publishing, 2007), para. 11.004.
889. (1726) Sel Cas Ch 61.

'This may seem hard, that the trustee is the only person of all mankind who might not have the lease; but it is very proper that the rules should be strictly pursued.'[890] A constructive trust has also been applied where a trustee or fiduciary purchases the reversion of a lease.[891]

317. The rule has been applied to other fiduciaries,[892] such as a personal representative,[893] a company director or an agent. In *Regal (Hastings) Ltd v. Gulliver*,[894] a company owned a cinema and set up a subsidiary to acquire leases of two other cinemas so that the whole lot could be sold as a going concern. The landlord refused to grant the leases unless the subsidiary's share capital was completely paid up. As the parent company did not have enough money to subscribe for all the shares, the directors subscribed for the rest. When the company was transferred to new controllers, the directors made a personal profit on the transaction. The new controllers brought an action against them to account for the profit and the court held that it was to be held on constructive trust for the company. Although the transaction had clearly been entered into in the best interests of the company, the court pointed out that the rule does not depend on the presence of fraud or *mala fides* but on the mere fact of a profit having been made.[895] In *Industrial Development Consultants v. Cooley*,[896] the defendant was the managing director of a company which offered construction consultancy services to clients. The company had been involved in negotiations with a potential customer which ended unsuccessfully. However, subsequently the customer awarded the contract to the defendant personally. He was required to hold the profits on constructive trust for the company.

II. Competition with Trust Business

318. The operation of the constructive trust in this general context is sometimes explained as being designed to prevent a trustee or fiduciary from putting himself in a situation where his duty to the trust or his fiduciary obligations and his own personal interests conflict.[897] To date, in cases where a trustee attempted to set up or succeeded in establishing a business in competition with the trust business the courts have either granted an injunction preventing him from doing so[898] or insisted that the trustee be removed from his position.[899] It is possible, however, that the courts could require such a trustee to hold any resulting personal profits on constructive trust, should an appropriate case arise.

890. *Ibid.*, 62.
891. *Gabbett v. Lawder* (1883) 11 LR Ir 295.
892. A fiduciary could be described as a person in a position of power or trust who is required to act in good faith on behalf of someone else.
893. *Kelly v. Kelly* (1871) IR 8 Eq 403.
894. [1967] 2 AC 134.
895. *Ibid.*, 144.
896. [1972] 1 WLR 443.
897. *Ibid.*, 453.
898. *Re Thomson* [1930] 1 Ch 203.
899. *Moore v. McGlynn* [1894] 1 IR 79.

III. Secret Bribes or Commission

319. A fiduciary[900] who accepts bribes or secret commission arising out of a transaction in which he is acting on behalf of the principal without the knowledge and consent of the principal, will, at the very least, be liable to account for the bribe or commission and may be required to hold it on constructive trust. Although certain earlier case law suggested that such a fiduciary was only liable to account for the bribe or commission,[901] the absence of a proprietary remedy may be crucial in determining whether the principal can recover against the fiduciary, in the event that the money was used to purchase property or if the fiduciary was declared bankrupt. More recent case law has rejected the earlier approach and imposed a constructive trust in such circumstances.[902]

IV. Receipt of Trust Property or Participation in a Breach of Trust

320. Although the imposition of a constructive trust in this situation arises in the context of a pre-existing fiduciary duty, the constructive trustee is actually a stranger to the beneficiary but has either received trust property from the original trustee or participated in a breach of trust by him. The imposition of a constructive trust in this context permits the beneficiary to pursue a 'deep pocket' in circumstances where the original trustee has been declared bankrupt or disappeared, so that pursuing him for an order for damages for breach of trust would be futile. As has already been mentioned, a purchaser of trust property will be bound by that trust or subject to the remedy of tracing unless he or she qualifies as a bona fide purchaser for value without notice of the trust.[903] The question which arises in this context is whether such a recipient of trust property who has since parted with it or its identifiable proceeds, can be held liable to the original beneficiary. As explained by Keogan, Mee and Wylie, '(t)he categorization of such a recipient as constructive trustee provides a legal mechanism whereby the recipient can be fixed with this type of personal liability'.[904] The Irish courts have, to date, imposed such a constructive trust if the person who receives trust

---

900. Note the liberal interpretation of the term 'fiduciary' adopted in *Reading v. Attorney General* [1951] AC 507 where a British Army sergeant was held to be liable to account to the Crown for the bribes he received by using his uniform and the privileges attached to it to carry out certain smuggling activities.
901. *See Lister & Co v. Stubbs* (1890) 45 Ch D 1. *See* , however, the more recent decision of Lord Neuberger MR in *Sinclair Investments (UK) Ltd v Versailles Trade Finance Ltd* [2012] Ch 453. Note that Lord Neuberger MR has since stated that the approach taken in *Sinclair* in this respect should be regarded as overruled, *see FHR European Ventures LLP v Cedar Capital Partners LLC* [2015] AC 250, 273.
902. *See Attorney General for Hong Kong v. Reid* [1994] 1 AC 324; *FHR European Ventures LLP v Cedar Capital Partners LLC* [2015] AC 250.
903. *See* para. 243 above.
904. *Law and Taxation of Trusts* (Dublin: Tottel Publishing, 2007), para. 11.022.

property had either actual or constructive notice of the breach of trust.[905] There is a dearth of Irish authority on when a stranger, often an agent of the original trustee, who has assisted in a breach of trust should be made personally liable by the imposition of a constructive trust. It has been argued[906] that the Irish courts should adopt the traditional English test[907] which requires the stranger to 'knowingly' assist in a dishonest breach of trustor be guilty of the 'unconscionable' retention of the benefit of the monies received.[908]

§3. No Fiduciary Relationship

I. The Vendor as Constructive Trustee

321. It has been long established that once a valid contract for sale has been entered into, the vendor is regarded by equity as a constructive trustee of the property until completion and the beneficial interest passes to the purchaser.[909] The decision of the majority of the Supreme Court in *Tempany v. Hynes*[910] introduced some confusion into the law on this issue by ruling that the beneficial interest passes only to the extent that the purchase price has been paid. Usually only a 10% deposit will have been paid at this point, which meant that a judgment mortgage registered during the period between contract and completion of the purchase could attach to the 90% beneficial interest retained by the vendor. This would result in the purchaser acquiring the land encumbered by this charge on the completion of the transaction. This approach created other difficulties and anomalies and based on a recommendation made by the Law Reform Commission in this respect[911] the position in *Tempany v. Hynes* was reversed by the Land and Conveyancing Law Reform Act 2009. Section 52(1) of the 2009 Act provides that the entire beneficial interest passes to the purchaser on the making of an enforceable contract for the sale or other disposition of land after the commencement date. This means that once the transaction has been completed by the purchaser, any judgment mortgage registered against the vendor's legal interest after the contract was entered into will no longer affect the land. It should be noted, however, that the vendor is a trustee 'in a qualified sense only'[912] and certain features of the relationship between the vendor and the purchaser seem inconsistent with the existence of a trust. For

905. *See Re Frederick Inns* [1994] ILRM 387; *Ulster Factors Ltd v. Entonglen Ltd (in Liquidation)* [1997] IEHC 34. Laffoy J has noted a divergence in approach between the United Kingdom and Ireland on when a constructive trust should be imposed in cases of knowing receipt, *see Fyffes plc v DCC plc* [2002] 2 IR 417; *O'Donnell v Bank of Ireland* 2014] IESC 77.

906. *See* Keogan, Mee & Wylie, *Law and Taxation of Trusts* (Dublin: Tottel Publishing, 2007), para.11.021.

907. Set out in *Barnes v. Addy* (1874) 9 Ch App 244.

908. *BCCI (Overseas Ltd) v Akindale* [2001] Ch. 437.

909. *See Lysaght v. Edwards* (1876) 2 Ch D 499, 506 per Jessel MR.

910. [1976] IR 101.

911. *Interests of Vendor and Purchaser in Land During the Period Between Contract and Completion* (LRC 49–1995).

912. *See Rayner v. Preston* (1881) 18 Ch D 1, 6 per Cotton LJ.

example, the vendor is entitled to retain possession of the land and is entitled to any rents and profits from it until completion. Also, the vendor is entitled to rescind the contract if the purchaser fails to complete or comply with certain terms of the contract, in which case the vendor will become the absolute owner again, free from any trusteeship. The vendor's position as trustee means that he is under a duty to maintain the property while he retains possession and will incur liability if he wilfully damages it. However, the risk of accidental damage passes to the purchaser once the contract has been entered into[913] unless the Law Society of Ireland *General Conditions of Sale* apply which stipulate that the vendor is liable for such loss or damage.

II. Mutual Wills

322. A constructive trust may be imposed in the context of mutual wills. It is not uncommon for a husband and wife to agree to make wills in similar terms and not to revoke them. The arrangement typically involves them leaving their entire estate to the other spouse, but if that spouse is already dead, to specified beneficiaries such as their children. If one party has died and the survivor alters their will or makes a new will in favour of someone else (e.g., a new spouse), equity intervenes and imposes a constructive trust to give effect to the original arrangement.[914] However, before such a trust can arise, there must be evidence that both parties intended to make a mutual will and that they intended the arrangement to be irrevocable.[915] It should be noted that there are no reported Irish cases on this issue and in other jurisdictions some uncertainty has arisen in relation to specific aspects of the doctrine of mutual wills, such as identifying exactly when the trust arises and what property is affected by the trust.[916]

III. The Mortgagee as Constructive Trustee

323. If a mortgagee retains a surplus after exercising a power of sale over mortgaged property, it must be held on constructive trust for whoever is entitled to the equity of redemption.[917]

---

913. *See Raynor v. Preston* (1881) 18 Ch D 1, where it was held that the onus was on the purchaser to insure against this risk and the purchaser was not entitled to any insurance money received by the vendor.
914. *See Dufour v. Pereira* (1769) 1 Dick 419; *Re Cleaver* [1981] 1 WLR 939.
915. *See Re Goodchild* [1997] 1 WLR 1216; *Curtis v. Birch* (2002) 29 EG 139.
916. *See* Biehler, *Equity and the Law of Trusts in Ireland,* 6th edn (Dublin: Thomson Roundhall, 2016), 276–277; Keane, *Equity and the Law of Trusts in the Republic of Ireland,* 2nd edn (Dublin: Bloomsbury Professional, 2011 para. 13.42–13.43.
917. Conveyancing Act 1881, s. 21(3); Land and Conveyancing Law Reform Act 2009, s. 107(2).

§4. The New Model Constructive Trust

324. Lord Denning, in a series of 1970s judgments attempted to develop, what he referred to as 'a constructive trust of a new model'[918] which would be imposed whenever justice and good conscience required it. It was typically imposed in order to render a contractual license binding against a purchaser of land.[919] However, since Lord Denning's retirement, it has been rejected by the English courts. As Dillon LJ commented in *Springette v. Defoe*,[920] '(t)he court does not as yet sit, as under a palm tree, to exercise a general discretion to do what the man in the street, on a general overview of the case, might regard as fair'.

325. Despite the trust's questionable status in its jurisdiction of origin, the new model constructive trust has been relied on by the Irish judiciary in a number of High Court decisions.[921] According to Keogan, Mee and Wylie, '(t)hese Irish decisions are open to criticism, with the new model constructive trust being used in each case to avoid analyzing more closely the difficulties in the plaintiff's case'.[922] It seems to be relied on 'as a last resort where a particular judge feels that the plaintiff should win but does not see how to reach this result through the application of normal legal principles'.[923] These authors doubt whether the device could survive a review at Supreme Court level.[924]

918. *Eves v. Eves* [1975] 1 WLR 1338, 1341.
919. *See Hussey v. Palmer* [1972] 1 WLR; *Binions v. Evans* [1972] Ch 359.
920. [1992] 2FLR 388, 393.
921. *See Murray v. Murray* [1996] 3 IR 251; *Dublin Corporation v. Building and Allied Trade Union [1996] 1 IR 468*; *Kelly v. Cahill* [2001] 1 IR 56; *Re Varko Ltd* [2012] IEHC 278.
922. *Law and Taxation of Trusts* (Dublin: Tottel Publishing, 2007), para. 10.011.
923. *Ibid.*, para. 10.013.
924. *Ibid. See also Re Custom House Capital Ltd* [2013] IEHC 559 where the High Court required evidence of fraudulent conduct to justify the imposition of a constructive trust. This marks a departure from previous authorities on the new model constructive trust, *see* Biehler, *Equity and the Law of Trusts in Ireland,* 6th edn (Dublin: Thomson Roundhall, 2016), 288.

Chapter 7. The Administration of Trusts

§1. General

326. The principal legislation governing the administration of trusts in Ireland is the Trustee Act 1893, as amended by the Trustee Act 1931 and the Trustee (Authorized Investments) Act 1958. The Law Reform Commission has recently published a Report[925] making certain recommendations in relation to the appointment, removal, duties and powers of trustees and it is expected that a Bill implementing these proposals shall be published in the near future. The position of a trustee has been described by Wylie as 'an extremely exacting one, and, all too frequently, a thankless one'.[926] It is often undertaken out of a sense of family obligation. However, the duties and responsibilities imposed on trustees are very onerous, with the result that professional trustees are becoming more popular in Ireland. Trustees who fail to observe their duties or exceed their powers will be in breach of trust and may be personally liable for any consequential loss or damages suffered by the beneficiaries.[927]

§2. The Appointment, Retirement and Removal of Trustees

I. Appointment

327. A settlor will often appoint more than one trustee although, at the moment, there are no minimum or maximum requirements. The Law Reform Commission has recommended that legislation should be introduced requiring the appointment of at least two trustees or a corporate trustee in a non-charitable trust[928] and at least three trustees or a corporate trustee in the case of a charitable trust.[929] Few restrictions exist in relation to who can be appointed a non-charitable trustee. For example, a beneficiary or a relative of a beneficiary may be appointed a trustee, although this is usually undesirable as it may lead to a conflict of interest. However, a corporation may only be appointed as a trustee if its memorandum and articles of association permit it. Also, since a minor can no longer hold a legal estate in land,[930] this effectively precludes his or her appointment as a trustee. In 2005, the Law Reform Commission recommended that statutory restrictions should be imposed on who could be appointed as a charitable

925. *Trust Law: General Proposals* (LRC 92– 2008).
926. Wylie, *Irish Land Law,* 4th edn (Dublin: Bloomsbury Publishing, 2010), para. 10.01.
927. *See* Keogan, Mee & Wylie, *Law and Taxation of Trusts* (Dublin: Tottel Publishing, 2007), Ch. 19 for a discussion of the liability of trustees and Ch. 20 which discusses the defences which may be available to trustees faced with a breach of trust action.
928. *Trust Law: General Proposals* (LRC 92–2008), para. 2.22.
929. *Consultation on Trust Law: General Proposals* (LRC CP 35–2005), para. 1.96.
930. *See* s. 18(1)(c) of the Land and Conveyancing Law Reform Act 2009.

trustee.[931] The Charities Act 2009 has implemented this proposal by setting out certain criteria which disqualify a person from acting as a charitable trustee and making it an offence to act as such a trustee while disqualified.[932]

328. The initial appointment is usually made by the settlor or testator in the trust deed or will. If none are appointed or those appointed predecease the testator or refuse to act, the court has jurisdiction at common law to make the initial appointment.[933] In the case of a trust of land, section 19 of the Land and Conveyancing Law Reform Act 2009 sets out a list of persons in order of priority who shall be trustees in the absence of an express appointment. The trust property is generally vested in these trustees as joint tenants so that when one trustee dies, his share in the trust property passes automatically to the remaining trustee(s) under the right of survivorship.[934]

329. The trust instrument will usually nominate a person to appoint new or additional trustees in the circumstances outlined in the instrument. Often, this power will be framed as exercisable whenever the person nominated deems it necessary, but where limitations are imposed they may be strictly construed.[935] There is also a statutory power of appointment[936] which may be exercised by the person or persons nominated to appoint new trustees, or if those nominated are not willing or able to act, or if none were nominated, it may be exercised by the existing trustees or the personal representative of the last surviving trustee. A crucial restriction on this statutory power is that it is only exercisable to *replace* an existing trustee who has died; remained out of the jurisdiction for more than twelve months; desires to be discharged from his duties; refuses to act; or is unfit or incapable of acting. If there is a need to appoint additional trustees in circumstances where a trustee is not being replaced (e.g., due to an increased workload), currently it is necessary to apply to the court for an order pursuant to section 25 of the Trustee Act 1893. Section 25 confers jurisdiction on the court to appoint new or additional trustees whenever it is expedient to do so and it is difficult or impracticable to do so without the assistance of the court. The Law Reform Commission has recommended that a non-judicial power of appointment should be introduced to facilitate the appointment of additional trustees.[937] It also recommended the revision of the list of circumstances outlined above in which the power to appoint replacement trustees may be exercised[938] and the extension of the categories of persons who may exercise the non-judicial power of appointment to include the liquidator of a corporate

931. *Consultation on Trust Law: General Proposals* (LRC CP 35–2005), paras 1.31 and 1.37.
932. Charities Act 2009, ss 55–56.
933. *Pollock v. Ennis* [1921] 1 IR 181.
934. *See* para. 65 above.
935. *Re Wheeler* [1896] 1 Ch 315.
936. Trustee Act 1893, s. 10.
937. *Trust Law: General Proposals* (LRC 92–2008), para. 2.49.
938. *See Ibid.*, paras 2.50 et seq. For example, it recommended the deletion of the statutory provision permitting the removal of a trustee because of an absence from the jurisdiction for twelve months or more, on the basis that a trustee could fully participate from outside the jurisdiction in our modern technological world. It also recommended that the statutory provision permitting the removal of a trustee on the ground that he is unfit or incapable of acting should be replaced with a number of clear and objectively definable grounds, such as where a minor has been appointed, or where a trustee is a ward of court or the donor of an enduring power of attorney, or where a corporate trustee is in liquidation or has been wound up.

trustee and the beneficiaries if they are *sui juris* and together absolutely entitled to the entire beneficial interest in the trust.[939]

330. The statutory power of appointment must be exercised in writing and is usually made by deed which includes a vesting declaration. Section 12 of the 1893 Act provides that such a vesting declaration in a deed automatically vests the trust property in the new trustee without the need for a conveyance. The court when appointing a new trustee is also empowered to make such a vesting declaration.

II. Retirement

331. No one is bound to accept the office of trustee and a trustee may disclaim his appointment, preferably in writing. However, once the trustee accepts the office, he may no longer disclaim and may only retire in certain circumstances. He may retire if the deed expressly provides that he may do so. He may also retire in the context of the appointment of a new trustee under section 10 of the 1893 Act or an appointment by the court under section 25 of the 1893 Act. Section 11 of the 1893 Act provides that he may retire by deed if there are at least two other trustees remaining and they consent by deed. It has also been argued that a trustee may retire if he receives the consent of all the beneficiaries, provided they are *sui juris* and between them entitled to the entire beneficial interest in the property. However, it is unclear whether this would require the winding up of the trust and, therefore, the Law Reform Commission recommended the introduction of a statutory power for such beneficiaries to direct an existing trustee to retire.[940] It also recommended that a trust instrument should not be capable of restricting the right of a trustee to retire and any such provision should be invalid.[941] However, it recommended the retention of the rule that a trustee should not be permitted to retire unless at least two trustees or a corporate trustee remains and they consent to the retirement.[942] If this consent is not forthcoming, a court application would be necessary.

III. Removal

332. The trust instrument may expressly provide for the removal of a trustee and the courts may remove a trustee in the context of making an appointment under section 25 or pursuant to an inherent jurisdiction to remove a trustee if he is acting dishonestly, incompetently or if his conduct is deliberately obstructive and the welfare of the beneficiaries demands it.[943] As has already been mentioned, this jurisdiction may also be exercised by the court where there is a clear conflict of interest between

939. *Ibid.*, paras 2.94 and 2.95. The Law Reform Commission acknowledged that this position could be reached indirectly under the rule in *Saunders v. Vautier* (1841) Cr & Ph 240 by the beneficiaries bringing the trust to an end and setting up a new trust with new trustees.

940. *Trust Law: General Proposals* (LRC 92–2008), para. 2.137.

941. *Ibid.*, para. 2.133.

942. *Ibid.*, para. 2.135.

943. *Arnott v. Arnott* (1924) 58 ILTR.

the trustee's duty to the trust and his own personal interests.[944] Finally, it has been argued that the beneficiaries may remove a trustee if they are *sui juris*, and between them absolutely entitled to the trust property. The Law Reform Commission has recommended the introduction of a statutory power of removal for such beneficiaries[945] and the enumeration of specific grounds justifying the removal and replacement of a trustee by the court, for example, the bankruptcy/liquidation of a trustee, or his conviction of an indictable offence or imprisonment.[946]

§3. The Duties of a Trustee

I. Duty to Ascertain the Nature of the Trust and to Safeguard the Assets

333. A trustee is under a duty to ascertain the nature and extent of the trust property and to ensure that he understands the terms of the trust. The trustee is also under a duty to safeguard the assets of the trust which means that he should demand payment of monies owing to the trust as soon as they become due and institute proceedings if this demand is not met within a reasonable time.[947] However, if the trust fund is small and likely to be easily dissipated if proceedings are brought, a trustee should avoid litigation unless there is a huge chance of success.[948] His duty to safeguard the assets also means that if he is selling the trust assets, he must obtain the best price. Sometimes, it may require him to act in an ungentlemanly or unethical fashion.[949] The trustee must distribute the trust property in accordance with the terms of the trust. If there are doubts about the whereabouts or continued existence of any of the beneficiaries, the trustees may seek a Benjamin Order.[950]

II. Duty Not to Delegate

334. Trustees are under a duty not to delegate their powers and functions and generally, if they employ an agent, they will be liable for any default on the part of that agent.[951] The principle of *delegatus non potest delegare* is not applied inflexibly as the proper administration of a trust would not be possible if a trustee was not free to delegate the performance of certain functions to professional agents, such as solicitors

944. *See Moore v. Mc Glynn* [1894] 1 IR 74, *see* para. 314 above.
945. *Trust Law: General Proposals* (LRC 92–2008), para. 2.151.
946. *Ibid.*, para. 2.156.
947. *Re Brogden* (1888) 38 Ch D 546.
948. If a trustee is considering bringing or defending an action, he should seek the approval of the court. Otherwise, he may have to prove that the litigation expenses were properly incurred before he can be indemnified against those expenses.
949. *Buttle v. Saunders* [1950] 2 All ER.
950. *See* para. 258 above.
951. *Turner v. Corney* (1841) 5 Beav. 515, 517 per Langdale MR.

and brokers. Therefore, a trustee may employ a professional as his agent where an ordinary prudent man of business would do so, and Wylie has commented that he may even be in breach of trust if he fails to do so.[952] In such circumstances, the trustee will not be held liable for the default of the agent.[953] It should also be noted that such an agent should not be entrusted with duties which are not normally undertaken by that class of agent.[954] The Law Reform Commission has recommended the introduction of a statutory power to delegate 'delegable functions' to 'authorized agents'. This power would be subject to a general duty of care and a specific duty to supervise agents.[955]

III. Duty to Act Without Remuneration

335. As has already been mentioned in the context of constructive trusts, a trustee is under a duty not to profit from the trust and to avoid a conflict of interest.[956] The restrictions on remuneration and the purchase of trust property can be viewed as specific applications of this broader principle. In general, a trustee is under a duty not to be remunerated for work carried out by him in his capacity of trustee. This is a harsh rule and has been applied even when the trustee has spent much time and energy performing his duties.[957] However, this rule is subject to a number of exceptions. The trust deed itself may allow for remuneration and if the settlor or the testator wishes to appoint a professional trustee, it is essential that the deed makes satisfactory provision for payment.[958] Although, the court has an inherent jurisdiction to order that a trustee receives payment, if the deed does not authorize any payment or to increase the level of remuneration authorized in the deed, this jurisdiction is exercised sparingly by the court in circumstances where considerable work had been done by the trustee.[959] At common law, a trustee is entitled to be reimbursed for expenses properly incurred in the administration and management of the trust at common law.[960] This right to indemnity in respect of costs and expenses has also been recognized by statute.[961] The position of a trustee who is also a solicitor is particularly contentious due to the suspicion that such a trustee may bring unnecessary litigation in the name of the trust if permitted to charge for his services. However, the rule in *Cradock v. Piper*[962] sets out that if a solicitor-trustee acts for himself and his co-trustees in litigation relating to the trust, and the expenses are no greater than if the solicitor had acted for his co-trustees alone,

952. Wylie, *Irish Land Law,* 4th edn (Dublin: Bloomsbury Publishing, 2010), para. 10.38.
953. *Speight v. Gaunt* (1883) 22 Ch D 727. *See also* the Trustee Act, s. 24, which indemnifies trustees in respect of acts and neglects by other trustees, bankers or brokers with whom trust money may be deposited unless guilty of wilful default.
954. *See Rowland v. Witherden* (1851) 3 Mac & G 568.
955. *Trust Law: General Proposals* (LRC 92–2008), paras 6.20 and 6.25.
956. *See* paras 315–318.
957. *Re Ormsby* (1809) 1 Ball &B 189.
958. Note that in England the basic presumption of gratuitous service has been reversed in relation to trust corporations and professional trustees, *see* Trustee Act 2000, s. 29.
959. *See Boardman v. Phipps* [1967] 2 AC 46; *Re Norfolk's Settlement Trusts* [1982] Ch 61.
960. *Courtney v. Rumley* (1871) IR 6 Eq 99.
961. Trustee Act 1893, s. 24.
962. (1850) 1 Mac & G 664. This rule was applied in Ireland in *Re Smith's Estate* [1894] 1 IR 60.

he is entitled to charge his normal fees. Finally, if all the beneficiaries are *sui juris* and agree to pay the trustee, such an agreement may be enforceable.[963] The Law Reform Commission has rejected the idea of introducing a statutory charging clause, on the basis that in most instances when it is appropriate and warranted, a charging provision is included in the trust instrument.[964] It was particularly emphatic in its rejection of a statutory charging clause for charitable trustees pointing out that the voluntary nature of charitable activities should be maintained to ensure public confidence in the administration of charities.[965] It did recommend, however, that legislation should be introduced allowing for the remuneration of trustees for non-trustee services.[966]

IV. Duty Not to Purchase Trust Property

336. In general, a trustee is not permitted to purchase trust property from himself and his co-trustees. This is known as the 'self-dealing rule' as the trustee is essentially the purchaser and the vendor. Megarry VC explained in *Tito v. Waddell* (No. 2)[967] that such a sale is voidable by the beneficiary, however fair the transaction. Although the situation seems to give rise to an irrebutable presumption of undue influence, the beneficiaries must take action to have the purchase set aside within a reasonable time. Otherwise, as is the case with all equitable remedies, delay will defeat equity. This rule tends to be strictly applied even to a trustee who has recently retired,[968] although if the trustee retired many years before taking part in the transaction the sale may be upheld.[969] Also, the rule will not be applied, if the trust instrument expressly permits it, if the court sanctions the purchase or all the beneficiaries (being *sui juris*) agree to the transaction. As Keogan, Mee and Wylie note, in such circumstances the trustee is effectively purchasing from the beneficiaries and so, logically, the applicable principles are those underlying the fair dealing rule.[970]

337. A less strict approach is taken where a trustee purchases property from the beneficiaries rather than the trustees. This is sometimes described as the 'fair dealing rule'. Although the presumption of undue influence arises because of the relationship, the trustee may be in a position to rebut that presumption. As stated in *Tito v. Waddell (No 2)*, the trustee will be required to demonstrate that he has taken no advantage of his position, that he made a full disclosure to the beneficiary and that the transaction is fair and honest.[971] This will be easier to prove if the trustee can prove that he gave full value for the property by producing an independent valuation. If the beneficiary

963. *Re White* [1918] 1 IR 19.
964. *Trust Law: General Proposals* (LRC 92–2008), para. 2.184.
965. *Consultation on Trust Law: General Proposals* (LRC CP 35–2005), para. 2.54.
966. *Consultation on Trust Law: General Proposals* (LRC CP 35–2005), para. 2.60.
967. [1977] Ch 106, 241.
968. *Wright v. Morgan* [1926] AC 788.
969. *Re Boles & British Land Company's Contract* [1902] 1 Ch 244.
970. *Law and Taxation of Trusts* (Dublin: Tottel Publishing, 2007), para. 15.016.
971. [1977] Ch 106, 241 per Megarry VC.

obtained independent legal advice this will also help the trustee's case. However, the absence of such a valuation or advice may not be fatal to his claim.[972]

V. Duty to Invest and Keep Accounts

338. Trustees are under a duty to invest the trust property with a view to ensuring a steady income for the beneficiaries currently entitled to an interest in the trust property while, at the same time, preserving the value of the capital for the benefit of those who may subsequently become entitled to an interest. They are only entitled to make investments expressly authorized by the trust instrument or those authorized by statute. If the trust deed is silent on the subject of investments, section 1 of the Trustee (Authorized Investments) Act 1958, as amended, specifies which investments are authorized. The Minister for Finance has the power to vary the list and the scope of permissible investments was expanded in 1998.[973] In 2002,[974] the restriction on the proportion of trust funds which may be invested in a single collective investment scheme was removed, although trustees are now required to take due account of an appropriate diversification of investments and to review the investment of trust funds every six months. Trustees are also under a duty to keep accounts in relation to the trust and, upon request, to allow the beneficiaries to inspect these accounts.[975]

339. As Meredith MR stated in *Re O'Connor*,[976] even if the investment is authorized by deed or by statute, the trustee is still under a duty not to act dishonestly, negligently or in breach of trust in investing on insufficient security. Therefore, a trustee is subject to a certain standard of care even when making authorized investments. This standard of care has been considered by the courts on numerous occasions. In *Learoyd v. Whitley*,[977] Lindley LJ adopted what is known as 'the prudent man of business standard'. This requires the trustee to take the care that an ordinary prudent man would take if he were making investments for the benefit of those for whom he felt morally bound to provide. This approach which seems to require the avoidance of speculative or hazardous investments was adopted by Murphy J in the Irish Case, *Stacey v. Branch*.[978] In that case, the plaintiff alleged a breach of duty on the basis that if the trust property had been let over a fourteen-year period, rather than maintained by a caretaker, it would have yielded a substantial rental income. Murphy J dismissed the plaintiff's claim stating:

> In selecting an investment he must take as much care as a prudent man would take in making an investment for the benefit of persons from whom he felt morally

972. *Smyth v. Smyth* (HC) 22 Nov. 1978; *Provincial Bank of Ireland v. McKeever* [1941] IR 471.
973. Trustee (Authorized Investments) Order 1998 (SI 28/1998).
974. Trustee (Authorized Investments) Order 1998 (Amendment) Order 2002 (SI 595/2002).
975. *Chaine-Nickson v. Bank of Ireland* [1976] IR 393, 396; *O'Cahill (Inspector of Taxes) v. O'Driscoll* [2005] IEHC 179.
976. [1913] 1 IR 69, 75–76.
977. (1886) 33 Ch D 347.
978. [1995] 2 ILRM 136. Note the critique of this decision by Keogan, Mee & Wylie, *Law and Taxation of Trusts* (Dublin: Tottel Publishing, 2007), para. 16.007.

bound to provided .... he must avoid all such investments of that class as are attended with hazard.[979]

340. The English case, *Bartlett v. Barclays Bank Trust Co Ltd*,[980] involved a professional trustee who had made a speculative purchase of property which resulted in a large loss to the trust fund. The beneficiaries succeeded in their claim against the trustee. The court mentioned that a higher standard of care is expected of a professional trustee which carries out the specialized business of trust management.[981] Where the breach of duty is alleged to have occurred as a result of a lack of initiative, it appears to be very difficult for the beneficiary to succeed. In *Nestle v. National Westminster Bank plc*,[982] the trustee (a bank) was unaware that it had a wider power of investment than it actually exercised. The beneficiary maintained that the trust fund should have been much more valuable than it was when she became absolutely entitled to it. The court held that she had not established a breach of trust on the basis of 'the prudent man of business standard' although it acknowledged that no testator would choose such a bank as trustee in light of what had happened. This decision has also been criticized as unduly lenient to the professional trustee in question and may no longer hold weight in light of recent English legislation which requires trustees to obtain and consider advice in relation to their powers of investment unless it is not necessary or appropriate in the circumstances.[983]

341. One issue which may cause confusion is the extent to which trustees are entitled to take into account non-financial considerations in making investment decisions. For example, are they entitled to make politically motivated or ethical investments by investing only in companies which demonstrate best practice in areas such as environmental protection or human rights? It is clear that trustees cannot refuse certain investments on political grounds if they would be more financially beneficial to the beneficiaries than other investments.[984] However, it would seem to be acceptable to pursue an ethical investment policy if the financial implications are equally beneficial from the point of view of the beneficiaries.

342. The Law Reform Commission has recommended the introduction of a statutory standard of care for trustees which would also apply when they are making investments. It would require the trustees to exercise such care and skill as is reasonable in the circumstances, having regard in particular:

(a) to any special knowledge or experience that they have or hold themselves out as having; and

979. [1995] 2 ILRM 136 at 142.

980. [1980] Ch 515.

981. *See also* the *obiter* comment of Harman J in *Re Waterman's Will Trusts* [1952] 2 All ER 1054, 1055 that a paid trustee is expected to exercise a higher standard of diligence and knowledge than an unpaid trustee.

982. [1993] 1 WLR 1260.

983. Biehler, *Equity and the Law of Trusts in Ireland,* 6th edn (Dublin: Thomson Roundhall, 2016), 500–501.

984. *Cowan v. Scargill* [1985] Ch 270; Martin *v. City of Edinburgh District Council* [1988] SLR 329.

(b) if he acts as trustee in the course of a business or profession, to any special knowledge or experience that it is reasonable to expect of a person acting in the course of that kind of business or profession.[985]

It recommended a different duty of care for charitable trustees, requiring them to act in the interests of the charity and in particular to:

(a) seek, in good faith to ensure that the charity acts in a manner which is consistent with its purposes; and
(b) act with the care and diligence that it is reasonable to expect of a person who is managing the affairs of another person.[986]

§4. The Powers of Trustees

343. The trust instrument will generally set out extensive powers to enable the trustees to properly administer the trust. Certain powers, intended to supplement such express powers, are conferred by legislation, such as the Trustee Act 1893. For example, in the case of a trust for sale or a trust conferring a power of sale, wide powers are conferred in relation to the conduct of the sale[987] and if a purchaser has been furnished with a receipt in writing by a trustee, such a purchaser is exonerated from liability in relation to the application of trust money.[988] In addition, trustees have a statutory power to compound liabilities,[989] to insure trust property out of trust income up to a certain limit[990] and to use trust income for the maintenance of minor beneficiaries.[991] The powers of trustees of land have been extended by section 20(1) of the Land and Conveyancing Law Reform Act 2009 which confers on such trustees the full power of an owner to convey or otherwise deal with the land, subject to any restrictions imposed by any legislation, the general law of trusts or the trust instrument. The Law Reform Commission has recommended the addition of new statutory powers and the extension of certain existing powers for trustees of property other than land[992] which shall probably be implemented by legislation in the near future.

---

985. *Trust Law: General Proposals* (LRC 92–2008), para. 3.15. This provision is modelled on the English Trustee Act 2000, s. 1.
986. *Consultation on Trust Law: General Proposals* (LRC CP 35–2005), para. 3.65. This proposal has not been implemented by the Charities Act 2009.
987. Trustee Act 1893, s. 13.
988. Trustee Act 1893, s. 20.
989. Trustee Act 1893, s. 21.
990. Trustee Act 1893, s. 18.
991. Conveyancing Act 1881, s. 43.
992. *Trust Law: General Proposals* (LRC 92–2008), Chs 6–11.

§5. The Variation of Trusts

344. Until recently, it was extremely difficult to vary the terms of a trust. The court had a limited jurisdiction to do so if an emergency situation, unforeseen by the settlor, had arisen and it was necessary to take action to salvage the trust. The court could also intervene to alter the terms of the trust to resolve a dispute between the beneficiaries. In addition, if all the beneficiaries were *sui juris* and in agreement, they could bring the trust to an end under the rule in *Saunders v. Vautier*[993] and set up a new trust subject to different terms. However, this rule could not be relied upon if there were minor or unborn beneficiaries. In the context of abolishing the rule against perpetuities,[994] it was envisaged that trusts could be set up which might last for a very long time and future generations of beneficiaries could find themselves locked into an arrangement which had become very unsuitable or inconvenient.[995]

345. Part 5 of the Land and Conveyancing Law Reform Act 2009 was enacted to improve the law in this area. It allows a trustee or a beneficiary to apply to the court for approval of an arrangement (varying, revoking or resettling the trust or varying the powers of the trustees to administer the trust) for the benefit of a 'relevant person' (i.e., someone who is unborn or is incapable of assenting to the arrangement due to a lack of capacity, or whose whereabouts or existence cannot be established, despite reasonable measures). Before approving the arrangement, the court must be satisfied that the application is not substantially motivated by a desire to avoid or reduce the incidence of tax. Such a restriction is not imposed by variation of trusts legislation operating in other jurisdictions[996] and the majority of applications elsewhere have been motivated by taxation concerns. As Wylie has noted, it remains to be seen what impact this restriction has on applications and it may depend on how active the Revenue Commissioners are in opposing applications.[997]

993. (1841) Cr & Ph 240.
994. *See* paras 53 et seq. above.
995. Law Reform Commission, *Report on Variation of Trusts* (LRC 63–2000), Introduction, para. 6.
996. *See* , for example, the English Variation of Trusts Act 1958.
997. *Irish Land Law,* 4th edn (Dublin: Bloomsbury Publishing, 2010), para. 10.82.

Selected Bibliography

Bell, A. *Modern Law of Personal Property in England and Ireland.* London: Butterworths, 1980.

Biehler, H. *Equity and the Law of Trusts in Ireland.* 6th ed. Dublin: Roundhall, 2016.

Bland, P. *Easements.* 3rd ed. Dublin: Roundhall, 2015.

Byrne, M. *Landlord & Tenant Law: The Commercial Sector.* Dublin: Round Hall, 2013.

Conway, H. *Co-Ownership of Land: Partition Actions and Remedies.* 2nd ed. Dublin: Bloomsbury Professional, 2012.

De Londras, F. *Principles of Irish Property Law.* 2nd ed. Dublin: Clarus Press, 2011.

Fitzgerald, B. *Land Registry Practice.* 2nd ed. Dublin: Round Hall, 1995.

Forde, M. *Commercial Law.* 3rd ed. Haywards Heath: Tottel Publishing, 2005.

Keogan, A., J. Mee & J.C.W. Wylie. *The Law and Taxation of Trusts.* Dublin: Tottel Publishing, 2007.

Lyall, A. *Land Law in Ireland.* 3rd ed. Dublin: Round Hall, 2010.

Maddox, N. *Mortgages Law & Practice.* Dublin: Round Hall, 2007.

Pearce, R. & J. Mee. *Land Law.* 3rd ed. Dublin: Roundhall/Sweet & Maxwell, 2011.

White, F. *Commercial Law.* 2nd ed. Dublin: Thomson Roundhall, 2012.

Wylie, J.C.W. *Landlord and Tenant Law.* 3rd ed. Dublin: Butterworths, 2014.

Wylie, J.C.W. *Irish Land Law.* 5th ed. Dublin: Bloomsbury Professional, 2013.

Wylie, J.C.W. *The Land and Conveyancing Law Reform Act 2009: Annotations and Commentary.* Dublin: Bloomsbury Professional, 2009.

Wylie, J.C.W. & U. Woods. *Irish Conveyancing Law.* 3rd ed. Haywards Heath: Tottel Publishing, 2005.

Index

The numbers here refer to paragraph numbers.

Index

Index

www.ingramcontent.com/pod-product-compliance
Lightning Source LLC
Chambersburg PA
CBHW071446230926
51846CB00001B/358
9789041194800